HOURS TO REMEMBER

HOURS TO REMEMBER

Reflections on life in South Australia 1889–1929 from *The Children's Hour*

HEATHER BONNIN

SOUTH AUSTRALIAN GOVERNMENT PRINTER

First published 1987 by the South Australian
Government Printer
282 Richmond Road
NETLEY SA 5037

National Library of Australia
Cataloguing-in-Publication entry
Bonnin, Heather, 1929-
Hours to remember.

ISBN 0 7243 6502 8.

1. South Australia — History. I. Title.
II. Title: The children's hour.

994.23

Wholly set up and produced in Adelaide,
South Australia

Designed by Grace Bock
Typeset by Paragraphics
Printed and bound by the South Australian
Government Printer

CONTENTS

For Bonnie and Catriona

We work to contribute to the land of which we are a part.
Dr Ainslie Meares 1976

There is more in mankind to admire than to despise.
Plato

PREFACE

This book is not a history of *The Children's Hour*, nor is it a social history of South Australia.

Rather, while paying homage to *The Children's Hour*, I have tried to convey an impression of earlier days in South Australia by using excerpts from the first forty years of the *Hour*'s publication—from 1889 to 1929.

Although those years represent only a little more than half of the *Hour*'s lifetime, selecting the material has still brought difficult decisions because so much seems worthy of inclusion. There are certain passages which must be included, but with a rich harvest to reap from the final choice will inevitably reflect the interests and attitudes of the author.

I have taken a large proportion of material from the very earliest editions from 1889 to the early 1900s because I suspect that much of the wonderfully interesting information contained in them is unknown to most South Australians, as it was to me. I hope that this unusual material may give some readers a greater understanding and appreciation of South Australia. Because this book is focused on South Australia I have not included any articles about the rest of Australia or descriptions of life in other parts of the world. I mention this so that readers will not think that *The Children's Hour* was parochial.

This, then, is a very personal book, both in the way it was compiled and in the reactions one may expect from those who read it. There are, for instance, many people living in the State who vividly recall *The Children's Hour* and their response will naturally be different from that of younger readers and others who have never heard of it.

The preparation of this book has brought me immense pleasure and a profound respect and admiration for those who shaped the colony of my grandparents' childhood. I inherited their efforts, being born in Adelaide where I have lived all my life. Perhaps it was from a desire to come closer to the life of my forebears that, except for one or two irresistible passages, I made my selection from the *Hours* between 1889 and 1929, for I was born in 1929!

ACKNOWLEDGEMENTS

I would like to express my thanks to the Director-General of Education, Mr J. R. Steinle, for allowing me to write this book about *The Children's Hour*, and for all his support.

I am indebted to many people for their assistance. First I acknowledge with gratitude the generous help and continued interest of Juliana Bayfield, Children's Literature Research Collection Librarian, State Library of South Australia; the guidance, encouragement and support of Garth Boomer, Chairman of the Commonwealth Schools Commission; and John Hutchins, Head of the Publications Section of the Commonwealth Schools Commission.

I also thank Sir Walter Crocker, Geoffrey Dutton, Kay Hannaford, Geoffrey Locke, Colin Thiele, Rosemary Wighton, Glenys Harradine and Elizabeth Kwan.

My special thanks go to my family for their patience and encouragement.

Heather Bonnin

INTRODUCTION

The Children's Hour was first published in Adelaide. Volume 1, Number 1, consisting of four pages, and costing a halfpenny, appeared in March 1889.

A year later, in July 1890, the *Education Gazette* gave the following information under the heading of 'Reading 131. General Principles':

> In order to further encourage a taste for reading a small paper *The Children's Hour* is published by the department for circulation among the schools.

At that time the colony of South Australia was fifty-three years old, and no one could have imagined the enormous influence this small paper was to have in the years ahead—not only in South Australia where it originated, but in the other States of Australia which later copied the idea, so that ultimately children across the continent received a school paper.

The monthly paper soon increased in size to twelve pages, then sixteen, and finally twenty pages. It continued until December 1963, by which time it was felt to have outlived its purpose. There were books in most homes, public libraries had been established for many years, and radio had long since proved to be a pleasing, as well as a powerful, influence. Above all, television was beginning to be within the reach of more and more households, tending to eclipse other media. *The Children's Hour* could not compete.

From the time the *Hour* began, many of South Australia's leading educators were regular contributors to it, but generally their articles appeared under pseudonyms, or carried only the author's initials, so it is now difficult to identify them. Tempting as it is, it is not possible to explore that aspect of *The Children's Hour* here. However, with apologies for many oversights, a few are mentioned whose personalities and contributions helped to shape the paper, and influenced the reading, and probably the thinking, of hundreds of South Australians.

It seems almost certain that the idea of *The Children's Hour* came from J. S. Hartley. In 1889 he was the Inspector-General of Education in South Australia; he is now held in high esteem as one of the State's most enlightened educators.

February 1897.

RECEIVED WITH THANKS.

ARTICLES, selected and original, from Henry Golding, Fred Graham, W. Skitch, Margaret Ryan, R. Sutton, Frank A. Dawkins, Mr J. Langdon Bonython, Miss Twiss, T. Bosch, Uncle Will and Austral.

1902.

MR HARTLEY.

I wish I was as near as the South Australian school children are to the grave of Mr Hartley; if I were, I would go and see it nearly every day. Our teacher stopped work this morning to tell us about Mr Hartley, what a good man he was, and told us to try and imitate him. When some of the Cororooke school children sent their exercises to the Ballarat Exhibition, Mr Hartley saw them, and said it was very good writing, so he took some over to South Australia, and asked the children to try and write like it. Mr Hartley has a beautiful monument erected by teachers and pupils of South Australian schools; it is made of pure white marble, and I think he well deserved it.

I am a pupil of Cororooke State School. A picture of our school appeared in your Third Class *Children's Hour* some time ago at Mr Hartley's request. We have taken much more interest in South Australia since then.

For many years the death of a prominent and distinguished Adelaide citizen was publicly noted with regret and deep respect, even in *The Children's Hour*, and this tribute to Mr Hartley came from an address given to the Flinders Street School in 1897, by Mr J. Langdon Bonython, the Chairman of the Adelaide School Board:

> The members of the Board have much pleasure in visiting the school, but it is a pleasure mingled with sadness. They cannot forget that on former occasions they have been accompanied by one who is not with them today. I refer, of course, to Mr Hartley. On one occasion he said to me 'I shall probably leave behind me no children, but I cherish the hope that something I may do will, when I am gone, continue to influence the world for good. In this way the childless may still live on'.

The Children's Hour seems to fulfil his hopes.

Mr Alfred Williams, who followed Mr Hartley as the head of the State's Education Department, took *The Children's Hour* in new and far-reaching directions. He was closely associated with the ideas of curriculum reform and 'new education' which emerged in the early 1900s. He felt most deeply the need to inspire in children a love of their country, and he believed that education should include learning for oneself—learning about the birds, trees, animals, plants and the Australian land. He linked these ideas with the development of a spirit of patriotism, and in *The Children's Hour*, which he strongly promoted, his influence can be recognised. Typical of the articles he encouraged were the series, 'Our Own Country', under the editorship of C. L. Witham from 1904 to 1906.

Mr B. S. Roach, whom Mr Williams appointed as Editor of the *Hour* in 1906, was Headmaster of the Walkerville School at this time. They were personal friends and shared the same ideals and views on education — particularly the commitment to Australia. They saw the *Hour* as not only a supplement to the recognised text books, but ultimately as a replacement of them in subjects such as literature, history and geography.

It is perhaps to Mr Roach that *The Children's Hour* is most indebted. His attitudes to learning, his personal ability and the contacts he had established meant that, as Editor, he was able to exert considerable influence on the thinking of his readers. While Hartley believed that children should consider themselves citizens of Greater Britain who lived in Australia, Roach and Williams held the strong conviction that as well as being British, children should be encouraged to regard themselves as Australian, and helped them to understand what that meant. Roach recognised, in particular, the important role of the British-born explorers in bringing a spirit of heroism to their new country.

Roach joined an expedition in Spencer Gulf, in 1907, for a short while, during which time he got to know a group of men, among them prominent South Australian naturalists and scientists. He also moved in literary and political circles, so that in addition to his recognition as an educator he had the respect and support of a wide and influential group of friends. As they generally shared his ideals and philosophies he was able to enlist their help as contributors to the *Hour*. Their names appear with their articles in some sections of this book. It was Roach himself, however, who wrote the wonderfully graphic accounts of the explorers.

In the *Public Service Review* of February 1913, Mr Roach's work not only as a lecturer in history and literature, but also as Editor of *The Children's Hour*, was referred to with the news of his promotion in the Civil Service. The following lines give some idea of the reputation which the paper had by that time gained:

> Mr Roach's splendid work in connection with *The Children's Hour* is well known and appreciated throughout the length and breadth of the state. He is well equipped for the important post he holds and has a deep knowledge of the child's mind and its development.

The names of the many others associated with education mentioned in the pages of this book, will generally be known only by those few readers who are familiar with the State's history of education. They can nonetheless be noted and appreciated for their part in that historic enterprise, *The Children's Hour*. Writers included Cymro, Mr Oliver Jones, who produced a lively and friendly letter every month. He also regularly presented a collection of puzzles and games—Puzzledom—which was begun by an earlier editor whose pseudonym was Sirius. Cymro appears to have been a warm and agreeable man. He occasionally signed his letters 'with kind love to you all'.

The Column for Girls was for many years conducted by Miss Marion Rees George, who later became the first headmistress of the first girls high school in Adelaide.

In her thesis *Making Good Australians*, Elizabeth Kwan says of *The Children's Hour*:

> Part of its appeal to children must surely have been its appreciation of their environment and circumstances. It spoke to them of their country, their people. Nowhere else could they readily find such material.

On the first page of the final number of the *Hour* in December 1963 the Editor wrote:

> Dear Girls and Boys,
>
> This is the last number of *The Children's Hour*. I am a little sorry to see the end of a publication which has served the children of South Australia for so many years. When the first *Children's Hour* was printed seventy-four years ago, it filled a long-felt need as there were very few books suitable for children. In these modern times, however, there is such a wealth of reading matter printed especially for children that it is felt there is no longer the need for *The Children's Hour*.
>
> It is interesting to recall that many well-known Australians have written for *The Children's Hour*: Dame Enid Lyons, Sir Keith Smith, Sir Marcus Oliphant and Sir Donald Bradman.
>
> I have just been browsing through the first *Children's Hour* and wishing that I could show it to all of you . . . Perhaps I can.
>
> Goodbye and Merry Christmas to you all.
>
> Yours sincerely,
>
> F. G. Kealley.
> *The Children's Hour* Editor.

It is now over twenty years since those words were written. Perhaps this book will at last, to some extent, fulfil Mr Kealley's wishes and in doing so remind those of earlier generations—and bring to the notice of present and future ones—of a very admirable and interesting South Australian enterprise.

CHAPTER ONE

BEGINNINGS

Setting out 'to encourage a taste for reading', in some instances *The Children's Hour* became the sole source of new reading matter, not simply for schoolchildren, but for their families as well. The paper was primarily intended for the State schools of Adelaide and the country districts, although some private schools for many years received it too. Most State schoolchildren were from working-class families, and it was an unheard-of luxury for many of them to buy the few children's books published in Australia or those imported from England (available in the shops of Adelaide in the late 1800s and early 1900s). Over the years, as the paper became more substantial both in size and content, it became a convenient source of material for teachers. Most articles were accurate, and some were particularly valuable because they were contributed by eminent writers in their field. But the simple pleasure the paper gave to a great number of people was almost as important as its educative value. Around the turn of the nineteenth century and onwards, there were hundreds of tiny schools of ten or fewer children scattered over the most remote parts of the State.

Below left: *1911. Bookabie School.*
Below right: *1917. Wickham's Hill School. Teacher—Miss Adeline Adcock. Photo: C. Burrow.*

The standards which most little schools aspired to, and often attained, is perhaps one of the most humbling and inspiring revelations of the early editions.

The separation of so many settlers from one another was, in one sense, out of character for a community like South Australia, based, as it was, on a strong sense of 'family'. A close bond between the people of this State existed, and remained a predominant and significant feature of life here for many years.

Indeed, a sense of paternalism, and maternalism, flowed through the first decades of colonial life in Australia. There are often respectful references in the earliest editions of *The Children's Hour*, to the Queen (and subsequently the King) and the Governor (and later to the Governor-General); this aspect extended to the Ministers of Education, the Director of Education, and School Inspectors. Almost without exception, they are depicted as not only authoritative, but warmly benevolent, and this may have helped further to sustain this feeling of 'family', which is a particularly South Australian characteristic.

As time went on each school grade was provided for by *The Children's Hour*, although articles were sometimes appropriate for two classes. But gradually the selection of material became more precise, as levels of comprehension were carefully considered. It must be realised, though, that the numbering of classes at that time did not correspond to the grading nowadays. For example, Class I was about the same standard as the present Grade III, there being 'Lower Junior' and 'Upper Junior' levels (roughly comparable to the Junior Primary of later years) before the Class I level was reached. 'Grades' were introduced in later years. The Grade VII and VIII publications demanded a degree of comprehension which made them very satisfying reading for adults.

At first, articles were mostly reprints from existing English papers and journals, such as *The Child's Pictorial* and *Aunt Judy's Magazine*, mixed with original contributions from teachers at various schools, or from the Editor. Excerpts from stories, frequently adventure stories, by well-known and popular authors of the time, such as Charles Kingsley, began to appear as early as March 1890.

In 1889 the following letter appeared in the September issue:

AUNT KATE'S CUPBOARD.

To the Young Readers of *The Children's Hour.*
My dear little Friends,

I have always been very fond of telling tales to children. Some of them all out of my own head, but most of them were told to me when I was a little girl or I read them in books. Most of these old stories are now what is called out of print and many of them I have never seen in print at all. So it occurred to me that I might write some of them down, and thus reach a great many more children than I can with my voice. My cupboard is my memory, and you are welcome to put the stories I tell you into your cupboards so that they may be brought out when they are wanted. If you like the first story you will be sure to have more from your sincere friend,

Catherine Helen Spence.

Miss Spence had other abilities besides her literary ones. She was to become influential in many areas of social reform in South Australia, particularly those concerning women and children. However, 'Aunt Kate's Cupboard' made only a brief appearance in *The Children's Hour* and it would be interesting to know why.

The wide circulation of *The Children's Hour* had another important social effect. It was a uniting influence. In a country which was strange in so many ways to its new settlers, where there were many small and far-flung settlements, it was important to encourage a feeling of belonging to the new land, as well as to each other. The first edition of the *Hour* seems to recognise this, and to be attempting this unifying role, in the following 'Views of Adelaide':

> We intend to publish from time to time pictures of the principal buildings of Adelaide, which may be interesting to children in the country. In this number we give views of the General Post Office and the Town Hall.

In each subsequent issue throughout 1889 photographs were featured. April presented Government House and Saint Peter's Cathedral; May, the Botanic Garden; in June a glimpse of the countryside near Adelaide showed the Gumeracha Bridge, and Gully View near Mount Barker. Then, in addition to several more views of 'The Gardens', there were photographs of the Lunatic Asylum, the Old Government Offices, the National Bank and the Imperial Buildings in King William Street. The early editions followed this pattern and included an item of interest about Adelaide each month. Sometimes a short description accompanied the photograph, making important buildings and gardens more interesting and appealing.

When, in May 1894, the new Angas Building of the Children's Hospital was opened, it was an occasion of both ceremony and celebration and the children of the Sturt Street School (in the city) and the North Adelaide School, took part in the programme. First they sang the 'Song of Australia' and 'God Save the Queen' and later they presented items on the lawns, for the entertainment of the invited guests gathered to watch from the balcony above:

> The Sturt Street boys gave an exhibition of marching and the North Adelaide boys executed the physical, martial and firing drill. The younger girls of the North Adelaide school gave pole drill, with poles trimmed with pale blue and navy ribbon—the colours of the School.

Pride in Adelaide's buildings was justified because by this time Adelaide had acquired buildings of an impressive standard and stature. When *The Children's Hour* entered South Australian school life in 1889, the building boom of what were later referred to as 'The Glorious Seventies and Eighties' had transformed much of Adelaide, as well as parts of the adjacent suburbs, from a simple colonial settlement into a promising municipality. It was acquiring an atmosphere of dignity, grace and elegance, and a sense of style, self-confidence and progress.

Even a brief look at photographs of the buildings around Adelaide between 1835 and 1900 arouses respect and admiration, as one recognises the good taste exhibited in much early Adelaide architecture. By the 1890s, as well as fine Government buildings,

1912.

ADELAIDE.

THE following verses appeared in an English paper. They are supposed to be written by a person, not learned, but who is very enthusiastic about the charms of Adelaide and its surroundings. The name Adelaide was borrowed from Queen Adelaide, the wife of King William IV, who was the British Sovereign when South Australia was founded. It was originally intended to give the name of Wellington to our capital city, but King William decided otherwise.

Streets a-running straight and wide, a-looking mighty clean,
Lying open to the plains, why! Adelaide I mean.
Ask me what I'm longing for? or where I'd rather be?
Drop me down in Adelaide, that's good enough for me.

League on league of wattle bloom a-bursting out in style,
Dandelions a-yellowing the paddocks by the mile,
Up and down and round the world wherever I may be,
Scent of Spring in Adelaide is good enough for me.

Scent of purple lucerne crops alive with honey bees,
Sweet perfume of orange bloom that drifts along the breeze,
Make your choice from all the world but leave, ah! leave to me,
Adelaide, so cosy-like, between the hills and sea.

London's full of loveliness, and London's full of care,
Shipping office full of folk a-going anywhere;
See a fellow rushing in, as mad as mad can be,
Shouting, 'Steerage, Adelaide!—that's good enough for me!'

1898.

OUR PICTURES.

THIS month our pictures are all of places within easy walking distance of Adelaide which are most enjoyable spots for boys' holiday rambles and picnics. In the spring and autumn months there are few prettier nooks in our hill glens than the waterfall at Burnside. In summer it is one of the coolest and most sheltered spots near our city schools, and although the waterfall is not at its best during the hot season it is always pretty and attractive.

To those boys who love a longer ramble, the Greenhill Road is one of the most lovely hillsides in South Australia. About half way between Burnside and the Mount Lofty Road there is a quiet-looking steep road to the left, which goes down into Slope's Gully.

This Gully, or glen, as I prefer to call it, is not only cool and secluded, but it is rich in beautiful rocks, rare wild flowers, ferns and sweet-singing birds. I hope all you boys and girls who visit this lovely glen will go there as friends and protectors of the latter, and neither disturb their pretty and cosy nests nor do them harm. Listen to their sweet songs, and to all the pretty things they say to you, or to the secrets they softly tell each other in the tree tops over your heads; but, if you want to sleep in peace when you get home at night, do not frighten or harm them.

For those who love a longer ramble still, I suggest the Greenhill Road to the top, and then turn to the right along the front of Mount Lofty. Just at this turn there are lovely views of the plains, with the silvery sea in the background to the westward, and to the east the beautiful and rich apple country around Summertown and Uraidla.

After boiling your billy on the summit of the mount, and enjoying a well-earned lunch and an hour's rest, please descend the mountain by the southern road, past the little castles of the late Sir Thomas Elder, and Sir William Milne, and you will soon find yourself on the main road from Crafers to Glen Osmond. Go on past the Eagle-on-the-Hill by the way, and should you feel very tired, when you reach the foot of the glen, you can get a comfortable tram ride back to the city. By the time you reach home, your boots will be a little thinner in the soles, but your legs will be stronger, and I hope your own souls better and purer for your day's holiday ramble amidst some of the beauties of God's very beautiful world.

there were banks and the offices of professional business people whose chambers lined Grenfell, Currie, Pirie and King William Streets. Adelaide's first shopping area in Hindley Street had spread further, into Rundle Street. Behind the elegant wrought-iron posts and balustraded balconies were the premises of tailors, hatters and mercers, boot shops, drapers and clothing stores. Many school supplies came from Rigby, publishers, stationers and booksellers, whose building in King William Street was three-storeyed.

Bridges spanned the River Torrens and later the railway lines, at Morphett Street, and the City Bridge divided King William Street from King William Road to the north. Horse-drawn carriages and trams clattered (and later, electric trams rattled) away from the square mile of the city, originally known as South Adelaide, towards the suburbs beyond. Villages, later to be suburbs, sprang up on the edge of the parklands, from the very earliest days of Adelaide's settlement. But one had only to go a short distance to leave town life behind, and be out in the country.

In 1898 the children of Adelaide were being encouraged to enjoy the neighbouring foothills, and the nearer slopes of the Mount Lofty Ranges—'The Adelaide Hills'—in their spare time. In the *Hour* the editors offered suggestions for a day out which sounded peaceful and interesting, even if the claim to be 'within easy walking distance of Adelaide' would raise eyebrows today! Appreciation of the countryside was encouraged in the early editions of *The Children's Hour*.

Adelaide, as is well known, had been imaginatively planned to have a spacious border of open land, called 'parklands', to frame a mile-square city, including open squares. To leave or enter the city in any direction meant travelling through the parklands, creating a subtle but unmistakable change of environment.

For many years the parklands were partly wooded, partly open land, fenced and gated in places to allow the grazing of cattle. In the crisp winters the grass was lush and green, while in the summer heat it was bleached to pale straw and the heavy brown earth crumbled dryly underfoot.

The Children's Hour tried to make sure that the parklands and open spaces were appreciated, although few people were probably conscious of this original feature of town-planning.

The emphasis was on contemporary life, rather than on the past. Occasionally there was an exception. In February 1904 the editors advanced from their generally parochial view and included this:

> It will help us to understand more clearly the story of 'our own country' if we first consider it as being only a part of the great island continent of Australia. It will further assist us if we can also consider Australia in its true relation to much older known parts of the world.

The discovery of Australia, let alone South Australia, was hardly referred to. Cymro's regular column, 'Facts and Fancies', slipped in one or two items, almost apologetically, in 1893:

> Captain James Cook the famous sailor was murdered by the natives of Ohwhyhee [*sic*] January 14th, 1779. In 1769 he visited New Holland and

gave it the name of New South Wales. He was accompanied by Sir Joseph Banks. The people of Sydney have erected a splendid statue to his memory.

Another entry states with simple directness:

On January 26th, 1778, Captain Phillip assumed the Governorship of New South Wales. He was therefore the first governor in Australia and likewise that is the reason why New South Wales is called the Parent Colony.

These little 'facts' were squeezed in among the 'fancies' such as: 'A boy was asked the feminine of tailor. Imagine his answer: dressmaker'. There were sentimental items too: 'Home is where there's one to love us, Home is where there's one to love'. Cymro ended this particular selection on a characteristically lighthearted note, with the old rhyme 'Solomon Grundy'.

It was in his letter headed 'Campbelltown, December 26th, 1896 (I am writing this on Boxing Day, or to be truthful, Boxing Night)' that he gave what seems to be the first account, in the *Hour*, of the arrival of South Australia's first settlers:

In our history lessons we read about the *Mayflower* which took the first settlers to America. Now boys and girls in this colony should remember the names of the first vessels that came to South Australia. In July 1836, the *Duke of York* arrived, and one day after came the *Lady Mary Pelham*. These two vessels carried the brave men and women who intended to make their homes in a new country. Of course when the ships arrived all were anxious to see who would be the first to touch the land. One jolly sailor called Russel took the youngest baby-girl in his arms, jumped into the sea, and raced the others to the sea-beach. He reached the water's edge first and standing in the water, he let the dear little baby's pink toes touch the white sand. The little girl's name was Beare, and I will try to find out her Christian name, and let you know in my next letter. These first settlers made a beginning at Kingscote, on Kangaroo Island, so that this town can lay claim to being the oldest town in our land.

1916.

TAKE CARE OF THE PARK LANDS.

RECENTLY, we have been informed, several children have been found picking olives from the trees growing in the Adelaide parklands, their intention being to make money by selling the olives. When detected these young offenders made various excuses for their wrong doing, though it is hardly possible that they really believed that they had any right to property not their own. The olives in the parklands belong to the Adelaide Corporation, and are sold on behalf of the funds in charge of that body.

The young transgressors must know that they would be committing a wicked act if they entered a private garden and, without the owner's permission, picked any flower or fruit. But their sin is even greater if they steal or destroy what belongs to the people as a whole.

During late years the Corporation of Adelaide has expended every year many thousands of pounds in beautifying the parklands. Bright flower beds have been laid out, shrubs and trees have been planted, and what once were bare paddocks have been changed into lovely gardens. All are free to walk in these pleasant places, the like of which were once enjoyed only by wealthy people who had gardens of their own. If, however, some of our young people cannot appreciate such great privileges they are not educated up to the standard of people who can be trusted amidst such beautiful surroundings.

Learn to take care of all property, either public or private, but, above all, take particular care of any that belongs to the Government or any other public body. He that destroys or steals public property is an enemy of all.

1905.

THE PEOPLE'S PARKLANDS.

To the boys and girls of South Australia—The parklands surrounding Adelaide and other towns and the trees and plants in the squares of all South Australian towns, belong to the people. The parks are your playgrounds.

You have a right to use them for your games, but try not to harm them in any way. Help, if you can, to keep them beautiful.

Do not let anyone kill or hurt the birds or break down shrubs and trees if you can prevent it. Do not stand or swing on the wire fences. Remember boys and girls! The parks and squares are yours. Think of them as your own property and protect them accordingly.

1912.
A Glimpse of the Adelaide Park Lands.
The spires of the Anglican Cathedral are to be seen in the picture. The City of Adelaide is encompassed by nearly 2000 acres of park lands, on which such games as cricket and football are played.

1893.

FACTS AND FANCIES.

THE City of Adelaide has five squares. Victoria Square was named after Queen Victoria; Light Square after Colonel Light, who surveyed Adelaide; Hindmarsh Square, after Governor Hindmarsh, our first Governor; Hurtle Square after Sir James Hurtle Fisher, first mayor of Adelaide; and Whitmore Square after Mr W. N. Whitmore, London Chairman of the committee that was formed in London in 1834 for the colonisation of South Australia on Mr Wakefield's plan.

People of South Australia are very proud of the City of Adelaide, which has the best situation of any capital city in Australia. It is built on a plain sloping gently to the sea. Behind the city is the beautiful Mount Lofty Range. The soil on which the city and suburbs are built is very fertile.

Colonel William Light was the great man whose name will be praised for ages for selecting the site of the beautiful city. Like many great and good men, he sowed the seed that others have reaped. His few years in South Australia were full of trouble and pain. Anyone who wishes to understand something about the early settlement of South Australia must know the life of Colonel Light.

However, towards the end of the year, another vessel, the *Buffalo*, arrived, having on board the first Governor, Captain John Hindmarsh, his family, officers for the new colony, and some more settlers. They landed on the long white sea-beach of Glenelg, and as it was a terribly hot day they took shelter under a big gum tree. A flagstaff was fixed, the sailors stood behind them, and the settlers were in clusters. The Governor had a big blue envelope, from which he took a big sheet of parchment, on which were written his orders from King William IV. As soon as the Governor finished reading the King's letter, the English flag was run to the top of the pole, the soldiers fixed their guns, the settlers cheered, and some blackfellows, who were wonderingly looking on at a safe distance, ran away as fast as their legs could carry them, when they heard the guns go off for the first time in their lives.

Cymro's human touch gave his letters great appeal, but in this description he concludes with some odd comments about the Aborigines:

> Whenever I think about that first day I cannot help feeling disgusted with our blackfellows, in-as-much-as they let their country go to the whites without a struggle.

But it was not until 1907 that the first detailed accounts of the founding of Adelaide merited a place in the *Hour*. An essay entitled 'The Founder of Adelaide' summarises the early life of Colonel William Light and then confidently asserts, 'And now we come to the most important event in the life of Colonel Light'; it goes on to describe the prominent part he played in forming the city's character, and introduces it with this brief summary:

> The discoveries of Captain Sturt, when he made his famous boat voyage down the Murray, and the writing of Edward Gibbon Wakefield had turned the eyes of English people to South Australia as a suitable land for making a new settlement. The position of Governor of the colony was first offered to Sir Charles Napier, a famous soldier, who afterwards distinguished himself in India. Napier declined the position and suggested that Light should be appointed. This proposal was not followed. Captain Hindmarsh was made Governor and Light was made Surveyor-General.
>
> Light was ordered to leave England before Hindmarsh, so that he might find a suitable site on which the capital city was to be built before the Governor and most of the new settlers arrived. As Light was a sailor as well as a soldier, he was given command of the *Rapid*, a small vessel that was to take him and about twenty others to South Australia.
>
> After a voyage of 104 days, the *Rapid* reached Kangaroo Island, and on August 20th, 1836, anchored near where the town of Kingscote now is. Light found that three other ships had arrived before the *Rapid*. They were the *Duke of York*, the *Lady Mary Pelham*, and the *John Pirie*. They had landed altogether ninety-seven settlers, who were mostly living in tents on shore. After spending eighteen days on Kangaroo Island Light decided that it was not a suitable place on which to build the city. He then sailed the *Rapid* across to the eastern shores of St Vincent Gulf and anchored in Rapid Bay. A fortnight was spent examining the country in the Yankalilla District, and then the ship was sailed farther northwards. By the end of September, Light had found the inlet on which the City of Port Adelaide is now built. On November 6th (a Sunday) the River Torrens was discovered by Mr Kingston, who was second in command of the surveying party. He afterwards became the father of a famous son, the later Right Honourable C. C. Kingston, whose statue is now being erected in Victoria Square.

1900.

HMS Buffalo.

At the beginning of December Light sailed the *Rapid* to Port Lincoln, and spent some days looking for suitable land on which to build the capital. The harbour satisfied him, but the land he thought unsuitable. He returned to Port Adelaide, where he landed and walked inland to Mr Kingston's camp on the Torrens.

On Wednesday, the 28th December, the warship *Buffalo* arrived at Holdfast Bay (Glenelg) from England. The Governor landed on the same day, and at the foot of a large gumtree, under the shade of which were gathered many of the settlers camped at Holdfast Bay, he told them that South Australia was a part of the British Empire. Light did not meet the Governor on that day, but remained at his camp near the Torrens.

On December 29th the Governor walked inland to Light's tent, and next day went with Light to see the land on which he had decided that Adelaide should be built. The Governor was pleased with the soil, but told Light that the city should be built nearer the sea.

Light knew that the distance of seven miles between Adelaide and its port was a great drawback, but near the place he had chosen for the city was a good supply of fresh water in the River Torrens, while at Port Adelaide there was no drinking water. He also saw that the rich soil around Adelaide would grow enough food to supply the settlers in the infant city.

A bitter dispute soon started between the Governor and Light, but the latter would not give way and say the city should be built on the coast. In January 1837, he started his men marking out the streets of the future city. Soon pegs driven in the ground showed where the broad, straight streets of Adelaide were to be. Six large open spaces, known as 'squares' were marked off within the city, to be places wherein the children of today can watch flowers blooming and hear birds singing, away from the crowded streets. Around the city Light had 2000 acres of land pegged out to be parklands, on which the boys and young men might play cricket and football and other games.

But Light passed through a very unhappy time. He was blamed by people for delays that he could not help, and the general quarrel between him and the Governor still continued. At last his health failed, and he gave up his position as Surveyor-General.

He built for himself a cottage near the River Torrens and named it 'Thebarton House'. It still stands, and its name has been borrowed by the important town which has grown up near it. In the garden near his house he spent many happy hours watching the growth of trees, flowers, and vegetables which he planted from cuttings and seeds sent him from Europe.

In January 1839, some bad news gave him a shock that may have hastened his death. During the long years he was roaming in strange lands, he had painted many pictures and written long notes dealing with what he had seen. These were intended to be used in writing a book about his life. He had packed them in several cases, which were stored in a building made of wood and thatched with straw. One hot day this place was burnt to the ground, and all Light's property changed to ashes. In the Adelaide Art gallery there are three watercolour pictures which Light painted during the first twelve months he spent in South Australia. Luckily he had sent them to some friends in England, and they were thus saved from the fire.

Light's troubled life ended on the 5th October 1839. The day before he died he had written to a friend telling him that he was sure he had picked the best site in South Australia on which to build the City of Adelaide. His dying wish was that his friends should write on a plate of copper that he was the founder of Adelaide, and bury the copper plate with him.

He was buried in the centre of Light Square, Adelaide. Over his grave is a monument, on the top of which is a surveyor's instrument telling the passerby that the great man buried beneath was a surveyor. From this brief account of his life you have also learnt that Colonel Light was a sailor, a soldier, an artist, a writer and the FOUNDER OF ADELAIDE.

Although early records of Light's life refer to his childhood at Theberton Hall, Lincolnshire, England, *The Children's Hour* made the common mistake of spelling it Thebarton—the misspelt name had somehow become attached to Light's cottage, which he had originally named Theberton in memory of his childhood home. The misspelling was perpetuated by the naming of the area surrounding his cottage, which became the suburb of Thebarton. (A move, in about 1980, to re-establish the correct name of Theberton was defeated.) Perhaps

Proclamation Tree at Glenelg.

the final chapter in the tragic story of Colonel Light's association with South Australia occurred much later, long after his death. In 1927 the Thebarton cottage was demolished. The *Hour* drew attention to this insensitive destruction. There were concerned people then, as now, it seems, who recognised the importance of preserving places of historic significance and who deplored the casual attitudes which allowed them to be lost:

> On the 6th of August last, the Mayor of Thebarton (Mr H. S. Hatwell) unveiled a bronze tablet that has been fixed to mark the site on which once stood Colonel Light's cottage. After the unveiling, the Lord Mayor of Adelaide (Sir Wallace Bruce) and Mr A. A. Simpson made speeches telling about Colonel Light and his old cottage. It was the house where that great man spent the last few months of his troubled life, and it was in one of its rooms where he died on October 5th, 1839. During the past twelve months the cottage has been pulled down to make room for a factory that has been built on its site. Changes must take place in a busy world, old buildings must be razed to give place for new ones; but all who like to study history will regret its passing.

The general tone of *The Children's Hour* implied that life for most South Australians was very good, even highly desirable. Seventy-one years after settlement the *Hour* asked its readers: 'Why did our forefathers leave their native land to form a new home in South Australia?' The answers followed: a war against France in the early part of the nineteenth century which brought crippling debt and deeply depressed social conditions to Britain. The 1820s and 1830s were described as:

> . . . perhaps the most miserable that the British working people ever passed through. Their wages were very low, their hours of labour long, women and children toiled more like beasts than human beings in crowded, unhealthy factories, or down in deep mines, and the price of food was very high. Those unhappy times are now often referred to as the Hungry Twenties and Thirties. There is little wonder that the working classes were discontented. They had little hope of raising themselves from their low position in their crowded land. No wonder they asked themselves whether they might not emigrate to a new land where they might live happier lives.

South Australia, by contrast, the article implied, was becoming a place of progressive ideas, a place with a future. It refers with justifiable pride and admiration to such achievements as the method of voting by ballot introduced in South Australia, which was followed by nearly every country in the western world; the Real Property Act, which was adopted by government, as a result of the efforts of Sir Richard Torrens; and it describes the establishment of that remarkable international link—the Adelaide to London Telegraph line.

Beginnings are important, and *The Children's Hour* readers were assured that there was certainly nothing to be ashamed of in their State's history:

> 1907.
>
> SOUTH AUSTRALIA.
>
> In looking backwards at the history of our land are there any facts that we may dwell on with pride? We should all be thankful that South Australia, unlike any other of the States of the Commonwealth was never

used as a settlement for convicts. Our early settlers were distinguished for their good conduct, and for the many reforms they introduced to make our land a happy one in which to live.

1916.
Colonel William Light, Founder of Adelaide.

CHAPTER TWO

EXPLORATION

'The literature of South Australian exploration is voluminous, instructive and much of it intensely interesting.' So states the second volume of the *Cyclopedia of South Australia*, published in 1909, adding that, 'From the landing of the earliest settlers to the present time [1909] the work of exploration has never entirely ceased and is still going on.'

This was the reason why *The Children's Hour*, during its first decades, would sometimes publish reports of journeys of exploration as they were actually happening, as well as recalling the honoured epics of the past.

The enormous and seemingly endless task of exploring the Australian continent can be sensed in a passage published in 1919, when *The Children's Hour*, reflecting on northern Australia, drew this analogy:

> Australia is like a house containing six large rooms, into one of which very few people ever enter. The rooms are the six states, the empty one being the Northern Territory. At the present time there are only a few thousands of white folk living there, but Australians are hoping that in a few years their vast empty Northern Territory will have many more people working in mines and on farms and stations.

It was inevitable that South Australia, because of its geographical position, would become concerned with solving the mysteries of the unknown interior. It followed that there would be close associations with the historic expeditions of the men one might call 'the professionals', such as Sturt, McDouall Stuart, Eyre, Giles and Warburton, whose achievements played a great part in filling up the 'blank' spaces on the map.

In colonial days children were exposed to tragedy, and were familiar with death in a way which seems, to later generations, both morbid and gruesome. But in an era when infant mortality was common, and maternal death in childbirth occurred in many families, there was neither much hope, nor any point, in avoiding the reality of death. Even so, the reports *The Children's Hour* gave of the Calvert Expedition must have been very moving to readers, adults and children alike.

1897.
Calvert Expedition — Funeral Caskets
Photo: Frühling, Adelaide.

1897.

THE CALVERT EXPLORING EXPEDITION.

Honour to the brave.

If you look at our picture this month you will see the above words attached to a beautiful wreath, which was sent all the way from Melbourne to be placed on the graves of the two lost explorers, Mr C. F. Wells and Mr G. L. Jones. The picture shows the two coffins as they lay in the Adelaide Exhibition building, awaiting the solemn funeral service, on Sunday afternoon, July 18th, when about 5000 people attended the service and followed the long-lost wanderers to their last resting-place in the North-road Cemetery.

Many brave men have died of hunger and thirst trying to find out what kind of country there is in the far central and north-west central portions of our great island continent, but perhaps none so well known to, and so deeply respected by us in South Australia as Mr Wells and his young companion Mr Jones.

If you draw a line on your map of Australia from the north-west boundary of South Australia to Shark's Bay in West Australia, and look upward from this line towards the River Fitzroy, you will see at a glance that that portion of the map is almost blank. Well, it was to try and find out what this part of Australia was like that this party, called the Calvert Exploring Expedition, was sent out. The party began work on the 16th of July, 1896, and concluded the first part of their task on their arrival at the Fitzroy on the 6th of November. On this journey they travelled over 1500 miles. More than 1000 miles of this terrible journey were over a dry sandy desert, and, as the weather was exceedingly hot, the whole party had a narrow escape from destruction. Mr Wells and Mr Jones had left the main party at a place called Separation Well, to make a sort of off-shoot exploration of unknown country, and were to join their companions at a place called Joanna Springs; but, as bad luck would have it, this spring could not be found, and, to save themselves from death by thirst, they had to leave their two lost comrades in the dreary desert.

After many fruitless attempts to find and succour them, after weary months of sorrowful waiting, the sad news at last came that the two

1896.

IN our own colony we have given a send-off to the Calvert Expedition, an exploring party which is to start from the Murchison in West Australia, and explore the country between that and the settled portion of South Australia. The work will be carried out entirely at the expense of Mr Albert F. Calvert, of London. He has planned the expedition in order to increase our knowledge of the land, the minerals, plants, animals, and natives of this, at present, unknown portion of Australia. Five years ago Sir Thomas Elder fitted out a similar expedition, which had to return before completing its work. Let us hope that the Calvert Expedition will be more fortunate.
With best wishes to you all,
I remain, yours faithfully,
Uncle Will.

brave fellows had been found amidst the burning sands, where first one and then the other had lain down to die. With his last feeble strength the elder of the two had buried the younger in loving lonely silence, perhaps with only the stars and angels looking on. So two more heroes have gone to rest, and to join so many others whose bones have been frozen by the North Pole's strand or been bleached by the burning sun and desert sands of Africa and Australia. Even in that terrible last hour, as he felt his life slowly ebbing away, young Jones, in his loving letter to his father and mother, must have been comforted by the thought that he was only one of a long line of brave Englishmen who have died for the good or the honour of their country, for we find him writing—

And how can man die better
Than facing fearful odds,
For the ashes of his fathers
And the temple of his God.

I would have all you boys try to remember these words, and think under what terrible conditions he wrote them, and let each one say to himself—'My country shall never want for a noble boy or a brave man'.

After so many brave attempts to find them had failed, the bodies of the two explorers (Messrs Jones and Wells), who were lost in the great desert of West Australia, have been found, and are to be brought back to South Australia for burial. Their camels had died, and the two unfortunate men had struggled on alone on foot, till they perished of thirst. It is touching to read that Charles Wells had, though weak and dying himself, dragged the dead body of his companion to a sand ridge and there covered it as well as he could with sand, afterwards crawling back to the shade of a tree to await the approach of death himself. It is a sad ending to the promising lives of two brave men. But all Australian boys should feel proud that our brothers still show themselves as brave and daring as those heroes of discovery and exploration who first disclosed the secrets of our continent; and every Australian girl's heart will be touched with pity, both for the fallen explorers dying in the vast wildness of sand, and for those left to mourn their loss.

The expeditions which had been made into South Australia and the Northern Territory were probably most interesting to South Australian children because personal links with the explorers could be established, even if at second hand. This was done very expertly by *The Children's Hour*. It is another example of the 'family' feeling and pride in the State so well fostered by its editors. For example, a personal touch comes in the accounts of both Eyre and McDouall Stuart with the mention of a flag embroidered in silk by the ladies of Adelaide, one given to each explorer as he set out from Adelaide.

The achievements of the best-known early explorers, like McDouall Stuart, also exhibited, as the editors would have well realised, the qualities of human endurance and courage so willingly accepted by readers of that time as stirring, admirable and morally uplifting. In 1900 the successes of McDouall Stuart were admiringly narrated, ending, however, on a reproachful note:

But in this colony there is as yet no memorial to Stuart. There have been several attempts to collect enough money for a statue to be placed in one of the streets or squares of Adelaide but so far only about £173

1907.

STURT.

ON the 9th of February Sturt and his companions reached the place where the Murray enters Lake Alexandrina. They had been thirty-three days on the water, and twenty-six days on the River Murray. The lake was named by Sturt after a young lady, who was at that time 11 years of age, living in England. Her name was the Princess Alexandrina Victoria. She afterwards became the great and well-beloved Queen Victoria.

A few days were spent examining the lake and the mouth of the Murray. On the Goolwa side the explorers disturbed immense numbers of ducks and black swans. As the boat approached, the swans rose, and the patter of their wings on the water sounded like the hand-clapping of thousands of people.

The voyagers tried to take the boat through the dangerous channel by which the Murray enters the sea, but on account of the shoals they were unable to do so. The party then walked over the low sandhills and saw the long unbroken line of breakers washing the shores of Encounter Bay. The men bathed in the sea and brought back a load of cockles, which were boiled and eaten.

The people of South Australia received Sturt very kindly. They gave a dinner in his honour, and he was given a high position in the Government service.

Sturt sent for his young wife, who was in Sydney, and built himself a comfortable cottage, near the seacoast, about six miles from Adelaide. He called his house 'The Grange'; it is still standing. Here his four children—three boys and a girl—spent many happy years.

There are many things to remind South Australians of this noble man, who was so skilful, so brave, and so unselfish. In Adelaide there is a street named after him, and we have a county and river which bear his name. In the Adelaide Art Gallery a portrait and a marble bust help us to recall his fine face. In the Public Library is his diary, written in a clear hand-writing, and there is also the thermometer he used to mark the great heat during the awful time he spent at Rocky Glen. Let us hope that South Australia some day will raise a statue to remind us of her greatest explorer.

has been raised. Perhaps some day the boys and girls of the schools will help and then Stuart's companions will not be able to say that we have forgotten the greatest of South Australian explorers.

Happily, by 1907, when another editor published a similar account of Stuart's journey, the statue had materialised.

The greatest of South Australian explorers was John McDouall Stuart. He arrived in our State in 1839; he was then 24 years of age. In Scotland, his native country, he had been trained as a surveyor, and he no doubt thought that he would find plenty of work in South Australia, where the land had to be marked out into sheep runs, farms, townships, &c.

Stuart was one of the men forming the party which Captain Sturt led on his last journey into the Barrier and Grey Ranges and the Stony Desert. You may remember how the men suffered when they were kept in the Grey Ranges by the severe drought. No doubt these trials taught Stuart many of the lessons of an explorer.

Captain Sturt always spoke and wrote in the highest praise of Stuart, who showed in many ways that he always thought highly of his great leader.

For several years after his return Stuart earned his living by searching for suitable land for sheep runs in the unknown parts of South Australia. Sheepfarmers who wished to take up new country employed him at this work. This was an excellent training for the great task he was yet to do.

It taught him to find his way over trackless sand or in thick scrub as easily as we find our way through the streets of the town in which we live. He learnt to tell at a glance whether the land he was passing over contained water for his men and horses, or whether he must push on to more likely country. He became, in fact, master of all the learning and the skill of the 'bushman'.

In 1859, with a white companion and a native, Stuart passed over the land dividing Lake Torrens from Lake Eyre, and, going westward, discovered the Stuart Range, in the midst of very dry country. He then turned southwards to the coast, and suffered great hardships from the want of water and food.

1907.
Captain Sturt's Cottage at the Grange.
Photo kindly supplied by Mr E. Paul Howard.

Once the party had over 100 miles to cover with only enough food left to make two meals. By eating the boiled leaves of a plant called 'pig's face', growing on dry, sandy soils, they gained enough strength to reach a sheep station; but the three explorers were in a very weak condition.

Next year the Government of South Australia offered a reward of £2000 to the explorer who would cross Australia from south to north.

Stuart, with Mr Kekwick and another white man, started on this journey. The little party had thirteen horses and a large supply of provisions. By March, 1860, they had passed between Lakes Eyre and Torrens, and had reached the point up to where the country had been explored by others.

After passing this country a strange-looking object came into view. It looked from a distance like a railway engine with a high chimney. When they came nearer they saw that it was a column of sandstone rising up from a low hill. The column is nearly the height of the tower of the Adelaide Post Office.

Stuart named this rock Chambers' Pillar, after a sheep farmer then living in Adelaide. Mr Chambers and his family had often shown many acts of kindness to Stuart.

In a few days, after getting past the Macdonnell Range Stuart reached the centre of the continent.

There was a high mountain near, which you will find on the school map marked as Central Mount Stuart, 4168 ft high. Stuart and Kekwick climbed to the top of the mountain, and built there a pile of stones, on which they fixed a pole, to which was nailed a Union Jack.

This flag had been presented to Stuart by Miss Chambers, and she had made him promise to fix it in the centre of the continent of Australia. When Stuart had fulfilled the wish of Miss Chambers, he and his companions gave three hearty cheers. At the moment they must have felt the joy that brave soldiers feel when they have captured from an enemy a long-held fortress.

Remember that the enemies Stuart and his men had to face were hunger and thirst. It requires quite as much bravery and skill to conquer such foes as it does to stand up to soldiers of flesh and blood.

On July 25th, 1862—exactly nine months after they had left Adelaide—Stuart gave his men a surprise. As they came up a valley the leader listened and heard a sound which he knew full well. Thring had ridden on ahead of the party, when suddenly he shouted, 'The sea! the sea!' The men made the wilds ring with three hearty British cheers. They had reached the winning post at last; their long journey northwards had ended, for as they rode forward they saw the beach and the calm waters of Van Diemen's Gulf. Stuart bathed his feet in the waters, and all the men gathered sea shells. A large tree was selected, and on its bark were carved the letters 'J. M. D. S.'.

On the trees was fixed a Union Jack, and then Kekwick and Waterhouse made speeches, in which they praised Stuart for at last having crossed Australia. Stuart replied. Then three cheers were given for Queen Victoria.

Next day the return journey was begun. Stuart, who had not enjoyed very good health during the journey from Adelaide, now became very ill. He was no longer able to sit on his horse so they made a litter, on which he was carried for over 600 miles. Often he wished that death

1907.
This Picture Shows how Stuart was Carried for About 600 Miles.
It is from a rough sketch by Mr Stephen King, kindly lent by Mr W. P. Auld.

would come to relieve his sufferings. You may imagine how hard was his lot in this homeward journey. He was nearly blind; the movement of the litter gave him intense pain; but he still skilfully guided the party back the 2000 miles to the settled districts.

When Stuart and his men reached Adelaide they were received as if they had been brave soldiers returning from a hard-fought battle which they had won. Thousands of people lined the streets and cheered and cheered again the sunburnt men as they once more rode their horses through Adelaide streets. They had been absent for one year and thirteen days.

Stuart was given £2000 and a large piece of land, and each of the men was also rewarded. Stuart did not long remain in South Australia, but left for England, where he died in 1866. He was buried in Kensal Green Cemetery, and his sister erected a monument over his grave, which bears the following inscription:—'To the memory of John McDouall Stuart, South Australian explorer, the first who crossed the Continent from South to the Indian Ocean. Born 1815; died 1866'.

About three years ago a marble statue of Stuart was erected in Victoria Square. The brave explorer is represented in the dress of a bushman; his gun is in one hand, his water-bottle slung over his shoulder, while his left hand is clasping a chart of some newly discovered country. He seems to be looking towards the fine Adelaide General Post Office. One might think that his eye is following one of the network of wires which leaves the Post Office and is carried to our Far Northern country—across mountain ranges and dry plains, over rivers and tropical vegetation—till it reaches Port Darwin. Thence it becomes a cable, and is laid under the sea; at length it reaches London, and carries every hour of the day news of great events happening around the world. The overland telegraph line was one of the advantages Australians gained a few years after the great journey of John McDouall Stuart.

In the first years of settlement an exploring party, which included the Governor himself, turned out to be an ill-fated expedition which determined the naming of Mount Bryan:

1927.

STORY OF HENRY BRYAN.

This is the story of a brave young man who, nearly ninety years ago, lost his life while exploring in South Australia. His name was Henry Bryan. In 1839, he and his brother Guy, had come from England, and were staying with Governor Gawler at Adelaide.

In December, 1839, the Governor and several others made a trip to the River Murray. They pitched their tents on a bank where the great river makes a big bend and turns southwards to flow down to the sea. The town called Morgan is now built somewhere near where the Governor's party pitched their tents.

Before the party had left Adelaide, some of the people were talking about a well-watered tract of country said to be north of the Great Bend in the Murray; other people were saying that this country was dry, and not fit for sheepruns. The Governor decided to see the country for himself, and learn what it was really like.

He took with him four men from the camp on the Murray. One of them was Captain Sturt, the brave explorer, who, nine years before, had brought the first party in a boat down the Murray. Another who went with the Governor was Mr Inman; in 1839 he was the head of the police force in South Australia. The other two members of the Governor's party were Henry Bryan and a policeman. The Governor had not intended that Henry should go, but he had pleaded so hard to be one of the five that the Governor at last took him.

On Tuesday, December 9th, the five left the camp at the Murray, and rode northwards into the unknown country. Two packhorses carrying food and two casks of water were led by the party. They had not gone many miles before they saw a high mountain, more than sixty miles away, rising up from the plain. The Governor named it Mount Bryan, after his young friend. When night came they camped thirty miles from their starting place.

The next day (Wednesday) they went along the plain, and the day soon grew very hot. The Governor became alarmed, because no water was found, and was about to order the party to return when they rode up a slight rise. To the northward they saw a sight that made them glad. It was a grand range of mountains, about 20 miles away. The Governor looked through his spyglass, and saw the country near the mountains was covered with lofty trees. They all saw and believed their eyes. Yet, really, there were no mountains, or trees, or water before them; all was as unreal as the country one sees in a dream. Before them was a mirage which so often has deceived travellers in hot, desert country.

For some hours they pressed on, and then suddenly the mountains and trees vanished, and with them their hopes of finding water. They could, however, see Mount Bryan, and even trails of smoke rising from it in several places. The smoke, the explorers said, came from fires lit by blackfellows in their camps, and water must be near where the blackfellows camped. So on the tired men and thirsty horses pressed to find water at the foot of Mount Bryan.

One of the casks carried by the packhorses was leaking, and the bung had come out of the other cask, and its water was lost. As the horses had had no water that day they were very weak. The Governor wished to return to the Murray by travelling through the night, when it was cooler; but his companions said, 'Where there are blackfellows there must be water. Let us push on to Mount Bryan, and tomorrow our troubles will be over.'

On the next morning (Thursday) Sturt and Bryan were left in charge of the tired and thirsty horses, while the other men walked towards the Mount to find blackfellows and water. They saw neither, though they did come to an old 'wurley' and the ashes of a camp fire. The Governor felt sure the blackfellows were near, perhaps hiding behind rocks and watching with their keen eyes the pale-faced strangers who were spying out their land. Still, no water for the thirsty horses that had been two days, and the men one day, without their having a drink.

On Friday night they began their return journey to the Murray, 65 miles away. The Governor, whose horse seemed to be better fit than the others, decided to push on ahead, reach the Murray and send back supplies of water, for the party that would be miles behind. Both Sturt and Inman begged the Governor to take Bryan with him for company, and the Governor consented. Bryan was in good spirits, having rested during the day. On Saturday morning the Governor's horse knocked up, and Bryan, who rode lighter, exchanged his horse for the Governor's. The Governor then rode on ahead.

While he was passing through a pine scrub a roaring hot wind rose, and the heat became so intense that the Governor was overcome, and had to lie down under a tree and rest. It was not until Sunday morning that he managed to reach the camp on the Murray; he and his horse were then more dead than alive.

The Governor was given food and drink, and, when he felt better, learnt, to his great joy, that Sturt and Inman had reached the camp. They had saved their lives by killing a horse and drinking its blood. But there was no news of Bryan.

On this Sunday several men went out to search for him, but saw no signs of him or his horse. On Monday, Sturt, Inman, and a black tracker followed the Governor's tracks until they reached the place where he and Bryan had parted. They then followed Bryan's tracks, and found that he had gone for about six miles, when he seemed to have dismounted, and taken off the saddle from the horse. He had also written a short note and spread it under the saddle. The note stated that he was going south and east. They followed his tracks for a short distance, and then lost them.

For several days they searched for him, but found nothing. How his life ended will never be known in this world. The grand mountain (3065 ft. high) will ever be a monument to the memory of Henry Bryan.

1906.

J. A. HORROCKS, OR SIXTY YEARS AGO.

One of the finest of the South Australian pioneers was John Ainsworth Horrocks, who was born at Penwortham Lodge, Lancashire, England, in 1818.

By the time he was twenty years of age he began to consider what occupation he would follow. The new colony of South Australia had been just started. Horrocks decided to try his fortune in the new land.

His father purchased for him 1000 acres of land from the London agents of the South Australian Government. The young pioneer made careful preparations for his new life by buying enough clothing to last some years, several guns, plenty of ammunition, and tools. He also engaged a blacksmith and some farm labourers to help him in his new home.

In the year 1838 Horrocks and a younger brother, Eustace, with the men-servants left the London Docks for South Australia. After a voyage of five months, during which they suffered much from the scarcity of drinking water on board ship, they arrived at Port Adelaide.

When they reached Adelaide they were very disappointed. Everything in the new town seemed to be in confusion. Those who had purchased land in London found that no land had been surveyed. Men who were eager to begin the work of clearing and fencing the land, so that they might grow wheat or rear cattle and sheep, had to remain in Adelaide. Governor Hindmarsh lived in a small wooden house on the banks of the Torrens, where His Excellency's two daughters did most of the household duties. Living was very expensive because all food had to be imported.

Horrocks was much distressed to find that he and his party had to live in idleness, and spend their money in the town when they might be doing work in the country. Mr Eyre, the explorer, told him of a place nearly 100 miles from Adelaide where there was some suitable land to make a farm. Horrocks and one of his men, a Mr Green, started for the new country, leaving his brother and the rest of the party in Adelaide. The two men steered their way by a compass and the stars till they arrived at the spot described by Eyre.

This locality was a few miles south of what is now the town of Clare. The scenery is even now considered to be the most charming in South Australia. From the high ranges runs a little river shaded by huge gum trees. In those days kangaroos and emus wandered about in large numbers, brightly coloured parrots screamed harshly from the trees, and wild flowers grew in great variety.

Horrocks found a large gum tree, hollow at its base. In this hollow tree he slept for several months. When he and Green had carefully examined the surrounding country, Horrocks decided that it was suitable for wheat-growing and the rearing of sheep and cattle. He named the place Penwortham, from his birthplace in England.

Horrocks returned to Adelaide, purchased a horse and cart, and, with his brother and the rest of his men, brought his belongings to Penwortham.

Soon he built a comfortable stone cottage for his homestead. He also purchased, at a very high price, some sheep, which had been driven overland from Sydney. In a few years they increased to a large flock. Other settlers followed and took up land near, so that in a few years he had many neighbours who were helping to increase the wealth of South Australia.

Horrocks made frequent journeys to Adelaide, where he noticed that there were many strong young fellows living in idleness who had not the courage to leave the town and face the work in the country. Many of them were invited by Horrocks to stay with him at Penwortham. When they saw how successful their host was in his work, they took up new country and became useful colonists.

Horrocks was now known to his guests and others as 'The King of the North'; and if to be a king is to show others the right way of living and to make his country better, as well as to rule wisely those who were under him, Horrocks deserved such a title.

After three years of hard work Horrocks found that he had prospered so well that he might take a trip to England to see his relatives and friends.

The wilderness he had found when he arrived at Penwortham had been changed by his industry into a valuable farm, on which were 9000 sheep; a vineyard and an orchard had been planted, and a fine stone house had been built. There were twenty-four white people living at Penwortham. Neighbours had settled the surrounding country. To mention a few of the names which are still remembered in the district, there were Mr Hughes at Watervale, Mr Gleeson at Clare, and the Messrs Hawker, who had a sheep-run at Bungaree.

He sang the praises of South Australia and took every opportunity of persuading young men to emigrate to it. He also collected money from his wealthy friends for the purpose of building a church at Penwortham (S.A.). He added a large sum himself to this money, and the pretty little church at Penwortham afterwards was built.

When he returned to South Australia he found that his property had been mismanaged in his absence, but, like a brave man, he set himself to repair these losses he had met.

In July, 1846, he left his sheep run to explore the country lying to the north of Spencer's Gulf. With him went a well-known artist, Mr S. T. Gill, several of whose sketches may be seen in the Adelaide Art Gallery. There were also five other men, including a blackfellow, in the party.

They took with them a camel—the first of these useful animals to be used in Australian exploration—six horses, and twelve goats. The latter were to be used as food. Two carts held the stores and baggage.

On the 2nd August the party camped at Mt Hughes's station, near to what is now the town of Gladstone. Here the camel bit one of the men, causing some severe wounds on his face.

The next day Mr White's station at Wirrabara was reached. Here Horrocks wrote a letter to his mother in England, little thinking it was to be the last he would write.

On the 7th August they came to the last station they would see before they plunged into the unknown wilds. This was a cattle station, situated near Mount Remarkable. It was owned by Messrs Malcolm and Campbell.

The party were now on the eastern side of the Flinders Range, and to reach the head of Spencer's Gulf it was necessary to cross the range. It would be a difficult task for the men to clamber on foot over these steep, rocky hills; but it was impossible for the horses to drag the drays over the range. While they were detained for several days repairing one of the drays Horrocks was shown by a blackfellow a cleft in the range, through which he managed to lead the party. This was the well-known Horrocks Pass, through which a road now connects the towns of Wilmington and Port Augusta. Those who travel through the narrow winding pass can understand some of the difficulties the party had when the road was not wide nor smooth enough for traffic. The pass is about five miles long.

In the wake of the epic, and now historic, journeys of discovery, came smaller, but important 'follow-up' scientific explorations. For, in the painful process of forging ways across the continent, a wealth of important information was uncovered and discovered, and although well documented at the time, it deserved far more attention than it could then be given.

Small expeditions were in many instances mounted and equipped by prominent Adelaide citizens, supported by the Royal Geographical Society.

To pastoral families, in particular, exploration was essential to the furthering of their investments. It was considered not only economically advantageous but character building as well.

Sons accompanied fathers, or deputised for them, or were sent off under the leadership of a respected and experienced explorer, to 'have the corners knocked off and make a man of him!' Some had the proud distinction of having their names bestowed on outback landmarks—lakes (which were usually salt, and frequently waterless, as were the rivers), peaks, hills, ranges, springs, waterholes, rocks and deserts, but rarely valleys, for so much of inland Australia is very flat.

The Children's Hour was two years old when a private expedition was undertaken by Mr David Lindsay on behalf of Sir Thomas Elder in 1891. This expedition, according to the *Cyclopedia of South Australia*, included 'a scientific staff of a surveyor, a geologist, mineralogist, meteorologist, naturalist and botanical collector, medical officer and photographer; there were, in all, nine Europeans and five Afghans, and the transport consisted of forty-four camels'.

The Horn expedition was referred to in 'News of the Month' in a *Children's Hour* edition of 1899:

> All members of this exploring party have returned to Adelaide having finished in about three months, the work of examining the country in the neighbourhood of the McDonnell Ranges. The expedition is said to have been examined and important results obtained, though it is stated that no discovery of gold bearing reefs has been made.

The *Cyclopedia of South Australia* gave more importance to this expedition, describing it as 'the most brilliant and learned scientific exploring party that ever ventured into the wilds of Australia'.

From time to time there are moves to alter long-established place names, in favour of those which appear, at the moment, to be more appropriate. Knowing and understanding the origins of names seems important if we are not to lose, or worse still, destroy, part of our history through ignorance and indifference. A great number of the Aboriginal names translated mean 'watering place', 'water-hole', or 'well'. This is not surprising in a State which is so dominated by its dryness. Water must have seemed as precious as gold—or, in South

May 1902.

A GREAT SAILOR ONE HUNDRED YEARS AGO.

THE *Investigator* sailed on July 18th, 1801, and by September 7th, 1801, Flinders sighted Cape Leeuwin, in West Australia. He next called at King George's Sound, and then crossed the Great Bight, and sailing eastward between the mainland and Kangaroo Island, he named the wide passage Investigator Strait, after his ship. He thus discovered South Australia, and named Kangaroo Island.

While sailing in the lower part of Spencer's Gulf he must have had very loving thoughts about the old home of his boyhood in far-away England, for he gave names to Port Lincoln, Boston Island, Boston Bay, Louth Island, Louth Bay, and Stamford Hill, all names of places near his native village in Lincolnshire, England.

Tuesday, the 23rd of March, 1802, must have been a bright clear day, for while standing on one of the bold headlands of Kangaroo Island, now known as Kangaroo Head, and looking up the smaller gulf, Flinders saw a high mountain, and named it Mount Lofty.

Many years afterwards this mountain became a landmark for ships sailing up to Glenelg and Port Adelaide, and a large white stone column was built on its summit to make it of more use still, and the Governor told us on Saturday, March 22nd, as he uncovered the tablet recently attached to it, that henceforth and forever it must be called the Flinders Column.

While sailing eastward, soon after he had discovered and named Mount Lofty, and when near to Port Victor, a French ship was sighted which was sailing in the opposite direction, hoping to claim the new land for France. Flinders at first got his ship and big guns ready for a fight, but finding out by flag signals that the Frenchman was only on a peaceful mission like himself, he put off in a small boat and paid a friendly visit to Captain Baudin. Flinders made him understand that he had already planted the Union Jack on the new land, and claimed it for the King of England.

The two captains parted in a friendly way, and as a meeting of two persons or two ships is sometimes called 'an encounter', Flinders named the fine bay in which the two ships had thus met, Encounter Bay.

This was on the 8th of April, 1802, as you will see from the tablet which the Governor unveiled on the Bluff just 100 years afterwards—on the 8th of last month.

1918.
Crossing Country Covered with Porcupine Grass.
The blades of this grass are as sharp as needles. They prick the horses' legs and cause them to bleed. The grass is sometimes erroneously called spinifex.

Australia's case, copper. It was often the purpose of an expedition to look for minerals, or water—or both!

1929.

NAMES ON THE MAP OF SOUTH AUSTRALIA.

Every name marked on a map once had a clear meaning. Frequently, however, in older countries, this meaning has been lost. It is easy to understand that the first meanings of many of the map-names on the map of England, for example, are no longer known: but even in South Australia, which is quite a young country, for there are people still living who were born before our State was founded, we are not sure why some of our map-names were given.

Many of them are those given by the blackfellows, and very beautiful names they are, for the blackfellows had a very musical language. Take the word Ulooloo, pronounced with the full vowel sounds. It reminds one of the notes the bush magpies carol in the early morning. Here are some other words that came from the blackfellows' language:—Onkaparinga, Yankalilla, Orroroo, Naracoorte, Caltowie, Kadina. It is to be regretted that there are not more native words on our map.

Then there are names given by the keen-eyed Captain Flinders when he stood on the deck of the *Investigator* and watched our coast unrolling like a vast map before his eyes. He used the names of towns and his friends in England, as well as the names of his companions on the ship to mark the capes, bays, islands, and hills that he saw. The land explorers, Charles Sturt, Edward John Eyre, John McDouall Stuart, when they were naming the mountains, rivers and lakes, also remembered their friends.

The early settlers desired to keep on the map the names of the Governor, or his wife, or prominent men of the time, and often towns were called after them. Hindmarsh, Gawler and Robe brings back the names of three early Governors: Hamley Bridge gets its name from Colonel Hamley, who for a year was our Acting-Governor: Port Augusta has taken its name from Lady Augusta Young, the wife of Sir Henry E. F. Young, the fifth Governor of South Australia: and Edithburg [*sic*] was named after the Lady Edith Fergusson, the wife of Sir James Fergusson (1869-73). The town of Gladstone borrowed the name of a great English Statesman: Hawker in the Far North and Morgan on the Murray each took the name of a well-known member of Parliament in South Australia when the sites of these towns were fixed.

1910.

THE DALHOUSIE SPRINGS.

Chris Giles
Normanville.

(The following account tells how Mr Giles and his companions discovered the Dalhousie Springs, which are south of Charlotte Waters and thirty miles east of the telegraph line.)

PART I.

On the 11th December, 1870, the main body of the expedition was in the valley of the Stevenson, the camps of all covering a distance of 30 miles. Mr Woods and some others, having been out in a north-easterly direction on the previous day, reported that the country in that direction had very much the appearance of 'spring country'—that is, it contained mound springs.

As to these curious features of the interior, we had seen many on our journey since leaving Lake Eyre. There are various reasons given to account for the origin of these springs. The most probable, it seems is that which supposes them to come from the vast supply of underground waters which we know are in that neighbourhood. The great heat of these springs shows that the water, after passing through a great depth below the surface of the earth where the heat is intense, has reappeared at the surface charged with mineral matter.

The mound springs are always surrounded by extensive areas, sometimes several square miles in extent, of dazzling white surface, very trying to the eyes of a traveller. This is caused by the water that runs away from the mound, evaporating and leaving behind the lime or other mineral with which it was charged.

Now to tell something of our travels.

A party—consisting of Messrs. Knuckey, Jarvis, Aldridge, Bee, and I—started on horseback from the camp to explore the country ahead of the main party. We would then be able to report whether the teams could travel over the new country which we had explored.

Of course, the weather was blazing hot, as might be expected by those who travel in this land during the month of December. We had gone about eleven miles, mostly over fairly good country, but also over some stony tableland, when we beheld a strange scene.

The level ground we had been traversing suddenly ended, and we found ourselves on the edge of limestone cliffs from 50 ft to 70 ft high. Below us were miles of waving green reeds, with at intervals pools of water surrounding island cones topped with reeds or acacia bushes. Far beyond these were dazzling white lagoons, which towards the south-east seemed to reach to where earth appeared to meet sky. The dazzling white and the vivid green formed a great contrast, and reminded me of the verdant islets in Torres Straits.

In places the cliffs were nearly vertical, but we found a suitable descent and soon reached the base of the cliffs, and came to the margin of the reeds. When we were at the top of the cliffs the reeds seemed only a yard in height, but now that we were near them they proved to be far above our heads as we sat on our horses. We measured them, and found they were 18 ft high in some places.

After cutting away the reeds with a tomahawk, so as to allow our horses to drink, we left them on the margin, and on foot began to enter the dense forest of reeds with the object of finding the spring-head itself. We had not gone far before we found that the firm earth was behind us. To our dismay, we were standing on a mere gridiron formed of roots of reeds, through and under which water of unknown depth was slowly flowing. I broke off an 18 ft reed and thrust it down to sound the depths of the water, but was unable to touch bottom.

1910.

THE NATIVES MET WITH IN THE OVERLAND TELEGRAPH COUNTRY NEAR CHARLOTTE WATERS.

Chris Giles
Normanville.

When wild in woods the noble savage ran.

Dryden.

1910.

THE ADELAIDE AND PORT DARWIN TELEGRAPH LINE.

DURING the year 1870 South Australia began a work which has been of the greatest benefit to all parts of the Commonwealth. In that year she commenced to lay a telegraph line, nearly 2000 miles long, across Australia from Adelaide to Port Darwin. From the latter place the wire—sometimes under the sea, at other times on land—reached London.

The construction of the Overland Telegraph Line cost South Australia nearly half a million of money. It was not completed until October, 1872, when the first messages were exchanged between London and Adelaide, a distance of 13 500 miles.

Sir Charles Todd, who died at the end of January last, planned and carried out the construction of the Overland Telegraph Line, which closely followed the track taken eight years previously by the explorer Stuart on his journey across Australia.

Amongst the principal helpers who assisted Sir Charles in this great work was Mr C. Giles now of Normanville. Subsequently Mr Giles held an important position in the Adelaide Post Office. Many years ago he wrote for a newspaper an account of the adventures he and his companions met with while in the interior of Australia. Mr Giles has kindly given us permission to make a selection from his writings, which we have adapted for *The Children's Hour.* Our readers will thus be able to learn from one who took an important part in carrying out the greatest work undertaken by South Australia nearly forty years ago.

Sir Charles Todd.
Born, 7 July 1826.
Died, 29 January 1910.

PART II.

The 'noble savages' gave us a considerable deal of trouble on our journey; but it is only fair to add that had they taken advantage of our weak points the result would have been more serious. Had they speared our stock, our further progress would have been stopped and our retreat through their country cut off. Every night we hobbled our horses and bullocks, but often by morning they wandered two or three miles from the camp. Several times natives were seen lurking amongst our animals whilst they were feeding, so it was not fear of these unfamiliar creatures that prevented the blackfellow from using his spear.

At first we saw little of the natives, though we had good reason to know that they saw a great deal of us. Our axes began to disappear in a mysterious manner, and the men's clothing hung at night on bushes to dry disappeared by the morning. Once a large heavy tarpaulin, quite new, vanished and was never seen again. Though we never recovered the missing axes, we saw traces of their work. While guiding a party of men to the River Finke I frequently noticed that the blacks had been before us, cutting down saplings with the axes they had stolen from us. Several times I was highly amused to notice in the broad sandy bed of the river that the native children had been playing at putting up telegraph lines: they had been imitating the work they had seen us doing.

Once we discovered some of our missing clothes in an unexpected way. In taking the first party to cut poles at the River Finke I struck the river in advance of the party and discovered a native granary or store of seed. On a rude platform built in the branches of a tree, 7 ft or 8 ft above the ground, was a number of bags of close netting. On climbing the tree to examine the bags I was astonished to find that they contained other bags filled with different kinds of seeds, stored for the dry season. The smaller bags were of various sizes, and consisted of the legs of our missing trousers and sleeves of our shirts—all tied up at the ends and filled with seeds.

When the men arrived they wished to confiscate the whole seed store, but I would not allow them to remove anything. I examined with much interest a net bag of a different shape from the others. From my knowledge of native customs gained from the time of my boyhood in the southern parts of the State, I recognised this bag to be the great medicine of the tribe. It contained the implements and charms of the *rainmaker*.

The principal object of the bag was a bundle of spun opossum hair. I unwound about 50 yds of it. Then there were 150 yds of spun human hair, wound very carefully round a pair of neatly made slippers, which were trimmed with the feathers of the white owl. Within the slippers, which had their upper parts placed together, were nearly 100 yds of spun human hair in two hanks. These were unwound, and at the end of each hank the Great Treasure was revealed. The first part of the Great Treasure had come from the south: the second part from the north. The first was a glass marble of the largest size used by white boys, and containing the usual coloured pattern in the centre; the second part was a mother-of-pearl shell with curious characters and marks engraved or cut upon the inner surface. I should very much have liked to keep the latter, for it was very interesting; but I was determined to take nothing, so I replaced the whole as carefully as I could.

Here was a marble probably from Adelaide—perhaps twenty or thirty years previously it had been a white boy's plaything; then it had in some way been secured by blackfellows, who had handed it on, probably by barter, until it had reached the central region of Australia. Side by side with the marble was a pearl shell from the north coast, originally obtained from the Malays, who for hundreds of years have sailed south from their islands to the coast of the Northern Territory to gather pearl shell.

By 1911 everyone was sharing, at second hand, in a new exploration adventure. South Australians were particularly proud that Dr Douglas Mawson, then a geologist at the Adelaide University, was taking part in an expedition to Antarctica. It must have brought a sense of wonder to children to think that he was 'one of us', as they read the stirring accounts of his exceptional courage, written in the *Hour* in the years that followed:

May 1911.

ANTARCTIC EXPLORATION.

At the present time England, Scotland, Germany, France, Norway, the United States, and even Japan have either sent, or are sending, expeditions to explore the lands around the South Pole; and there is yet another expedition that we hope will soon start. Money is being raised in Australia to fit out a party of our own men, who, led by Dr Mawson, of the Adelaide University, will help to learn in far southern lands, those secrets that since the beginning of the world have been hidden from man.

Now, let us learn something about the magnetic poles. These are two places on the earth's surface—one to the far north and the other to the far south of the globe—either of which attracts one of the two ends of a compass needle. In 1831 the north magnetic pole was located by Sir James Ross in a peninsula to the north of Canada. Further on in this article you will read of how, two years ago, the south magnetic pole was located by three members of the Shackleton Expedition, and how they took possession of it as part of the British Empire.

The members of the Shackleton Expedition were carried to the lands near the South Pole by the ship *Nimrod*. This vessel had been strongly built for the seal trade in the seas north of Newfoundland, so that she was well able to withstand the rude blows she would meet with from the ice in southern seas. Before she left England in July, 1907, she was inspected by the late King Edward who was accompanied by Queen Alexandra, and the present King (then the Prince of Wales), and several other members of the royal family. Queen Alexandra presented a Union Jack to Sir Ernest (then Lieutenant) Shackleton, and asked him to hoist it on the most southerly land he reached, and King Edward pinned on the leader's breast the Victorian Order.

Five months later the *Nimrod* was leaving Lyttelton, a port on the eastern coast of South Island, New Zealand, for antarctic lands. She had on board fifteen members of the expedition, amongst whom were three who had come from Australia, their names being Professor David, of the Sydney University; Dr Mawson, of the Adelaide University; and Mr Bertram Armytage, of Victoria. On the *Nimrod* also were ten hardy ponies which had been brought from the cold, bleak plains of Manchuria in eastern Asia. They, like most ponies, were full of tricks, but they rendered good service to the expedition. The following were their names:—Socks, Queen, Grisi, Chinaman, Billy, Zulu, Doctor, Sandy, Nimrod, and Mac. There was also taken a motor car, which did not prove so useful as it was expected to be.

On New Year's Day, when the *Nimrod* sailed out of the harbour of Lyttelton, thirty thousand people were there watching a regatta, but

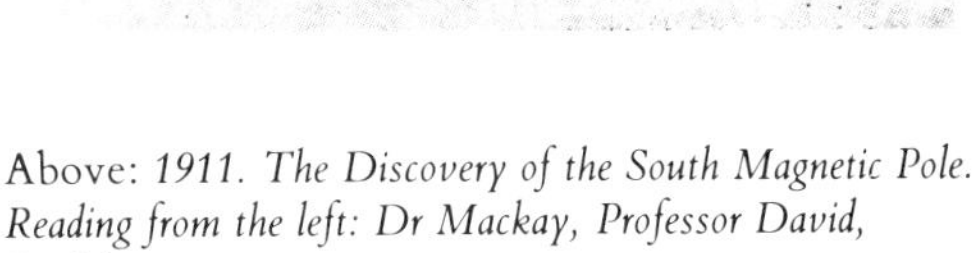

Above: *1911. The Discovery of the South Magnetic Pole. Reading from the left: Dr Mackay, Professor David, Dr Mawson.*

Right: *May 1911. A Summer Scene in Antarctica. Penguins listening to a gramophone.*

all sports were stopped for the people to watch the little ship move slowly out of the harbour, with the Queen's flag flying from the foremast. Guns were fired, whistles sounded from every steamer in the harbour, and the thousands of people who were watching waved farewells and cheered again and again. When the *Nimrod* came abreast of the *Powerful*, the flagship of the Australian fleet, the band of the latter played the well-known tunes 'Hearts of Oak are our Ships,' and 'Auld Lang Syne,' and the nine hundred blue jackets on the *Powerful* gave mighty cheers. It was a grand send-off to the fifteen explorers.

On the 16th January Dr Mawson found by instruments he carried that they had reached their goal; beneath their feet was the south magnetic pole, to which one end of every compass needle points. The grand old Union Jack was fixed to a short flag-pole. Heads were uncovered in the frosty air while Professor David said, 'I HEREBY TAKE POSSESSION OF THIS AREA NOW CONTAINING THE MAGNETIC POLE FOR THE BRITISH EMPIRE.' Then they gave cheers for King Edward, and Dr Mawson fixed his camera so that he could pull the shutter with a string and took a photograph of the dauntless three who had braved dangers and hardships to add the south magnetic pole to the Empire.

They tramped back to their tent some miles away and, after having a little cocoa, a biscuit, and a small lump of chocolate, they got into their sleeping bags, faint and weary, but feeling that they had earned a long sleep.

We cannot spare space to tell much about their return march of 250 miles to the coast, during which they suffered many hardships. On February 4th, when they were feeling very depressed and everything looked hopeless, a loud boom sounded through the still air. Dr Mawson shouted, 'A gun from the ship,' and rushed out of the tent, followed quickly by Dr Mackay and Professor David. Helter-skelter they ran over the ice on which they were camped—Dr Mawson's long legs giving him the lead in the race—and saw the dear old *Nimrod*, less than a quarter of a mile out at sea, steaming towards them. But the truth of the old saying 'There's many a slip 'twixt the cup and the lip' came home to one of them. Dr Mawson suddenly disappeared into an opening of the glacier. 'Mawson's fallen into a deep crevasse. Look out; it's just in front of you!' shouted Dr Mackay to Professor David. The two men looked down the opening and saw their companion twenty feet below. They ran back and brought the sledge harness, one end of which they dropped down the opening for Mawson to hold while they tried to pull him to the surface. But his weight was too much for the efforts of both men, and it was not until some sailors from the *Nimrod* landed and gave a long and strong pull that Dr Mawson was lifted out of the deep crevasse.

The rest is soon told. The *Nimrod* carried the whole party back to New Zealand, whence the members separated and travelled to their homes. Their leader became Sir Ernest Shackleton, and in his interesting book *The Heart of the Antarctic* has told the story of the expedition in a manner that will interest boy or girl readers.

By the late 1920s, the aeroplane was soaring across Australian skies, bringing with it excitement and glamour, and pointing to a new way of opening up the continent, although the increasing part air travel would play in Australian life in later years could not have been imagined. But the magic of flight soon made gripping reading. In the *Hour*, as early as 1928, an imaginary visit to Ayers Rock was undertaken in part by aeroplane. This legendary landmark is now known throughout the world, and attracts thousands of visitors each year.

Reading the article with its accompanying picture is rather like looking at a photograph of a famous person taken in childhood. One can recognise the original features but time, fame, and exposure have brought changes.

A year later came a description in *The Children's Hour* October issue of an exciting and almost unbelievable event. It had taken place a month or so earlier, and was described as 'a remarkable exploring

1928.

GREAT ROCK IN A THIRSTY LAND.

DURING the past months the newspapers have been telling us about people who have formed parties and made trips into Central Australia. Let us follow their example. We will call it the Grade IV Party.

We will catch a train going to Oodnadatta, the station farthest north in South Australia. The train leaves the Adelaide Station on Thursday morning at 8 o'clock, and arrives at Oodnadatta at 9.30 on Friday evening. It has travelled 688 miles.

At Oodnadatta we shall find that the railway is being extended to Alice Springs, and that already the new line is being used up to Charlotte Waters. Perhaps the makers of the line will allow the Grade IV Party to ride from Oodnadatta to Charlotte Waters. There we shall find fewer than a dozen people living in that faraway town. It is in that part of the Commonwealth now called Central Australia.

Let us now leave the new railway line and travel 250 miles to the westward. As there are no roads and the country is very dry to travel over, we will hire an aeroplane to carry us. In two or three hours if all goes well with our aeroplane, we shall see ahead of us a rounded mass rising high above the plain. On first catching sight of it, we shall think it is a mountain; but when we get closer, we find that it is a huge rock. Its great size makes it one of the wonders of Australia and perhaps of the world.

In the light of the setting sun, the rock glows with a bright red colour; the scrub at its base is green and beyond the scrub, stretching north, south, east or west as far as the eye can see, is yellow sand. Some day a great artist will paint a picture of it in its true colours, the rock, scrub, and sand, covered with the bluest of skies and a wonderful picture he will make of it.

As we come nearer to the rock we still notice that its surface is smooth and shiny, except in some places, where deep furrows or gutters are hollowed out of its sides. For thousands of years the rain in the wet season has fallen on the top of the rock and poured down the sides, making rounded holes along the furrows as it rushed down to the ground.

The rock was discovered about fifty years ago by the explorer, Mr W. C. Gosse. He named it Ayers Rock after Sir Henry Ayers who at that time, was a well known man in South Australia.

1928.
Ayers Rock.
From a distance of several miles.

feat carried out in Central Australia'—an expedition conducted by aeroplane:

1929.

LOOKING DOWN ON CENTRAL AUSTRALIA.

Last month the newspapers contained accounts of a remarkable exploring feat carried out in Central Australia. The leader of the party was Mr C. T. Madigan, MA, University of Adelaide. Mr Madigan is a South Australian who has crowded many stirring adventures into his life. In 1911 he went with Sir Douglas Mawson to explore a part of the great Continent that surrounds the South Pole.

Let us now describe Mr Madigan's adventures in Central Australia. The first explorers who led expeditions into this country were Eyre, Captain Sturt, McDouall Stuart, and Burke and Wills. Could these brave men have been raised from their graves to see the Madigan expedition last August, they would have marvelled at the new way of exploring. They would have heard a loud humming, and, when they raised their eyes, seen two monsters, each shaped like a huge dragon fly, speeding through the air at a rate that in a race would leave the Adelaide–Melbourne express far behind. Perhaps these old explorers would think they were looking at a pair of those extinct monsters—part lizard, part bird—that once flapped their mighty wings as they flew over parts of the earth's surface. We who live in this wonderful world of today know that these monsters were aeroplanes. They were lent by the military authorities in Melbourne, as were six trained men—a pilot for steering each aeroplane, two mechanics to attend to the machinery, a wireless operator to send and receive messages and a photographer whose camera was frequently pointed downwards to take pictures of the moving scene below. Through the kindness of Mr Madigan who remembers years ago when he sat in a schoolroom reading a copy of *The Children's Hour*, we have been able to reproduce several of the photographs taken.

The two aeroplanes started from Point Cook, the military aerodrome near Melbourne, and reached Broken Hill on the same day. Explorers in the olden days, equipped with horses and camels, would probably have taken as many weeks as the aeroplane took hours to accomplish this journey. The next 'hop' was from Broken Hill to Marree, a town on our North-South railway. Thence the explorers flew to Birdsville, passing

1929.
The Two Wapiti Aeroplanes Lent by the Royal Australian Air Force.

over the tracks on which the drovers bring down cattle from Sir Sidney Kidman's stations in Queensland, and viewing on their right the country where in 1861 Burke, Wills, and King staggered along, the first two to die, and King to suffer terribly until Howitt's party rescued him. Birdsville is a small settlement on the River Diamantina, in Queensland. It was used as a jumping off place for the party to fly to Alice Springs, the capital of Central Australia, and since last June the northern terminus of a railway connecting it with Quorn.

Readers should find Oodnadatta on our map and imagine it to be the apex of an immense triangle stretching northwards towards Alice Springs and eastwards towards the Queensland border. The area of the country within this triangle is about 30 000 square miles; in other words, it is equal to a square marked on the earth's surface, with each of its four sides 173 miles long, or the length of an airline drawn from Adelaide to Port Augusta. One of the main objects of the expedition was to examine this country, which has hitherto been a blank on our maps. No one had succeeded in crossing it. Our map shows that the aeroplanes crossed it while flying from Birdsville to Alice Springs, and also that the next flight from the latter town was eastward and back to the starting place. The explorers looked down on this immense tract of country and saw that it was made up of row after row of red sandhills, bare, desolate, and waterless. It was a silent sea of sand that had waited for untold ages for human eyes to look on it, and find it was, in the words of the Bible, 'an abomination of desolation'. No sign of life was noticed; even a lizard seems unable to exist in what may be described as 'The Dead Heart of Australia'. The explorers did not alight; had they done so the probability is they would have remained there, imprisoned in the sea of red sand. The landing wheels under the aeroplane which move it along the ground for its run-off before it rises would never have gripped the loose sand. Altogether 5 hours and 10 minutes were spent in three flights over this forbidding tract of country, and about 3000 square miles were examined from the air.

The aeroplanes, using Alice Springs as their starting place, were then flown to allow the party to examine the westward end of the MacDonnell Range. The zig-zag course taken is marked on our map. During the flight Mr Madigan's trained eyes were glancing downwards, and he was taking notes of the valleys, gorges, and rocks he saw below. In the other aeroplane the photographer, using a special camera, was constantly exposing films. When they are developed and arranged in order the result will be an air-view of about 150 square miles of rugged country that had not hitherto been carefully examined. One wonders what the wild blackfellows, some of whom must have been crouching with fear among the rocks, thought of the huge bat-like aeroplanes droning overhead.

The third important question which Mr Madigan set out to answer on this expedition was to find the real nature of two immense areas marked on the map as Lake Eyre and Lake Torrens. Together they cover 5000 square miles of our far-north country. Three large rivers—the Cooper and the Diamantina from Queensland and the Finke from Central Australia—are shown on the map as flowing into Lake Eyre. We know that these rivers, especially the Finke, reach the lake only when they bring down heavy floods, and, in that dry country, floods are very infrequent; indeed, they are often years apart. It is fourteen years since the Finke came down in flood. We also know that in that hot country evaporation is enormous, it being over eight feet in a year. Yet some people have thought they saw distant waters gleaming in these lakes, and even islands covered with green vegetation. Others have guessed that the waters in the lakes have welled up from below, and have come

1929.
A Typical Sandhill in Central Australia.

from the great artesian basin that extends to the westward of Lake Eyre. At times the aeroplanes came down to within twenty feet of the surface, when, as Lake Eyre is 39 feet below sea level, the explorers were moving through the air lower than the surface of the water in Spencer Gulf. While they were flying so low, the explorers noticed the aeroplanes were raising clouds of dust from the surface of the lakes; indeed, at one time the landing wheels of each aeroplane actually touched the surface of what the map indicates as water, but which is really dry land. Neither lake contained water. Tracks of stray camels were noticed in many places. Our huge lakes on the map are actually vast depressions that can be crossed on foot by any energetic man. He will, however, require to take a supply of drinking water with him, for he will find he has undertaken a hot trip.

Mr Madigan has shown that on our map the two vast lakes should no longer be coloured blue.

The great days of flying adventure had begun, and the exploits of airmen became the favourite topic of many young readers. *The Children's Hour* now included articles about aviators like Sir Ross Smith, and Parer and McIntosh who were flying across the world from England to Australia, when less than a hundred years earlier the journey had taken weeks and weeks by sea, and an expedition through the bush from Adelaide to Aldinga had been regarded as a risky adventure!

Exploration inspired admiration, whether it was on land, sea or air, but if it belonged to South Australia's history, or was achieved by South Australians themselves, it merited a special place of pride in the *Hour*.

The *Cyclopedia of South Australia* (Vol II, 1909) says of South Australian exploration that it is:

> . . . replete with adventure of many kinds, tinged with romance, and in places, darkened by tragedy. In this work the highest qualities of manly courage, fortitude and perseverance have been displayed. Heroism, fidelity, resourcefulness, and the true British determination have rarely, if ever, shone more brightly than in the deeds of the men who have dared and overcome the perils of the Australian bush.

The editors of *The Children's Hour* would have agreed.

CHAPTER THREE

THE BUSH

December 1929.

THE BUSH.

Here was the bush—the wide flat landscape of all shades of brown and purple shot with vivid green, the bright sun, the heavenly freshness of the morning air filled with scents from the soil and the vegetation, the brooding stillness broken only by the fluting of the Australian magpie, most musical of all bird sounds. I never felt happier than at that moment.

(*Sunny Australia.*)
Archibald Marshall.

In Australia 'the bush' and 'the outback' have been accepted as symbols of this country and in other parts of the world many people think this is really what Australian life is mostly about. It is true that out of seemingly endless and unpromising deserts a mythology has been created, much of this country's literature and art has flowered, and great wealth has been won. Yet, for most of us, the life which goes on beyond the towns and cities is little understood and seldom experienced. In 1889 when the first *Children's Hours* were being read this was perhaps even more true. In Australia, country people have always been different from city people in ways which have nothing to do with class or wealth. From the first days of European settlement many were prepared to face conditions of loneliness and harshness in strange surroundings. Isolation, for most, was inevitable, and sometimes almost intolerable. It was a continuing hardship for many years as this letter in *The Children's Hour* makes apparent:

1926.

LIFE IN THE FAR NORTH.

Gwenith Davies.

I Live in the Far North with my father and mother, and our life is very quiet. The nearest town to us is Quorn, and it is not very large. My mother said that we are lucky to be near the railway, because we can see a train and a few people sometimes. If you could come to where we live you would see a small station and a township, and many of us live here because there is a school or because men can work at the railway, post office, or the store.

1897.

EARLY DAYS.

Lizzie M. Fidler.

(The first part of 'Early Days' is now reprinted, with the second part added, at the request of many readers of the Third Class *Children's Hour*.—Ed.)

HAVE you ever thought what a lonely hard struggle our grandmothers and grandfathers had in the 'early days' of this colony? Perhaps some of you have, but very few of you present-day boys and girls know anything about them, though I expect you would like to know a little.

Well, just try to imagine how you would feel if, instead of trains and trams to take you here, there, and everywhere, you were jolted about in a bullock-dray, ploughing along through mud a foot deep and bogged in ruts in winter; smothered with dust and eaten with flies in summer.

If you lived any distance from Adelaide, your nearest neighbour was from two to ten miles—just as the case might be—away from you. Your store was from five to twenty miles; very seldom nearer than that. Dear me! You could not 'pop in' and match this piece of silk, or that piece of ribbon; and, as for dress stuff at 1s 11¾d the dozen (as we see it advertised now), such a thing was not dreamt of. Neither could you on a burning hot day 'send round' for some nice ripe oranges or bananas; no, indeed! You could *wish* for them right enough, but *get* them you could not. And these are but trifles compared with what had to be endured from wild dogs and blacks.

Every day seems the same here, because we do not have much fun, and only one picture show came last year. Only three times a week there is a train, and this brings a few people to go out to the sheep and cattle stations to work, or to go a long way up the track by mail car.

Some days you will see men called Afghans loading up a mob of camels with stores to be taken a long way up the track towards Queensland. The stations which are nearer the line send in donkey teams with white fellows for their things, and the boss comes in sometimes in his motor.

One day in the year we have a race meeting, and many people come from the places far away. They reach here in buggies and motors, and on horses. The men look very brown from the hot sun, and they rarely wear collars or coats. One man told me that he had not seen a train for ten months, and he had been on a sheep station more than a hundred miles away back.

The stations are very big, and it takes three days for the men to go round some stations to look at the animals. These men have to camp out and ride about on the hot sand all day. It is hard for them in the dry times when the dams are dry, and it must be nice when the manager tells them to get the sheep together and bring them slowly to our township to truck them to Adelaide.

(The foregoing account, which has been adapted, was written by a girl pupil in Grade V, Farina School. It secured first prize in a school's exhibition held last May.)

It has been claimed that there were as many as 800 'bush school teachers' at that time, generally single women with as little as six months' training, and sometimes little other academic background. They frequently arrived at their daunting posts with a battered suitcase of their own books—the basis for their teaching of literature. They were books of varying literary merit—a typical collection might have comprised Charlotte Bronte's *Jane Eyre*, *Robbery Under Arms* by Rolf Boldrewood and *For the Term of His Natural Life* by Marcus Clarke. They generally formed a very limited library and more was certainly needed.

So the arrival of the *Hour* each month was looked forward to with particular excitement by people in the 'bush'. The children took the magazine home to be enjoyed by the whole family. Enlivening their minds and broadening their outlook, as well as simply cheering their spirits, it broke the monotony of hardship and loneliness which must have seemed to many all that life could offer, particularly in the remote areas where news was spasmodic and visitors few and far between.

It is still remembered by many with nostalgia. One man can clearly recall the smell of the paper and the printing ink, as the new editions were unwrapped.

The sense of belonging to one another was fostered, and probably grew, in South Australia, with the regular inclusion in the *Hour* of letters from teachers and schoolchildren dotted about the whole of the State—which then included the Northern Territory.

As early as 1892 the *Hour* published letters from children under the heading 'Scholars Corner'. This was continued for many years, letters frequently coming from children living hundreds of miles from Adelaide. In 1897 Angola Underdown wrote:

SHORT DESCRIPTION OF OODNADATTA.

> Oodnadatta is a small town 688 miles from Adelaide. We have a train once a fortnight—on a Sunday. We have a nice railway station, two stores, one hotel, and a butcher's shop. The drought, which lasted about three years, has just broken up. We have had two and a quarter inches of rain, and the grass is coming up nicely. The creeks are all running, and goats and other stock will soon have plenty to eat. Station owners were sending horses, cattle, and sheep as far as Blood's Creek, because they were dying for want of food and water, so, of course, everyone was glad to see the rain. A private house and the Government goods shed have been burnt down within nine months. The latter fire was first seen about 5 o'clock in the morning, and was a dreadful sight.

There is an enviable freedom about life in the bush and the children's letters were generally fresh and natural. They seemed to love and respect their surroundings. Through their letters a contact was made, the loneliness and the hardship were perhaps understood, and at the same time a great deal of valuable and often fascinating information was given to the city readers. For instance, the peculiar beauty of the land could be glimpsed and the secrets of unfamiliar plants and animals shared. Country children are nurtured by nature which adds a particular richness to life in a way not always experienced by city children. Gertrude Johannsen wrote in 1925:

> Lately we have found many emus' eggs. One of these eggs holds as much as a dozen fowls' eggs. Its contents will fill a large frying pan. The shell is dark-green in colour, and its surface is rough.

The changes that were occurring were recorded too—even at far distant Charlotte Waters, in Central Australia. Soon photographs of schools became a continuing feature. These were, in some instances, touching illustrations of the loneliness of both the landscape and the lives of many outback schoolchildren. So the paper developed in a way which brought together the varied and numerous ways of life within the State.

July 25th, 1892.

LIFE ON A STATION.
TO THE EDITOR.

Dear Sir—Thank you very much for the kind letter you sent me on the 2nd of July. You said in your letter that the children who live in town who read *The Children's Hour* would like to know something about life on a station. First I will tell you where the station is, and then I will tell you what it is like. Yartoo is among the Gawler Ranges, so of course there are hills all around us, and very pretty they are too, with great boulders and trees, and bushes of every kind. When we go for a walk we see kangaroos and wallabies, and hundreds of rabbits. There are some wild parrots too, also some wild turkeys. One day I caught a wild cat in one of my traps. It had such a beautiful yellow skin. My father often catches dingoes in his traps. He skins them and the skins make nice mats. Since the rabbits have become so numerous the dingoes have increased very much. They kill a great many sheep and lambs. There are a good many blacks who get their living by

September 5th, 1925.

A LETTER FROM CENTRAL AUSTRALIA.

DEEP WELL STATION,
VIA CHARLOTTE WATERS.

Dear Friend,

WE live right up here in Central Australia, 50 miles south of Alice Springs. We are right on the Overland Telegraph Line and have a telephone. If they build the railway line to Alice Springs, it will be laid about five or six chains from our house, but now our nearest railway is 300 miles away.

Our home stands on the foot of a hill and there are hills all around us. Our home is called 'Deep Well', because we have a well 210 feet deep, and all around it are nice big green gum trees and pepper trees. On one side of the house we have a little garden of our own and in it we grow lettuce, cress, onions, and barley. We are not milking cows just now, but we milk goats instead.

When there is a good season there are many turkeys and sometimes emus and kangaroos about. We live on a cattle station. The cattle go about as they like and some of them get wild. About once or twice a year they are gathered together for the little calves (we call it mustering). The calves are then branded or marked, and then let go again until they are grown up and fit for market.

As we live far away from everywhere and our nearest neighbour is living 23 miles away, we cannot go to a public school, but we get our lessons by the fortnightly mail and do them at home. Our school is called the Correspondence School. I think it is more interesting than other schools.

That is all for this time, and I hope you are in the best of health.

Kind regards from,
Your sincere friend,
Gertrude Johannsen.

Right: *1914. Poonindie School.*
Teacher—Miss A. J. Archer.

kangarooing. I could tell you a lot more, but I think this letter is long enough.

I am etc.

Fred A. Crawford
Yartoo. July 25th, 1892.

For forty years or so the *Hour* had a vast distribution—even the smallest settlements had a school, and it was customary to print photographs of country schools in each monthly edition, and that, in itself, made a bond between all the readers. As time went by, many schools of only a few pupils were closed, when transport between towns became easier and smaller schools joined together to form one larger school. But sometimes schools disappeared because the towns themselves disappeared. Rectangular school buildings still stand in varying states of dilapidation in a few desolate parts of South Australia. They are pathetic reminders of struggling pioneer farming communities, long-since abandoned.

In some parts of the 'North' *The Children's Hour* would have been delivered by camel train. For a long time settlers in the North were largely dependent on the exceptional stamina of these desert animals

Below right: *1911. The School Children at Hergott Going for a Picnic.*
Photo: Miss Hiddle.

Below: *1916. Desks for an Out-back School.*
Bringing a desk to Mulka, a remote school 120 miles from Hergott.
Photo: Miss L. Bridgland.

to convey supplies through the rough country and the merciless heat of the parched land. The camels were imported from India and Afghanistan, and they were usually driven and tended by Afghans. Although the need for supplies—which even included school desks—to be delivered by camel has long since gone, it is still possible to meet descendants of the Afghan camel drivers in parts of the outback.

In 'A Letter from Central Australia', from Gertrude Johannsen once more, and written in October 1926, she remarks:

> I suppose very few of my friends down south have seen a camel team. We have seen a team of nearly 60 camels pass our place. They are loaded with goods, and have come up from the head of the railway line, which is 300 miles away from our home. The camels are tied one behind the other. The young camels walk along beside their mothers in their team.

It was not only through children's letters that the bush was brought to the city. Articles were regularly written by teachers, and others who contributed to the *Hour*, telling of visits to distant places throughout the State. Sometimes, as in the case of a long article entitled 'Melrose and Orroroo', written and published as early as 1898, one is conscious of both prosperity in the colony, and pride in the recounting of it. It must have made cheering reading, especially for those then living in less hospitable and less rewarding parts of the State. In 1898 one writer said of Melrose:

> It is one of the oldest towns in the North, and forty years ago was of greater importance than it is now. Situated at the foot of Mt Remarkable, and well supplied with water, it was the centre from which the stores were provided to carry to the sheep and cattle stations of the north. But when the country was thrown open to the wheat farmers, and the railway lines were constructed without touching Melrose, its importance dwindled. The principal source of employment is a large brewery, from which beer and temperance drinks are sent far and wide over the North. Near the town are some fine gardens, where fruit-growing is extensively carried on.

And of Orroroo he wrote:

> It is situated near the banks of the Pekina Creek, a little stream of inestimable value to the people around, as through the hottest summer it gives an unfailing supply of water. The Pekina Creek, which you see in the picture, just breaks through a gorge in the hills, passes Orroroo, and then loses itself in the Walloway Plain. The northern railway is carried over this creek by a bridge of four spans. The creek contains one splendid swimming hole, which during the hot months presents a very lively scene after the school has been dismissed and the boys have found their way to it.

In 1924 Mr W. M. L. Adey, who was a well-known figure in South Australian education circles, wrote a long article to the *Hour* following his visit to the west coast of South Australia. It began:

> The part of South Australia usually referred to as the West Coast is not so well known as it should be. At the present time there are few people living on it, but those who are have great faith in the future of their district.

There was plenty of evidence of 'great faith'. Faced with the challenges of the bush, the strengths and weaknesses of men and women quickly showed up, being proved, cruelly yet simply, by their very

1895.

THE SALT LAKE.

THE Salt Lake situated near Cameron is a very fine spot indeed. It is seven miles long. The salt is so thick that a waggon and team will go across without breaking it. In the winter the salt goes to water. People about here put sheeps' heads and other curious things in it to be crystallised. They leave them in for a long time, and when they take them out they look very pretty. In the winter, when the salt has melted, boats are launched, and great amusement is to be had by the people of the surrounding districts. Boating parties are often formed, even in winter, for the mere delight of a row. There are two islands on which they used to bury people. There is a small township near, and at the front there are large hills, known as the 'Hummocks Range.'

Clarice Davis
Cameron School.

1903.

A REAL DUSTSTORM.

by F. J.

NOW, when in your favoured parts of the country a high wind raises clouds of dust on an unmade road, a fallow paddock, or a sandbank, the nuisance is soon wholly or partially checked by wheat fields, grass paddocks, or scrub. Try and think of a big, sandy, fallow paddock hundreds of miles each way, and extremely dry, and perhaps you will be able to imagine in what huge, dense clouds the dust would gather. That is what the North was like, and no matter which way the wind blew it brought with it tremendous quantities of sand, so that we had severe duststorms at least five days a week on the average.

Now and then, however, the dust seemed to make a special effort, and it is one of those terrible days that I intend to try and picture for you.

The day after lessons began for this year the children in a small northern school had just commenced their afternoon's work when huge banks of dust were seen gathering in the south. The breeze had been blowing from the north-west with moderate force, but suddenly it changed to the south and increased into a fierce gale. Then the dense mass of dust began to approach. Extending as far as the eye could reach, and far more inky than many a thunderstorm, on it came, rolling over and over, and constantly changing colour with the changing light.

Doors and windows were hurriedly closed, and then it was upon us. The sky was free from clouds, but no sign of either sky or land was to be seen. Darker and darker it grew, while the wind whistled through the key holes, and drove the fine particles through every crevice—up through the floor boards, through the ventilators, and under the windows and doors—until we gasped for breath, and felt real pain on our chests every time we breathed.

survival, or in some instances by their ruin. The people of the outback knew much harsher influences than did their friends and relatives in the towns and cities, from whom in time they could be seen to differ intellectually, spiritually, emotionally, and physically.

For in South Australia, the driest State of the driest continent on earth, the outback is more immediate, more accessible than in most other States. The first country townships of the earliest days have in many instances by now become suburbs of Adelaide, but once away from the rolling fecundity of the Mount Lofty Ranges, the lush river flats of the River Murray, or the park-like paddocks and forests of the South-East, the bare bones of the land are soon exposed. It is easy to appreciate that, for the mostly British settlers, the cruelty of drought and the horrors and hazards of dust-storms and bushfires were a shocking and often bitter revelation. Their farming experience in European conditions ill prepared them for the harsh and alien environment of South Australia. Many gave up, finding the land and the droughts impossible to master:

1897.

NORTHERN DUST STORMS.

As I have not seen anything about the dust, in *The Children's Hour*, I thought I would write and tell you about it. The first dust storm was on the 8th of January, and my sister was caught in it. She had our dog with her, but she could not see him at her feet, it was so dark. There was total darkness for ten minutes. The next we had was a beautiful sight as it was coming. We wished our minister, Mr White, had been out here to take it with his camera; it would have been a grand addition to his northern views. The dust was much worse, and lasted longer. There was another last Thursday. The dust has been so bad on the Willochra Plain that it has soaked up all the water in the tanks and dams. We had 350 points of rain this week. Nearly all the cattle and sheep about here are dead.

Lillie Gillis
Boolcunda East.

In 1865 the Surveyor-General, G. W. Goyder, had warned that there was a recognisable rainfall line running from roughly west to east in the Lower North of South Australia, above which the land could sustain only grazing, not cropping. In 1902 this was explained in *The Children's Hour*:

Years ago Mr Goyder, a surveyor, noticed a bush called the salt bush growing in the North. At last he thought this bush grew only where the rain was very light, or not regular. He drew an imaginary line across South Australia, marking off the salt bush. This line has been named after him—Goyder's line of rainfall. You can mark this line on your maps. Start at Port Augusta, follow the railway line as far as the Burra, then across to Morgan. That line will be nearly correct. North and east of it is the drought-stricken country.

Despite Goyder's advice, the sowing, growing and reaping went on in the Upper North of the State, but South Australia's is a capricious climate, and in 1903 the *Hour* gave this gloomy information:

To the east of the range, (The Flinders) however stretches a vast plain. Before the disastrous drought set in this was annually covered with splendid crops and waving grass, and indeed prospered much more than many of the southern districts. But the absence of rain changed all this. For years the crops had been light and last season there were none at all, so that the only way you could tell a paddock from the road was to observe whether it was enclosed by a fence.

The cleared land, stripped of natural vegetation and with no planted crops to hold its red soil together, slowly blew south in great clouds, swept up by the hot north winds of summer:

1903.

DROUGHT-STRICKEN NORTH.

The farmer who lives to the north and east of Goyder's line, in the North, needs a good heart and a mind packed full of hopes. In some years the rain comes down so often that the farmers' hopes are raised. The grass springs up—beautiful grass, fattening grass, green grass; the saltbush puts on a lovely pale-green colour, the seed pods clinging thickly to the stems. Then the horses and cattle have springs in their toes; the farmer's son puts on father's big boots and walks on the young saltbush, just to hear it crack and crunch. The farmer works with a joyful heart—ploughing, sowing, and reaping his crops—sometimes counting his chickens before they are hatched. He will say, as he smokes his pipe at the close of a hard day, 'I will buy a cart and send the children to school, that new dairy shall be built for mother, the buggy shall be painted, and many other things shall be done'.

A few good years and then a drought. What a difference there is! The crops can't grow; the saltbushes are turned into dry sticks, with a few small, tough, dusty leaves clinging to them, the trees lose their fresh colour, and the grass and small plants die off. Then comes the wind. Northern people say there is more wind during drought years. The grass and small bushes being out of the way, the wind catches up the loose soil more easily. The dust rushes along sometimes in clouds, then in whirlwinds, and sometimes like a sea of dust.

The horses seem to have forgotten how to lift up their heads and tails, or to snort and gallop round the paddock when anything strange comes along. Instead of that, they plod slowly round searching for the bits of grass and eatable bushes, fighting the flies all day long. They often swallow a lot of sand, and that kills some of them. The men have to break down branches of sandalwood for food, straw has to be taken off sheds, cut up, and given to the stock. The dams are all dry, and water has to be carted for miles every day. The horses are too poor to go on with any extra work, and the farmer has no money to buy food for them. Sometimes the farmer's wife and children have bread and treacle for breakfast, bread and treacle for dinner, and then, as a change, treacle and bread for tea. The cows give very little milk, and for want of food some go dry.

There are many square miles of land with not even the sign of grass or bush. Some sown paddocks have shown small patches of light green, but you have to stand a long way back to see the green. Farmers have sown for seven or eight years and reaped nothing. Other farmers have reaped just enough to sow next year, and a few lucky ones have reaped a little more than enough for seed.

Such dust storms made life in the drought-affected areas of the North unremittingly uncomfortable and depressing. It took considerable fortitude and stamina to face up to the continual job

1896.

SCHOLARS' CORNER.

A DUSTY DAY.

ALTHOUGH Yunta has no great cricketers or cyclists to break records, still a record was put up here on Friday, April 10th, when we had the biggest, strongest, longest, and worst dust storm that has ever swept over South Australia. The people in the township had to burn lights all day long. The dust started at 9 o'clock in the morning and lasted till 5 o'clock in the evening. The dust was so fine that, even when all windows and doors were shut, it got into the house, and you could not see the other end of the room. It was impossible to set the table to have dinner; all that could be done was to have a piece of bread and walk about the house, holding a handkerchief up to your mouth to keep the dust out. At the railway station the dust was heaped up to about 3 ft high. The railway men had to be taking the dirt off the lines all day to let the trains in. The railway signals were of no use. The porter had to walk down to the train to tell the engine-drivers that the signals were down, and the train could come on. The school was in a terrible state, and it took nearly two hours to clean it. The dust was an inch thick all over the floor. The coachdriver left the township about 9 o'clock in the morning, and only got about a mile out. He could not see the road for the dust. He had two passengers on board. He had to get out of his trap and lead his horses. One of the passengers also got out of the trap and walked behind it. While he was walking along, the cape of his overcoat blew over his head, and while he was taking it off he lost sight of the trap, though it was only a few yards away. The passenger went walking along till he bumped against one of the houses. He asked the people inside where the hotel was, and they told him. He then went along till he got into a verandah, and waited till the coachdriver came and got him. I think you will agree that this beats all previous dust storms.

J. Wack
Yunta.

1929.

THE BREAKING OF THE DROUGHT.

THE breaking of the drought in 1902 I shall never forget to my dying day. I happened to be staying at a big station in my district. All day long a change had been in the air; the glass had been falling lower and lower, and our hopes rising higher and higher. But hopes had been so often raised in the past only to be disappointed that we dared not build much upon them. Over and over again in similar circumstances, the end had proved to be nothing more than a terrific dust-storm, followed by a few points of rain, quite insufficient to do any good at all.

But this time, at last, our hopes were to be fulfilled. As the storm drew towards us across the dusty plain, accompanied by peals of thunder and vivid flashes of lightning, we could presently see the rain descending in torrents from the bosom of the overhanging clouds. And at last it burst upon us, and, better still, continued all through the night. Since that night, I have always felt that the world can contain no other sound or smell which can compare with the sound and the smell of the rain at the breaking of the drought. For it was, indeed, the breaking of the drought.

That storm was followed by others, and in a few weeks' time an almost incredible change had taken place over the face of the country. Before the rain came, doleful prophets had said that, when it did come, it would be too late, that the whole surface of the soil had been destroyed in the long years of drought, and the grass seed must all have perished long ago; but all such gloomy predictions were falsified; and, within a couple of months of that first rain, almost the whole of our district was green with grass and herbage. And during the year of plenty which followed, in some paddocks, which during the drought were as bare as a macadamized road, one rode through grass high enough to tie over the withers of one's horse, so fertile is the soil when the rain does come.

(*A Parson in the Australian Bush.*)
C. L. S. Matthews.

of cleaning houses, clothing, and children, as often as three times in a week during the hottest summer months, helped by nothing more sophisticated than tubs, mops, brushes, brooms and dusters, with water, used very sparingly. For a pioneer bush woman, the well-kept appearance of her house and her family was an endless challenge and a source of great pride. The high standards these women maintained are apparent in many—though not all—of the school photographs included in the *Hour*. Spick and span, the boys in starched collars and polished boots, and the girls in starched white dresses and pinafores (and sometimes starched hats as well!), they stand in rows—sometimes as few as seven or eight children—against an almost identical backdrop—a small stone school building, a corrugated iron watertank, and perhaps a straggle of thirsty little gum trees, set starkly in a dusty plain.

Articles in the *Hour* celebrated the end of droughts too. The children who lived in the city and were unacquainted with the dramatic change the rains bring to the outback must have marvelled to read of it. But to anyone who has seen the flowering of the desert, such an account in the *Hour* is a reminder of this miracle.

Personal tragedy was common in the bush, and in *The Children's Hour* stories of heroism and human suffering lost nothing in the telling, and no details were thought too gruesome for the child-readers. Such things were facts of life which many of their contemporaries, and possibly they themselves, might very well experience.

July 1893.

A BUSH TRAGEDY.

The writer of this story lives on a station called 'Chandada' on the West Coast of SA and as an extremely sad and pathetic incident occurred here about four months ago, the facts of which as yet have not been published, I will now try and tell them to my young friends.

Perhaps some of my readers may remember the intense heat of the 23rd and 24th of December last year (1892), as by so doing they can thoroughly understand the terrible agony experienced by a child lost in the scrub, deprived of water and food.

My father was awakened about midnight on 28 December by a messenger, stating that a little boy aged three years and eight months had wandered away from home and could not be found. My father and others started as early as possible next morning to search. They had a distance of about eighteen miles to go first. Some went out on horseback and some walking; they had also blacktrackers. They followed the child's tracks for about eight miles out and my father picked up one of his little boots which he had laced up on one side. They could see where the poor little thing had fallen over porcupine bushes. He must have wandered about all night, as they could see where he had laid down in several places but could not rest for the ants. One black and a lubra who were with my father, were untiring in their efforts in searching even crawling along on their hands and knees where the tracks could scarcely be seen. At last at about 6 o'clock in the evening the lubra discovered him, called out to my father, who in turn called out to the little child's father. He came running to them and picked him up in his arms, but the poor little darling was quite dead, and just covered with ants. He had come back within two or three miles of his home in his wanderings.

We should never have recognised him again. His face was all bruised and scratched with falling down and the little foot from which the boot came off was bruised and cut with the porcupine and sticks.

The father and mother took him down to Streaky Bay, about thirty miles distant from here, and he was buried in the cemetery.

Maggie Godlee
Chandada Station.

1896.

A LOST CHILD.

R. H. H.
Port Germein.

On Wednesday, April 22nd, 1896, David Pillion, a little boy 3½ years of age, son of Mr M. Pillion, of Baroota North, was lost in the bush.

It is supposed that he left home with the intention of meeting his brothers on their way back from the Baroota Whim school, and being too early, and missing the children, had kept going on and on in the direction in which he expected his brothers to come.

On the children's return from school without him, the mother and other members of the family became alarmed, and at once started to search in the scrub and bushes in the paddocks round the school, thinking perhaps he had lain down and was sleeping.

Hour after hour went by, and all through the night the mother's voice could be heard calling 'Davie'. But they called and hunted and searched in vain, for the morning came, and there was no trace of the lost child.

On Thursday morning, as the children met for school, they were formed into search parties to assist the older folk in again scouring the scrub where the child was supposed to be, when word came that he had passed a farmhouse several miles away about sunset the night before.

A stray child, 3½ years old, several miles from home, no hat, no boots, crying for mother, and yet some folks are so intent upon minding their own business that they let him pass away into the scrub or into the swamps, to wander alone all through the dark night!

On Thursday many of the neighbours joined in the search, and, with the assistance of two black trackers, he was traced into the Winninowie swamps, where it was feared he might have fallen into a creek, or been drowned by the rising tide. However, as the tracks of his little bare feet showed that he had safely crossed the swamps, the party had strong hopes of quickly picking him up. But after passing the swamps, owing to the hard and stony nature of the ground, the greatest difficulty was experienced by the trackers.

For several miles now, to the eyes of the white folks, not a trace of the little bare feet was to be seen; and had it not been for the black trackers the party would no doubt have worked on the old theory, that any person when lost in the bush will keep travelling round and round in a circle. If this had been done, the child would probably never have been found alive. But whether it was owing to the keenness of their eyesight or to the instinct peculiar to their race, the blacks kept pushing onward, slowly but surely, mile after mile, until at last a patch of soft sand would be crossed, where the little footmarks would convince the anxious searchers that they were not on a false trail.

On Friday morning at daybreak Mounted Constable Blake, of Port Germein, with about sixty others, took up the search, and it was determined that, if possible, the little fellow should be found before many more hours had passed. He was soon traced into Nectar Brook Creek. On the north side of this creek a vermin-proof fence is erected, supposed to be proof against wild dogs. Owing to the hard and stony country here, not a sign could be found of his having crossed this fence. Many of the searchers were of the opinion that after having travelled so far without food or water it would be almost impossible for him to climb over it. Again strong hopes were entertained of finding him in the creek, and the party were not satisfied until every yard of ground and every tree and bush along the creek had been examined; but though the footmarks were very distinct where he had crossed it, the child himself was not to be found.

On Friday evening, when the sun went down, the blacks had lost the tracks, and the party having searched in vain were almost disheartened. The poor father's head was bowed down with sorrow, and the poor mother's grief was all the more heartrending because it could not find vent in tears. It was most pitiful to see them as the night set in, and they knew that their child would have to pass his third night out in the cold, unwatched and uncared for, except by that kind Providence who at all times appears to watch over and protect even the most helpless of His creatures.

While the party were searching the creek, the black trackers had also disappeared, and no one seemed to know where they were. But, as the darkness set in, they returned with the welcome news that they had picked up the tracks at some distance on the north side of the vermin-proof fence. As it was now too dark to follow the trail, it was arranged that fires should be lighted by those who camped out. Many from a distance were kindly invited to stay the night at farmhouses close by.

On Saturday morning at daybreak, according to arrangement, the two Port Germein trackers started on horseback from Mr Willoughby's, near Limestone Well, to try and pick up the tracks on a cross road about two miles north of where they were last seen.

The trackers, who were followed by a number of the search party, after riding several miles, dismounted, left their horses on the road, and went through the paddocks northward. The party behind, expecting that the tracks had been picked up, followed, but for some distance the ground was so hard that even the footmarks of the trackers could not be seen.

Still following until the ground became softer, at first appeared the footmarks of the trackers, then straight along between them the faint print of the little bare foot. This was followed to Mr Moseley's vermin-proof fence running east of Limestone Well. This fence was even more formidable than the two others already passed; surely it would stop him! No sign of his having got over it; and the ground again being too hard for the trackers several hours were spent in vain searching back among the bushes and trying to pick up the tracks. Still he was not there, and he had not turned back. The fence was cut, and again forward, across Horrock's Creek, a couple of miles further north, and there, about eighteen miles from home, was the lost child, in a hollow place in the ground, lying flat on his back, one arm across his forehead, the other hand holding the end of his brace, which he was chewing. He had his eyes open, and appeared to be quietly watching the party, as though he was himself afraid of being seen. Mounted Constable Blake picked him up and gave him small sips of weak brandy and water, while some of the others lit a fire, and made a big smoke to signal the glad news to the rest of the eighty to one hundred men and boys, who were searching the hills and creeks and flats for miles around.

As the glad news was signalled, a great shout went up. The father jumped for joy, while to the mother it seemed as if her boy was given back from the dead.

The poor little chap, though quite sensible, was just about done up, and, if not found, would probably have ended his short journey of life alone where he had lain down, having been three days and three nights without food or water. Though he had travelled about eighteen miles or more, across creeks and ditches, and had by some means got over three vermin-proof fences, capped with barbed wire, and no doubt travelled part of the distance by night, he had gone all the way, as nearly as possible, in the one direction.

It is now about four weeks since Davie was found, and, though for about ten days he was unable to walk, with the attentive treatment of a kind father and mother he has now fully recovered, though no doubt he will carry through life, like a horrible dream, the remembrance of his long, rough and lonely journey.

It is in the accounts of such searches that the earliest references to Aborigines appear in the *Hour.* Their amazing skill at tracking turned many a potential tragedy into a celebration. They are the unsung heroes of several successful search stories in the *Hour*, and readers today may find it strange that so little gratitude for their efforts is expressed. There is no evidence of animosity or intentional cruelty toward Aborigines in these passages. The attitude of settlers from any European country towards the natives of the country they were settling would at that time almost certainly have been the same as that of the early settlers in Australia. It was taken for granted that the black trackers would bring their knowledge and skills to the aid of the white man, to make possible these joyous reunions.

The Aborigines who drift in and out of descriptions of outback life in the earliest issues of *The Children's Hour* are sometimes regarded rather like animals—useful, but inferior, or curiosities to be observed with indulgent patronage:

> Let me tell you something about the little black children in our country. We white children do not play with them because they are very rough. They have little boomerangs which they throw at each other. They often throw stones at little birds.

So wrote Gertrude Johannsen once more.

In 1916 a woman, by then quite old, recalled her first Australian Christmas, fifty years earlier:

> In those days the blackfellows were many, and they often came to the station. Once or twice they took some flour and sugar from an outlying hut, but on the whole they behaved well. Sometimes they camped near the station, and at night would show us a weird corroboree, which made my blood run cold when I first saw it. A few sticks of tobacco was the payment we gave them for the night's entertainment.

There are ironies and pathos too, when lines like these appear in an article about Penola, entitled 'Our Own Country':

> The Aborigines are all extinct, the last one 'Yallum Jackie', who was king of his tribe, died in the Adelaide Lunatic Asylum quite recently.

1895.

FACTS AND FANCIES.

Cymro.

MANY children came down from the country schools to see the exhibition of the Chamber of Manufacturers. Of course there were other attractions and one little girl who was gazing open-mouthed at the bronze statue of our Queen Victoria, exclaimed with disgust, 'Well, I never thought our Queen was a black woman.'

He lived for many years on Yallum Estate, and was cared for by the late Mr John Riddock.

It is, then, unusual to find the Aborigines portrayed with any obvious admiration in the early publications of the *Hour*, but this description of duck-hunting seems to have been written by someone with not only a knowledge of the custom but a respect for the Aborigines too:

1896.

HOW THE BLACKFELLOWS CATCH WILD DUCKS.

One has often heard the expression 'going on a wild goose chase', which means trying to do something when there is very little likelihood of being successful. I should say that looking for mushrooms in the month of February would be 'going on a wild goose chase'.

'Chasing wild geese' may not be a very profitable occupation, but the tribes on the River Darling have found that hunting wild ducks not only affords them considerable amusement, but often provides their 'lubras' and 'piccaninnies' with an excellent supper.

At certain seasons of the year immense flocks of geese and ducks sweep down the Darling, never venturing in their flight too far from the stream. On such occasions the tribes who dwell on the banks of the river are all alive with excitement, yet their plans are carried out quietly and without fuss. There is no banging of guns to frighten away the timid birds. The dark inhabitants of the Australian bush resort to all kinds of cunning devices to procure food, but the following plan shows a great deal of ingenuity, and requires much skill and patience. A suitable spot on the river having been chosen, where a gum tree grows on each side, a net is suspended by a rope from tree to tree till the lower end of its meshes just touches the water. The rope is not made fast to the trees, but each end is held by a patient blackfellow, who takes care to be so hidden that the ever watchful eye of the wild duck cannot by any chance perceive him.

A number of the tribe now make their way up the stream, keeping well away from the banks. As soon as a flock of ducks is observed the blacks cautiously approach the water, and commence to drive the birds down the river towards the net. At first one would imagine the wary game would escape by soaring over the obstacle, so high is their flight. But no. The natives take advantage of the extreme timidity of the poor birds, and just at the right moment cause them, by a cunning device, to swoop right into the trap laid for them. How do they do this?

Well, listen. The wild duck is extremely afraid of its natural enemy the hawk; but as this bird of prey only attacks its quarry on the wing, the timid ducks, on perceiving their pursuer, make a rapid descent to seek refuge in the water. The natives are well aware of this habit, and have devised a plan to make the foolish duck believe that a real hawk is pursuing them. The men who are stationed at the net have provided themselves with several pieces of hard flat triangular-shaped bark. These they hurl into the air right above the flock of ducks, just as they are approaching the net. Their dexterity in throwing the boomerang enables them to cause the pieces of bark to somewhat resemble the quivering of the hawk when it poises on the wing. In order to carry the deception still further, the blacks imitate the peculiar cry of the hawk. Thinking their real enemy is pursuing them, down swoop the whole flock of ducks right into the meshes of the trap. The top rope is immediately let go, and the net is allowed to fall completely over the bewildered birds. The natives, who are all excellent swimmers from their childhood, at once dive into the water, and each secures a couple of the half-drowned victims. These, when killed, are thrust, feathers and all, into a heap of hot ashes; and when sufficiently cooked are pulled out fizzling and spluttering. The burnt skin and feathers are then scraped off, and the delicious morsels are eaten with considerable relish.

J.A.K.

An article included in a publication of 1921 is an early attempt at acknowledging the white man's debt to Aborigines and emphasising their loyalty.

March 1921.

THE AUSTRALIAN BLACKFELLOW.

There may be some of our readers who have never seen any of the blackfellows whose forefathers were once the only folk living in South Australia. Every year they are getting fewer in the settled districts. To see them in large numbers, living as they did when the first white settlers landed, one must travel far into the backblocks of this State.

Learned men have been puzzled to know where the blackfellows lived before they settled in Australia. As they were unable to write, they have left no history books to tell us.

In several other countries where the British have made settlements, they have had to fight long and costly wars with the native people. This was not so in Australia. Our blacks were not very troublesome to the early settlers. Australia has not had a native war such as was fought against the high-spirited Maoris in New Zealand, or the Kaffirs in South Africa, or the Red Indians in North America.

Several of the explorers received noble help from their black comrades. Kennedy, who, in 1848, led a party to Cape Yorke [*sic*] Peninsula, took with him a black boy named Jackey. When his master fell, speared by savage blackfellows, Jackey kept the enemies at bay while he buried Kennedy's body in a shallow grave. In the old church of St James, Sydney, there is a marble tablet, telling of brave Jackey's deed. Edward John Eyre, during his terrible journey along the shores of the Great Australian Bight, would have probably died had it not been for the help of his black servant, Wylie. Another great Australian explorer, the late Lord Forrest, of Western Australia, had a black companion named Tommy Windich (*-dik*), who travelled with his master for thousands of miles over unknown country. Lord Forrest saw that Tommy did not suffer want in his old age, and when the faithful fellow died, his master placed over his grave, near the shores of Esperance Bay, a tombstone, on which are carved boomerangs and spears, and a short account of Tommy's deeds.

The first serious articles about Aborigines had mostly concentrated on the life of tribal Aborigines—how they dressed, hunted, and crafted their weapons and artefacts. They were portrayed very much as the 'Noble Savage'. But gradually this changed:

1927.

THE BLACK TRACKER.

Is the Australian blackfellow intelligent? Some people have said that he is not, because, they add, before white people came to this country the blackfellows were unable to build houses or grow their food; they

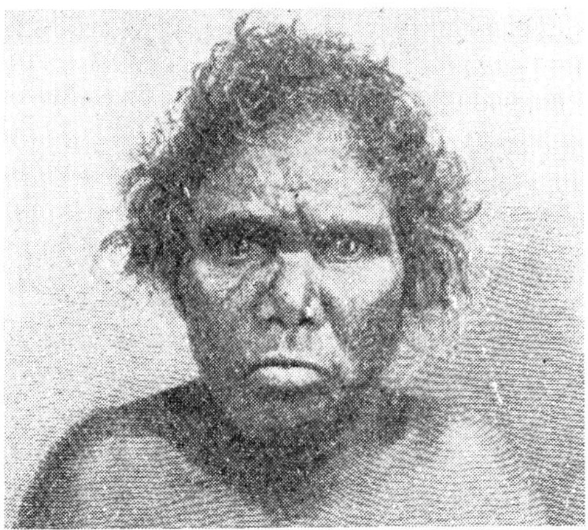

Top: *1921. An Elderly Blackfellow.*

Middle: *1921. An Australian Black Woman.*

Above: *1921. A Blackfellow's Grave.*
In some parts of Australia the dead bodies were placed on a rude platform.

(*These illustrations were reproduced from* The Picturesque Atlas of Australia.)

wandered over the land, hunting the wild animals, and never remaining long in one place.

If, however, these fault-finding people were dumped down from an aeroplane somewhere, say, in Central Australia, they would probably perish from hunger and thirst, whereas a blackfellow, if dropped down in the same country, would find his way to the nearest waterhole, and live on the animals he caught while reaching it.

Here is a story about a clever black tracker. It recently appeared with the letters A. H. T. It is retold in simpler words. Many years ago Freddy, a blackfellow, was paid to destroy dingoes on a sheep station near the River Darling. On the same station there were other workers who trapped the dingoes, but Freddy did not catch them in traps; he followed up the wily dingoes and shot them.

One evening Freddy returned to the station and told us that he fired at a dingo and hit it on its left hind leg, but that it had managed to get away into the scrub. As it was late, Freddy said, he had not followed the dingo, but next morning he would be on its tracks, and then there would be the end of Mr Dingo.

I was very curious to see the way Freddy tracked his prey, so next morning I went with him. Soon after we started he picked up the tracks of the dingo, though, I must confess, that I was unable to see a trace of them. I asked Freddy if he was sure that he was on the dingo's tracks.

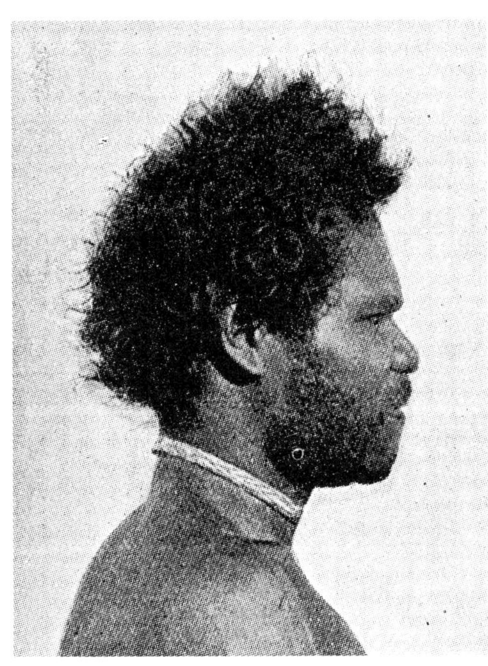

1925.
Young Man of Coastal Tribe.
Note the cane necklet.
(Photographs marked Spencer and Gillen are taken from Across Australia *by Sir Baldwin Spencer and F. J. Gillen.)*

'Yes, boss', he answered, and, pointing near the trunk of a tree, he said, 'Two and a half hours ago dingo rested near this tree'. It therefore seemed that Freddy was able not only to follow the tracks, but to tell the time the dingo was near a certain tree. As we went along I pointed out several trees—they are mostly the sheaoaks in this country—and asked, 'How long since dingo passed here, Freddy?'

Freddy's answers were, 'Two hours', 'One hour', 'Half-hour', 'Twenty minutes', as the case might be.

Then Freddy halted, and, in a quiet tone, said, 'Boss, you wait here. Dingo passed this tree only five minutes ago'.

I halted, and Freddy went on quietly alone. A minute or two later the report of his gun was heard. I went forward and saw the dead dingo, and, sure enough, its left hind leg had been slightly wounded. Freddy's wonderful eyes had noticed that in limping along its left foot had left a faint impression.

March 1925.

A NOBLE BLACKFELLOW.

The following story tells about a noble blackfellow who, some fifteen years ago, was living in the Northern Territory. He was known by the name of Neighbour. The white man who probably gave it to him must have guessed well the nature of this blackfellow, for he was the right sort of neighbour to be living near a person in trouble.

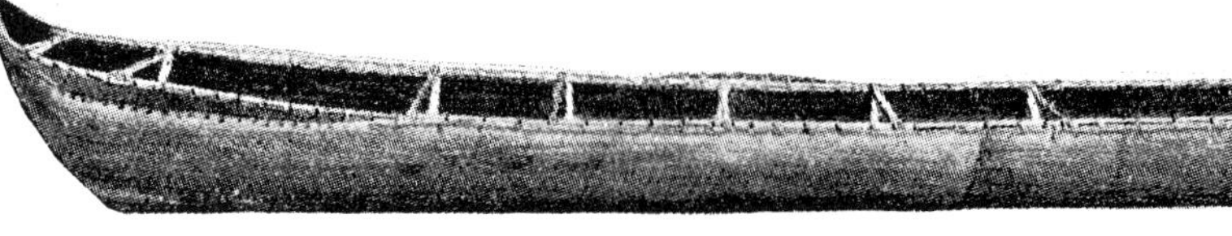

1925.
A Bark Canoe Used by the Coastal Tribes in the Northern Territory.
Spencer and Gillen.

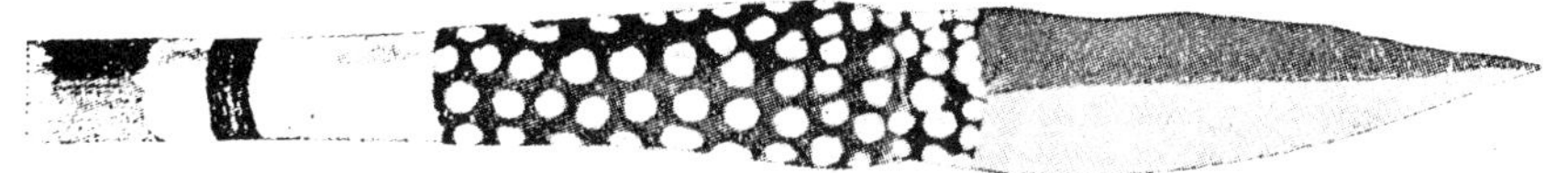

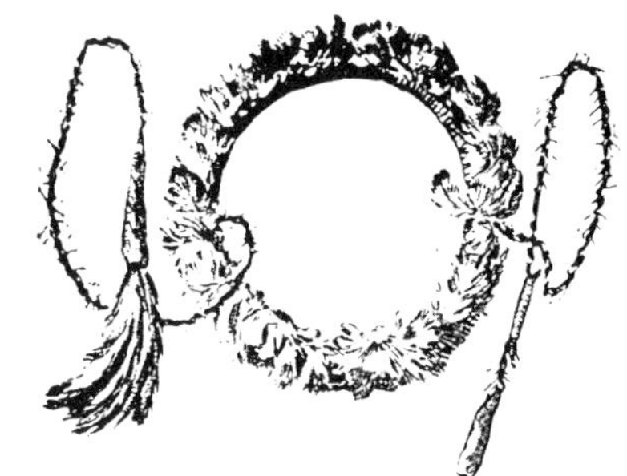

1925.
Decorated Spear-head Used by a Tribe in Northern Territory.
Spencer and Gillen.

1925.
Armlet Decorated with Cockatoo Feathers.
Worn by Blackfellows in the Northern Territory.
Spencer and Gillen.

Neighbour was one of a party of four blackfellows who had been brought into Pine Creek to stand their trial in a court of law. They had broken into a lonely hut on a cattle station, 230 miles away. Poor, simple blackfellows! They knew no more about right and wrong, according to a white man's way of thinking, than a wild dog knows when it snatches at a leg-of-mutton hung on a tree by a traveller's tent.

However, the law must be obeyed, and it was proved that the four blackfellows had broken into the hut. Three of them were given a slight punishment, but the judge pardoned Neighbour, because while he was being brought to the court he had done a noble deed.

The four prisoners had been arrested by Mounted-constable Johns. To prevent their escaping he had padlocked a chain around each of their necks, and then fastened together all the other ends of the chains so that the four blackfellows were bound each to each.

The party travelled many miles and reached the River Roper, which they found was swollen with a high flood. Mr Johns unfastened the chains binding them to each other, made each coil his chain around his neck, and ordered them to swim across the river while he on horseback swam after them. The blackfellows, who had been reared in a country of long rivers, were able to swim like ducks, and they soon reached the other bank.

But the trooper was not so fortunate. His horse, caught in the strong current, was turned over with its rider. When Mr Johns came up to the surface of the water, he was stunned by a kick from the frantic horse.

The man, senseless, was swept down the roaring flood and in a few minutes would have been drowned, but Neighbour, who was watching Johns from the bank, saw at a glance what was about to happen to his captor. Neighbour ran along the bank, coiling his chain around his neck as he did so. When he came near the drowning man, he plunged into the river, and after a hard struggle in the water was able to bring the trooper to the bank. Nor did that finish the act of kindness, for Neighbour ran at full speed over a distance of three miles to get other assistance for Johns.

1925.
Australian Aborigines in Chains.

So it was that at the trial we have already read about, the judge praised Neighbour for doing a noble deed and allowed him to go unpunished. Moreover the judge said that the King himself would be delighted if he heard the story of how Neighbour had saved the trooper's life.

The matter did not end at the court. The late Sir George Reid, who then represented Australia in London, told King George about Neighbour's brave deed and the King was pleased to confer the Albert Medal upon Neighbour.

This is a much-prized medal, which was first given by Queen Victoria to mark a brave deed performed in saving life 'at Sea or on Land.' Neighbour was the first Australian blackfellow to receive this distinction.

In March 1892, at the end of the summer, an article in 'News of the Day'—a regular column in the *Hour*—strikes a grimly familiar note:

During the second week in March the hills to the east of Adelaide have been blazing with very big bushfires. On the night of the 7th the scene was very grand, the darkness of the night allowing the blaze to be easily seen. These fires have been burning in the direction of Norton's Summit and have kept the people busy in their attempts to prevent the mischief from spreading. Marble Hill, the Governor's country seat has not escaped, for we have heard of Lord Kintore and his household turning out to help in beating out a fire in their neighbourhood, a task which is by no means a cool or easy one.

(Another Governor of South Australia, Sir Robert George, was not so fortunate and only just managed to escape with his household and family when the Marble Hill 'country seat' was almost totally destroyed by bushfire about seventy years later.) Fire is an integral, even essential part of Australia's character, and the destruction it brings has been part of the bushman's experience since the first settlers arrived.

1889.

A BUSHFIRE ON YORKE PENINSULA.

(*An Excerpt.*)

That last cruel fork of fire carried away with it the sight of those sweet blue eyes, and left behind a terrible, terrible agony, that the poor girl bore with clenched teeth and hands, a pain so great that she could not reply to the loud shouts of Katie, Katie, where are you? that, in the voices of father and brothers, came over the bare and blackened field.

They found her there, her face pressed against old Barney's head, her hands, for support, clasped around his neck, half fainting, but afraid to stir, for, for her, the light was gone for ever. Lift her tenderly, father, brothers lead the way to where a mother waits for her child. Home and Possessions were saved but alas for that which is dearer than all!

They took her to Adelaide and left her at the hospital, but all the clever doctors could not give back to Katie what the fire had taken away, and though she suffered terribly, when she knew that she would be blind for life, she tried hard to be patient, that her sorrow might not make it worse for the dear father and mother. She was helped in her endeavours to be good by a kind lady who came to see her to talk to her and teach her how to do many useful things with her hands. At last this lady persuaded Mr Dean to let his little daughter go for a year to the Blind School where she proved to be quick to learn and so ready to help others that when she went home her cheerful ways were sadly missed by all the poor sightless friends she left behind. And now the neighbours say that no one seems to live such a busy, happy life as Katie Dean, for she has learned the secret that it is only the idle useless people who are really unhappy and that the more one does to make other people glad the lighter one's own heart will be.

One of the early Australian classics, popular with both Australian and English readers, was a book entitled *The Recollections of Geoffrey Hamlyn in Australia*, written by Henry Kingsley. His account of a bushfire, taken from that book, was included in the *Hour* in 1906. It has been revealed, by a recent editor of Henry Kingsley's works, that he was advised to avoid any coarseness of expression or vulgarity in *Geoffrey Hamlyn* so as to make the work acceptable in the drawing rooms of the time! This may account for the 'un-Australian' flavour of the story. Here is an excerpt:

> There was nothing much to be done but to sit in the verandah, watching and hoping for a thunderstorm. James and I sat there late, not talking much. We knew that if we were to be burnt out our loss would be very heavy, but we thanked God that even were we to lose everything it would not be irreparable, and that we should still be wealthy. Our blood mares and our racing stock were our greatest anxiety.

How different such a story is from those narratives based on personal experience which made up so much of *The Children's Hour* and gave it much of its character:

1916.

MY FIRST CHRISTMAS IN SOUTH AUSTRALIA.

On a hot November day, more than fifty years ago, I first came to Adelaide. I had left my parents in Scotland, to work on a new sheep station, owned by my uncle, in South Australia.

I stayed for a week with my aunt at Fullarton, where I remembered having my first taste of loquats from a beautiful tree in the garden there. Then I crossed St Vincent's Gulf and was landed at my uncle's sheep station.

Several years before I came to South Australia my uncle had started this sheep-run on Southern Yorke Peninsula. It was a very wild land then, and for several years afterwards. Before I begin the real story I intended to write, I might tell my readers something about this country.

In those days the blackfellows were many, and they often came to the station. Once or twice they took some flour and sugar from an outlying hut, but on the whole they behaved well. Sometimes they camped near the station, and at night would show us a weird corroboree, which made my blood run cold when I first saw it. A few sticks of tobacco was the payment we gave them for the night's entertainment.

But to me, fresh from Scotland, the most wonderful sight was to see the flocks of kangaroos that bounded along over the flat country. In what we called the 'whip-stick' mallee were many swift wallabies, and in many parts of the limestone country were to be seen the deep burrows of shy wombats.

The walls of the station house were built of pieces of timber sawn flat, and over them was a roof of thick thatch. In summer the thatch made a very cool house. The galvanized iron now used for roofs makes much hotter rooms, but in summer, as will be seen farther on in this story, the iron is safer. The rooms were whitewashed, both inside and out, and the floors were of earth which had been frequently sprinkled with water and thus made hard.

Well, to go on with my story, I had lived on this out-of-the-way station for more than a month when Christmas Day came. I was feeling a bit homesick. The flat country around me looked so strange. The grass was dry, and the earth looked brown and baked, and I wished I was back on the bonnie blue hills of Scotland.

Christmas Day came in hot, one might almost say red-hot. On the station we had made up our minds to have a real old-fashioned Christmas dinner. The cook had mixed a big Christmas pudding, which was to be boiled over a fire lit some ten or twelve yards away from the house. I was told to attend this fire, and watch the pudding boil, while the cook baked the meat in an oven in the kitchen.

The day seemed to be getting hotter, when my fire of mallee sticks was blazing fiercely, and the pudding in the pot was bobbing up and down in the boiling water. I looked down the plain and saw a whirlwind start. On it moved, whirling round and round like a graceful dancer in a ballroom. It seemed to be coming towards the house, but that did not trouble me, because the country was wide enough for it to miss us and pass on.

However, I was wrong, for the whirlwind came at me like an express train, swept over my fire and the house, and went onward towards the south of the run. Little thinking of what mischief had been done, I began to place the scattered sticks together to rebuild the fire.

Soon, hearing a crackling sound, I looked up at the house. The thatch was burning in two or three places. In less than a minute it was a blazing mass, and the cook had run out to see what was the matter. In a quarter of an hour the house was in flames, and our Christmas dinner inside was much 'over-done'.

We had the Christmas pudding left, and ate it to pretend that we would have our Christmas dinner, but it was not a very pleasant one. I shall always remember my first Christmas in Australia, and how that wandering whirlwind spoiled our dinner and burnt down the station-house.

Personal anecdotes have generally provided the raw material which is smoothed, shaped, and embellished in the telling and retelling, and passed down through families, generation by generation, to become legend. The stories may ultimately bear little resemblance to the original tale, except that an essential basic message will be there.

Some of the 'bush' stories in the *Hour* are told with a simplicity and artlessness which is reminiscent of the naivety of folk tales:

January 1892.

A TEAMSTER'S EXPERIENCE.

(*A True Story.*)

In the year 1840 my father was travelling with a load of copper from the Burra to Port Adelaide. When he reached the River Light, just where the new Lenswood bridge now spans it, he had a very strange adventure. Soon after sunset one very hot summer day, the bullocks were unyoked and turned out to rest and feed, while my father gathered some sticks of wood, lit a fire and boiled his billy.

The tea was soon made, and with a large pannican of tea and a piece of damper, he made an excellent supper. (A damper is bread made without either yeast or powder, and baked in hot ashes.) He then rolled himself in a blanket and laid (sic) down at a safe distance from the fire, intending to sleep for an hour or two. Being very tired with his long day's work, he over slept himself, and in the meantime the bullocks wandered off. When he awoke he set out to look for them, leaving his mate at the camp to bake another damper. As he followed the bullock track through the scrub, he cut down some long supple branches from the trees to provide a new lot of whip handles, which were greatly needed. Just as he was in the act of cutting one, he heard a rustling in the bushes behind him on the dead leaves that were strewn all around.

On turning his head in that direction he beheld a terrible sight. There were two furry animals, about 5 ft in length, standing erect on their long powerful hind legs and thick tails, while the forelegs were small and appeared more useful as hands than for walking, and from a kind of pocket below the breast of one of them two bright eyes were peeping. They were looking at him as if they wondered what business he had in their part of the scrub. Father did not know what the animals were, and in his fright, he thought they were quite big enough to kill and eat him. He ran to a tree, so that if they chased him he could climb it and get beyond their reach, but they just stood gazing quietly at him. At length, my father clapped his hands and shouted, this startled them, and they hopped off into the scrub. When he got back to the camp he described the animals to his mate, who, looking very wise, said with a laugh,'Oh! they were only kangaroos'.

Father has seen many kangaroos since then, and often hunted them with dogs, for their skins are valuable and their tails when well boiled make very good soup, but he was never frightened by them again.

Agnes Gasmier
Finniss Point.

Despite many changes which have come to the outback, there is probably no part of South Australian life where so many values remain unchanging and unchanged:

1897.

A DROVER'S LIFE.

Not withstanding the trials and discomforts of a drover's life, there is much in it that recommends it to strong and healthy youth. If you look about you on a sale day in large market towns, such as the Burra or Adelaide, you will no doubt be able to see many drovers near the sale-yards, of all ages from youth upward. They are unmistakable with their top-boots and leggings and their stock-whips.

'Which would you sooner travel with—horses, cattle, or sheep?' I asked a drover of experience.

'With cattle', replied he, 'for when we've had them on the road for a few days they'll settle down and will hardly require any watching'.

The cattle drover must know the best roads or tracks to take, where water may be obtained, and also the best camping places. For the first few nights after leaving the station—their home—the cattle are very restless, and the drover and his men get very little sleep, for the mob requires careful watching, but by-and-by the cattle will settle down, and when camping-time comes they contentedly lie down and rest till sunrise. On a cold frosty night a drover will sometimes rouse up one of the fat cattle and will lay his blanket in the warm place where the beast had been lying, and will soon be comfortably asleep, while the poor bullock will move sleepily off to another place with a grunt, as much as to say, 'That's very kind, I'm sure!' If the cattle have been long without water and they approach a creek which has perhaps been set running by a storm, then they are off, and it is useless to try to stop them.

The sheep drover must travel more slowly, and he must have one or two good dogs with him. If the flock to be sent to market is very large it is generally divided into smaller flocks, each in charge of a drover. When a flock is about to pass through a run notice must be sent to the owner, who generally sends a boundary rider to see the shepherd safely through; for if by chance some of the station sheep were near the track the travellers might get mixed, or 'boxed' and this would necessitate the whole flock being drafted, that is to say, one lot sorted from the other, which, of course, would cause a great loss of time, besides a considerable amount of trouble.

Again, in travelling through wild-dog country the drovers must watch very carefully during the night. Some drovers take a light kind of fence with them, and if they camp in an open place they are then able to make a light yard within which to pen their flock. But sheep droving is very tedious and generally very dusty work, and it requires great patience and good temper to be successful.

A mob of horses is very hard to manage until a good distance from home, as sometimes a knowing horse will suddenly double round, and, before the drover knows what is the matter, the whole mob will be on the road back, the poor drovers galloping after them, and the Pack horses at the rear kicking up their heels as much as to say 'Here's some jolly fun!' In this way the drover will sometimes have to travel ten or fifteen miles before he gets his mob well in hand again.

The knowledge of the bushman is no myth and *The Children's Hour*, by depicting South Australian country life in so many forms over so many years, brings forth some of the wisdom implanted there. We begin to see how, over a period of many years, a pattern for bush life has been imprinted through the tough school of experience, through trials and errors—as well as successes.

The truths learnt and passed on by the early bushmen will not be quickly abandoned, nor forgotten.

CHAPTER FOUR

NATURE

> We anchored in Rapid Bay, in front of the most beautiful prospect imaginable . . . A party from the vessel went on shore and on their return gave a most enchanting account of the country, which everywhere resembled a gentleman's park—grass growing in the greatest luxuriance, the most beautiful flowers in abundance and the birds of splendid plumage.

So wrote Mrs Robert Thomas in her diary while on board the *Africaine* which reached South Australia in November 1836. Ten days later, at Holdfast Bay, she wrote with the same enthusiasm for these new surroundings where she was to make her home:

> The birds here are of beautiful plumage. White and black cockatoos were in abundance, the former with a large yellow and orange coloured crest, sometimes pink. Parrots, or rather parakeets as they would be called in England, for they were very, very small, were of every variety of colour. Also there were wild ducks and flocks of geese, with occasionally a black swan flying.

This strange land on the other side of the world brought the first settlers countless new experiences, which included the enjoyment of new flora and fauna.

A sense of excitement and optimism rippled through their letters and diaries. They would often comment on the beauty of the land, the 'park-like' landscape, wishing that their near and dear in England could enjoy it too. Occasionally some were disappointed to find depressing wind-swept sandhills, and for others the summer was almost unbearably hot. But most people seemed eager to discover the country and enjoy all it had to offer. The Adelaide Hills quickly became the most popular place for walks, picnics, and family outings, and appreciation of nature seems to have been a characteristic of the early colonists, whether it was the simple pleasure of day-to-day observation or serious scientific study.

There was an economic value in this. In places where the right information about the nature of the land had first been gathered, agriculture and horticulture, and even towns and buildings, were more likely to be prosperous.

1898.

THROUGH MY SPECTACLES.
THE SOUTH-EAST PLAINS.

By M. C.

THREE huge columns of blue-black smoke curl and ascend, and ascend and curl, as it were in dumb protest against the flames below, which are hissing and crackling as they devour the green shrubs.

This cleared land is very fertile in places. In the last season from cleared land on these plains 20 bushels was not the highest yield by far. Behind the smoke is a broad orange belt, softening into old gold, and then into a splendid yellow-green. This belt stretches out for miles on each side, and blended in with it, streaking and splashing it on the one side, is a mass of brown flame, while on the other side a mixture of purple and ruby strive to darken its glow. As I look it changes, ever changes, and by-and-by the great world-painter's colours will be exhausted, and the brush laid down and the canvas veiled, and we shall say, 'Lo, the night cometh!'

Already my ears catch the swish of w high overhead, and looking up, I watch one of the sights which I shall always associate with these south-eastern plains.

You remember the hills I wrote of last February? Well, they are behind me, and from them in the day time certain birds fly across to the plains. They are happy hunting grounds for them. Driving along in the cool morning air, it is no uncommon sight to see half a dozen large eagles soaring and circling over the plains. There the rabbits have less shelter, and are easier to catch, and there also the young lambs are bleating. But the magpies are the most constant frequenters of the plains, and at eventide they begin to think of their homes on the range, and fly back there again.

Three sail by. Now here's a regular flight, quite twenty. Far away are a straggling company; you can count them one by one as they pass. Again come three pairs. For a quarter of an hour or more they fly overhead, all on swiftest wings of speed, as if they knew the 'sunset gold' would soon be changed to 'twilight grey', and wanted to lay claim to good conduct by getting home before dark.

It is a pretty sight in the calm of the evening to watch those rushing wings, and to catch now and again the short warble—with the exquisite sleepy sound in it—the most delicious note, I think, from a magpie's throat, and only heard at eventide.

Although it was customary for botanists and other scientists to accompany expeditions of discovery, many of the explorers themselves made detailed observations of the country and its flora and fauna, which they recorded in notes and sketches and collections of specimens.

Exquisite drawings of native plants, birds and animals were converted into meticulous and scientifically accurate engravings. *The Children's Hour* printed its illustrations from such engravings until photography became available.

In 1834, two years before colonisation, a South Australian Literary Society had been formed in London, whose members were 'gentlemen intending to emigrate'. It became the South Australian Literary and Scientific Association.

On their arrival, a few colonists with an interest in natural history each began their own private collections of specimens. Then, in 1838,

1898.
The Native Companion.
From Birds of Australia *by kind permission of Charles Stuart & Co.*
G. T. Broinowski, Fecit.

the Natural History Society of South Australia was set up, and soon books and specimens were being donated to form a public library and museum. The Royal Society began a South Australian branch during the first years of the colony, and before long the South Australian Institute was established. This ultimately consisted of the Natural History Museum and the Public Library, and later the Art Gallery. By 1864 the Institute Building had been built on North Terrace. So intense was the interest in the affairs of the Institute in its early years that its social gatherings would be attended by a thousand or more people!

It is interesting to compare an article published in June 1893 with one written thirty years later, in August 1923:

June 1893.

EXTINCT ANIMALS OF AUSTRALIA.

A most valuable discovery has recently been made in the north-east of our own colony of the bones of enormous extinct animals. The place where these remains have been found is Lake Mulligan, which lies in a desert region, north of Lake Frome, containing salt lakes of which Lake Mulligan is the chief. The discovery was made by Mr Hurst who was sent out by the governors of our Public Museum, and seems to be a most valuable one, as three complete skeletons have been found of the diprotodon, an animal like a kangaroo in form and habits, only of a gigantic size between that of a rhinoceros and an elephant. In addition to this, some of the bones of an enormous wombat have been discovered, the animal when alive being as large as a bullock. Altogether 2000 bones have been unearthed, and, as these are on their way down, public curiosity will only be satisfied when they are placed in the museum. It is interesting to know that some of the animals whose bones have lain so long undisturbed are probably quite new to science.

August 1923.

A GIANT WOMBAT.

We know that hundreds of thousands of years ago, ages before the blackfellows came to Australia, there were great numbers of pouched animals living in our land. These animals were very much larger than many of the native animals are today.

There were kangaroos which stood 11 ft in height and weighed six times heavier than the largest kangaroo of today. There were wallabies 9 ft high and three times heavier than the gray kangaroo we see now. The opossums were of the size and weight of a large bear.

But to people of our State the best known of these animals of the past was a giant wombat, the bones of which have been found near the Burra, at Yankalilla, at Hindmarsh, and in Lake Callabonna.

Lake Callabonna is in the Far North, at the northern end of Lake Frome, and, like all the lakes in that part of South Australia, it contains little water except during floods. The country around is dry and barren. Some years ago great numbers of bones of the giant wombat and other large animals were found in the salt mud of this lake.

These bones were carefully collected from the mud and taken to the Adelaide Museum, where clever men have been able, after much care, to arrange the bones as a skeleton of the giant wombat.

This skeleton is now to be seen in the Adelaide Museum.

July 1924.

THE SOUTH AUSTRALIAN MUSEUM.

ON North Terrace, Adelaide, there is a handsome group of buildings forming three sides of a square. One of them is known as the South Australian Museum. From its basement to its third storey this building is filled with wonderful things. A printed list of them would take up the space of many *Children's Hours.*

The Museum is open to visitors every weekday except Tuesday, when it is closed for cleaning. It is also open on Sunday afternoons. No charge is made to those who visit the Museum. All that is asked of them is to behave properly.

All boys and girls visiting Adelaide should try to spend some time in this great building. There they will learn much that cannot be taught properly from books.

They will also be able to purchase packets of post cards, each containing a picture of something to be seen at the Museum. A packet of six cards costs sixpence.

June 1919.

A HUGE WHALE.

OUR readers have probably learnt from the daily newspapers that last October a very large whale was stranded on the West Coast. It has been secured for the South Australian Museum. Mr Edgar R. Waite, the Director of the Museum, has kindly written the following article about whales. No doubt many of our readers have paid visits to the Museum, where there is to be seen a wonderful collection of natural history specimens. They will hope that the time is not far distant when Mr Waite will be able to show the huge whale skeleton to visitors.—Ed.

August 1908.

THE HYDATID.

R. H. Pulleine.

THE hydatid tapeworm is found in several parts of the world, but it is most abundant in southern Australia and Iceland. Here are two countries separated by a great distance, situated in different zones and therefore different climates and yet both are suitable for the growth of hydatids. Why should this be? The answer to this question is that both countries are alike in having many sheep and many dogs. Many of the dogs in South Australia are infected with three kinds of tapeworms of which the hydatid tapeworm is by far the smallest.

The Children's Hour was thus born into a community which was aware of the scientific awakening and increasing knowledge of the time. The editors were able to build on this interest which was to become a tradition characteristic of South Australia.

In the late nineteenth century it was not unusual to find research and scientific observation being undertaken voluntarily by enthusiastic and enlightened amateurs. The South Australian Museum benefited from such help, and the *Hour* benefited too. Every monthly edition contained articles about natural science in some form. These were very often contributions by experts and people of eminence in their field who were willing, even eager, to further interest and knowledge in subjects dear to them. The articles written by the editors themselves were not always scientifically correct, so instruction by generous and serious scholars was very valuable. This practice was established largely as a result of the efforts of Mr B. S. Roach in his time as Editor. In the 'new education' of the early 1900s, nature study had an important place. Much store was set by a child's personal experience in observing her surroundings. Children were taught that this country was worthy of respect, and full of interests, and were encouraged to discover all they could about it.

Mr James Aitken, who wrote on birds in the *Hour* for some years, pointed out not only similarities but differences between Australian birdlife and that of birds in other parts of the world.

1918.
What Is It?
Photo: F. J. Butler, Parilla.

An example of professional interest in the *Hour* is seen in the natural science articles contributed by Dr R. S. Rogers, MA, a supporter of Mr Roach.

June 1909.

NATURE.

OUR SOUTH AUSTRALIAN ORCHIDS.

I ought to tell you that so far as South Australia is concerned almost all our orchids grow from bulbs. There is a tall handsome orchid, often called the 'wild hyacinth', which is one of the exceptions to this rule. In tropical countries most orchids are parasitic, that is to say they live on other plants and are to be found growing on trees. In this State we have only one orchid which has this peculiar habit and it is found far up in the interior or near Lake Eyre.

Dr Rogers gave a lead to others writing for the *Hour*. The following piece has an interesting conservation angle:

November 1910.

NATURE.

The bush is now rich with orchids and boys and girls who have of late been reading the very able descriptions of these wonderful plants, written by Dr Rogers, have trained their eyes to see the fantastic blossoms that lift themselves on long slender stems; or in other words, boys and girls have cultivated the 'orchid eye'. There has been a development of 'orchid love', it is to be hoped, with the training of the, 'orchid eye', for these strange flowers that fascinate every flower-collector, and it is also to be hoped that this love will not allow the flower-hunter to destroy the flowers that he proposes so much to admire. The true flower-lover does not pick many of the same kind, but only one or two of each variety for his collection. He knows full well that every flower destroyed means so much less seed for the following year. The method of gathering the flowers is most important, there being a wrong and a right way of picking orchids, for they spring from bulbs or tubers. If the flower stalk is simply pulled up out of the ground the upper part of the tuber is injured and it is unable to produce flowers again. Such a method of pulling the flower and stalk up is the wrong way. The right way is to pinch off the flower stalk just above the surface of the ground in order not to injure the tuber. The writer who is also an orchid admirer desires the boys and girls of the fourth and fifth classes to instruct the younger children how to pick an orchid, and trusts that the future collectors will not gather orchids in a wholesale manner, as one does roses, violets, and those flowers that produce many blossoms on the one plant. Be content with one or two specimens of each kind. Remember that for thousands of years the orchids in Australia have been free to flower and increase without being plucked by white people, and yet orchids are rare plants. If, then, these multiply so slowly they will certainly soon disappear altogether unless we all determine to pick fewer, and admire them where they grow.

Dr Rogers also enlisted the help of the readers of the *Hour* in collecting, and forwarding to Adelaide—transit expenses paid!—sleepy, or stump-tailed lizards. His reasons for wanting them were not stated, but there is another glimpse of the prevailing attitudes towards conservation in his comment: 'As these harmless creatures are very numerous in our Northern Areas there will be no danger of seriously diminishing their numbers by complying with this request'.

1909.

FOR NATURE STUDENTS.

A GENTLEMAN who is interested in the study of wild flowers of the State, and who wishes to encourage pupils of the schools in the same delightful study, has offered three prizes, each of one guinea, for the best collection of orchids made during the next twelve months, beginning with the present month of May 1909.

1909.

FOR NATURE STUDENTS.

IN *The Children's Hour* for May 1909, it was stated that three prizes, each of one guinea, were offered to orchid-collectors. The donor was Dr R. S. Rogers MA, of Adelaide, who in three subsequent numbers of *The Children's Hour* wrote the most complete and popular account of South Australian orchids yet published. Dr Rogers has recently sent to the Education Office a cheque for three pounds ten shillings and sixpence from which four prizes have been forwarded to the prize-winners named in the following letter. Dr Rogers has the collections of orchids, which he will give to the collectors, or to any person appointed to represent them, who will call at 63 Flinders Street, Adelaide.

August 1916.

THE 'DEADLY' SNAKES
OF SOUTH AUSTRALIA.

Edgar R. Waite, FLS.
(Director of South Australian Museum)

(Mr Waite is one of the highest authorities on the subject he has dealt with in the following article. In 1898 he published a valuable book entitled *Australian Snakes*. He came to Australia in 1892, and, after filling a high position in the Australian Museum at Sydney, was Director of the Christchurch (NZ) Museum until his appointment to his present position.—Ed.)

HOW many kinds of snakes are there in Australia? is a question I am frequently asked, to which, if in the humour, I may reply 'three kinds'. As, however, something further is obviously expected, I add 'harmless, venomous and deadly'.

There are about 100 different species of snakes in Australia, of these 30 are non-venomous and the rest venomous; but of the latter only a very few are really deadly. It follows, therefore, that if we know the deadly kinds, we need not trouble to learn the others, excepting as a matter of interest.

There is no easily ascertained character by which harmless and venomous snakes may be distinguished. The largest snakes—say over 8 ft in length—are pythons, and are therefore harmless; but mere estimate of size must not be accepted, for snakes are usually reckoned to be very much longer than they really are. A reptile estimated at 7 ft will probably dwindle to 5½ ft when placed alongside the tape.

With one notable exception, small snakes—say 18 in. or under—are, even if venomous, not dangerous to man. It is always well for uninformed people to give snakes a very wide berth, but definite knowledge may save much trouble. If the snake by which one is bitten is known to be venomous, methods of treatment may be applied and, if it is known to be harmless, much anxiety may be prevented.

Yet there were sometimes editorial articles which must have pained the more professional writers by their non-scientific approach. They adopted a style which endowed birds and animals—even plants—with human responses and reactions, and, worse still—speech! In 1904 a piece appeared entitled 'Apple Trees in Love' by a contributor named Henry Ward Beecher:

> We have seen human creatures whose ordinary life was dutiful and prosaic; but when some great excitement or grief, or, more likely, of deep love, had thoroughly mastered them, they broke forth with a richness of feelings, an inspiration of sentiment, that mounted up into the very kingdom of beauty and for the passing hour they glowed with the very elements of poetry. And so to us seems an apple tree. From November to September it is a homely, duty-performing, sober, matter-of-fact tree; but September seems to stir up a love heat in its veins.

It is more likely that an apple tree 'seemed' to children in 1904 much the same as it would to children today—a source of delicious fruit, or a good place to climb—and one wonders why the editors included such an extravagant passage.

Other contributions referred to 'Mr and Mrs Willie Wagtail' or to 'Mrs Swallow's husband' and 'her babies'. Children in stories sometimes held imaginary conversations with birds and animals, as in 'The Little Pink Shell' written for Class II in 1903:

> Alice's breath went away, so that she could hardly find voice to answer. 'What do you mean? Who are you?' 'I am your sponge,' said the soft gurgling voice, 'And my little pink shell has clung to me through all my sorrows and hard times, do not drag her away.' 'I won't, if you want to keep it,' said Alice, 'but what do you mean by your sorrows and hard times? I treat you quite well, I am sure. Sponges are made on purpose for people to use, you know.' 'Indeed they are not,' said the sponge, with some anger. 'They are made to live free and happy at the bottom of the sea, with myriads of living creatures, far from the reach of man.' 'Oh, do tell me about it,' cried Alice . . .

A monthly feature which continued for years was 'Our Bird Letter'. Written in the first person, and signed 'Willie Wagtail', it was headed, 'Honeysuckle Arbor' or 'Hollow Branch, Old Gum'. Although it sometimes resorted to the technique of giving birds human speech, which was sometimes inappropriate, it provided good information on local birdlife. The letter was the mouthpiece of the Bird Protection Club, and on occasions Willie Wagtail spoke very plainly:

> Most of the big trees that remain are dying at the top, and are looking sickly and unsightly. What is the cause? Some folk say that it is the result of the climate. This is not correct, but then some people blame the climate for their own faults. I can tell you the real cause, because every day I am in the tree tops and able to observe just what is happening . . .

The study of birds was given the greatest attention of all nature study in *The Children's Hour*. Mr A. D. Edquist, who had been sent to Melbourne to train as a nature study teacher for the South Australian Education Department, established the Bird Protection Club which attracted a membership of hundreds of children throughout the State. Lists of the schools belonging to the club were published in the *Hour* and each of their members was allotted a number.

The custom of shooting birds and robbing nests had generally come to be regarded as an acceptable and inevitable pastime for boys, to the sorrow of those concerned for the protection of birdlife. The situation was considered serious enough to prompt a ministerial rebuke in the *Hour*:

1898.

THE EGGS OF MAGPIES.

The Hon Minister of Education wishes teachers and scholars to understand that every effort should be made to protect our Native Mapgies and their nests. He learns with much regret, from the Secretary of the Native Birds Protection Society, that large numbers of native magpies' eggs are taken every year, and he desires to impress upon all our readers that taking these eggs is a breach of the law as well as a cruel and wanton destruction of a beautiful and most useful bird.

The Bird Protection Club was a commendable and successful attempt to change children's attitudes. One of its great virtues was that anyone could take part in it, and the country children, so often at a disadvantage through isolation, had better opportunities to note and study a wide variety of birds than the city children did. Each year an essay competition was held and the winning club was awarded a large silver trophy (second prize, a collection of books). In country schools the club would sometimes have no more than five or six members, but their dedication and enthusiasm often made them the winners. A photograph of the winning club appeared in the *Hour* each year. The group, including the teacher, would be clustered proudly around the coveted trophy or books. The winning essay would be published beside the photograph.

1911.
Narridy School Bird Club.
Winners of First Prize (the Silver Cup) in 1911 Competition.
Teacher—Miss Kathleen Bethune.

1921.

GREYCOAT'S PRAYER.

A TALE OF THE WALLABY FOLK.

W. Hessel Hall, MA.

GREYCOAT was a scrub-wallaby, and a handsome fellow he was. He came from an ancient family, too, far older than that of any Pharaoh of old. His small head, fine features, and tiny hands told of delicate breeding and dainty ways. His thighs were the thighs of an athlete, with muscles—in the best of training—that could carry him fast and far. Each curved toenail was an excellent sword, and terribly sharp. They were dangerous weapons when the great muscles delivered their blow. And exceedingly useful tools when he wanted to dig for roots, like Paddymelon, his tiny friend.

When feeding, he walked leisurely with a plompity-plomp and a plompity-plomp; but when startled, he lifted his head and flew over the plain, measuring its width with great bounding strides, his family all lived their happy life, till the awful drought began to grip the land. And the grass, all dry and powdered, was lifted by the wind and carried far away. And the squatter's dam was dry. And the sun looked down on the bottom, where he had never looked before, and baked it hard, till great cracks yawned where the soft clay-mud had been. And Greycoat pined. Softears grew weak, and Joey was likely to die, for want of water to drink.

'Twas then, in their sorest need, that Greycoat prayed. He had no words, or voice, to pray, but hollow sides and shrivelled tongue—the symbols of their need—these cried for him, with prayer more eloquent than many prayers chanted in great cathedrals dim.

In proof, such prayers were heard—the answer came—a voice within that spake in the wallaby tongue: 'Dig, Greycoat! dig! there is water beneath the sand!' So Greycoat began to dig in the sandy bed of the creek, and Softears aided, too. And Dingo, their foe, drew near, and for once forbore to hunt, and joined the search.

And as they dug, stronger and stronger the scent of water grew. The sand grew damp; yet, still they dug, till, from every side, the precious water flowed at last. First Dingo drank, then all the wallabies quenched their thirst. Then homeward they did go, plompity-plomp, plompity-plomp.

No words were said, but all gave thanks. By sparkling eyes, by springing gait, and loosened tongues, they all gave thanks to the Giver of every good and perfect gift.

(The Commonwealth School Paper.)

1899.

COLUMN FOR GIRLS.

I KNOW some ladies who will not wear hats trimmed with those long delicate white feathers called ospreys, because the greatest cruelty is practised in obtaining them. Let us all try to do our little share, though it may be a very small one, in preventing all cruelty to, and unnecessary destruction of, the creatures which God has made so beautiful and endowed with such wonderful instinct, as well as tender love for their young.

I heard a story once of a kind lady who was scolding a small boy for robbing a bird's nest, while at the same time she was wearing a bonnet in which the chief ornament was a lovely little bird with slender wings and long tail. 'How sad the poor mother bird will be', said the lady to the young nest-robber, 'when she returns and finds all her dear children gone'. 'Oh, she won't know anything about it', said the smart boy; 'she's dead. That's the mother you have in your bonnet.'

December 1898.

THE PROTECTION OF BIRDS.

SINCE we printed our special notice on the protection of our native magpies in the November *Children's Hour*, Mr Tepper of the Adelaide Museum brought to this office a pretty little swallow which he had picked up in the parklands one Sunday with both wings cut off. It would seem that this very graceful and useful bird had been cruelly killed just for the sake of its wings. This being so, we beg most earnestly that all our gentle-minded girls and ladies will refuse to wear any hat or bonnet which is trimmed with any part of a bird.

October 1911.

OUR BIRD LETTER.

HOLLOW BRANCH, OLD GUM.

DEAR Girls and Boys—Nowadays it is a joy to live in South Australia; one feels so secure since over 6000 boys and girls have pledged themselves to protect, and not to kill us for our pretty feathers. At one time, especially on Sundays, it was a common thing for me to see parts of my relatives in the hats of people going to church. The sight always made me sad, and I wondered what the minister said to the girls and boys, and if he taught them how wrong their conduct was.

June 1911.
Whistling Eagles.

By 1904 there were legal constraints on the handling of birds, as laws for the protection of wildlife had been introduced. A list of the protected birds was printed in the *Hour,* and was accompanied by this advice:

1904.

BOYS AND GIRLS, TAKE CARE OF THE BIRDS.

Most kinds of birds are your sweetest and best friends. They are not only beautiful creatures, but they make our glens, woods, and fields bright and cheerful with their sweet songs and merry calls and chatter. Were it not for the good and useful work the birds do you would not be able to live at all for any great length of time in our beautiful world. Remember this and always guard them as your good friends . . .

Readers were provided with a statement of the 'new law', part of which said:

It is illegal to kill, wound, possess, sell, offer to sell, or export any Protected Bird; or to take, destroy, or sell the eggs of any Protected Bird; or to sell or offer for sale the skin or feather of any Protected Bird, or any article made therefrom, or in which the same is used.

Penalty, from one to twenty-five pounds, and in addition, the prescribed value of the bird.

1914.

THE WAGTAIL.

Dr R. H. Pulleine.

The wagtail is found all over Australia, and wherever he is found he is the friend of man. One of his names, 'The shepherd's companion,' aptly describes him, for he loves to follow sheep and cattle, when he perches on their backs and searches for food on the surface of their bodies.

The wagtail belongs to the great family of fly-catchers, and has a wide mouth with strong bristles on each side. He is wonderfully skilled in catching insects on the wing, and may often be seen hovering like a little hawk in the middle of a cloud of flying-ants. It is a very interesting sight to see him dart out time after time from a neighbouring tree, hover a moment, and return with his prey.

The wagtail has two notes, or calls. One is a shrill rattling chatter, which it utters when surprised or alarmed, and the other is a sweet plaintive little song of four notes which it sings chiefly in the evening.

Wagtails are most daring, and love to tease cats. Last year, at the back of my house in North Adelaide, wagtails were nesting. On walking down the lane behind the house I disturbed a cat, which ran away swiftly. In a moment one of the wagtails flew down and sat on its back, where its mate instantly joined it. The cat galloped off with its two riders and ran under the door of a neighbouring stable, actually brushing the birds off its back as it went out of sight.

Can anyone call to mind any other of our birds at once so familiar and so full of character. There are many more beautiful birds, and some with sweeter songs; but, judging on points, our little wagtail is the king of the lot.

1904.

PROTECTED BIRDS.
FIRST LIST.

Birds Protected During the Whole Year.

1. Blue Doves, Thickheads, Shrike-tits, and Bell-birds
2. Bower-birds
3. Butcher-birds and all species of Crow-shrikes
4. Cape Barren Geese
5. Cuckoos
6. Diamond-birds (or Pardalotes)
7. Fantails (or Wagtails) and Fly-catchers
8. Herons, Bitterns, and Egrets
9. Ibis and Spoonbills
10. Laughing-Jackasses and Kingfishers
11. Magpie Larks
12. Mopokes and Night-jars
13. Native Tits
14. Owls
15. Nut Piping Crow-shrikes (or Native Magpies)
16. Pipits and Larks
17. Reed Warblers and Bush Larks
18. Robins
19. Sea-gulls
20. Stone Plovers or Night Curlews
21. Superb Warblers, Emu Wrens, Blue Wrens, and Wrens of all species
22. Swallows and Martins
23. Swifts
24. Terns (or Sea Swallows)
25. Tin-tacks and Ephthianuras (white-fronted Chat)
26. Tree Creepers
27. Thrushes
28. Wood Swallows

February 6th, 1911.

THE ROYAL SOCIETY FOR PROTECTION OF BIRDS.

(The following letter from the Duchess of Portland has been received by Mr Edquist, who has kindly handed it to us for publication. It shows the great interest Her Grace takes in the subject very dear to the hearts of members of our Bird Protection Clubs.—Ed.)

Welbeck Abbey, Worksop, Notts.

DEAR Sir—I am sorry not to have before now acknowledged your interesting communication received last autumn. As President of the Royal Society for the Protection of Birds I am delighted to know of the progress made in Australia, and especially pleased to hear of the formation of so many School Bird Protection Clubs.

We watch with great interest all that is done in the colonies, and we never forget that Australia was one of the first in which a branch of the British Society for the Protection of Birds was formed. That was in the days before bird and tree celebrations were started in England.

Bird observation is a most delightful occupation for both old and young, and the children who join your School Clubs are to be congratulated. Please tell them that I hope they will all be loyal and true members, and that they will derive as much pleasure and profit from the study of the protection of birds as do thousands of young people who in England now join in bird and tree competitions as school cadets.

In our society's annual report for 1910, which is now being printed, there is a paragraph devoted to an account of what is being done in the schools of Australia, and I think we all feel very proud that you should have thought our methods worthy of imitation and our leaflets suitable for reprinting and distributing.

With every good wish for the success of the Australian Bird Protection Club.

I am, yours truly,
Winifred Portland.

1909.

AUSTRALIAN BIRDS.
THE PIGEON FAMILY.

James Aitken.

ONE of the finest birds living in our scrubs is the bronzewing pigeon. It is still to be found in large flocks in many parts of South Australia where few people are settled; but today there are many young Australians, living in towns, who have never seen these birds, though the grandparents of the same young people saw bronze-wing pigeons flying about in the same districts in hundreds.

In the early days observers of birds noted that, excepting the bronzewing pigeon, there was an absence of other wild pigeons and other wild fowl in the bush near the coastal districts of southern Australia. As explorers went farther inland they saw several different kinds of bronzewing pigeons, and also doves. Farther inland still was seen the fruit pigeon, so called because it lives on fruit. Its plumage matches the colours of the trees on which it lives so well that it is a difficult task to see this bird.

Bronzewings, doves, fruit pigeons, and others help to make up a large pigeon family for Australia. Learned men who have studied this family tell us that our tame pigeons at first came from the blue-rock pigeon—a bird still to be found in large numbers on rocky cliffs in Europe and Asia. Here it builds its nest in caves or on ledges of rocks. Thousands of years ago men captured some of these birds, and from them have descended the house pigeons of today. Tame pigeons are kept in hundreds by the people of India about their temples. These same people think it a very pious deed to spend money, which they can ill afford, in buying grain to feed the temple pigeons.

SECOND LIST.

Birds Protected during Specified Period.

From June 1st to December 20th, both inclusive—Emus, Swans, Wild Geese (except Cape Barren Geese), and Plovers.

From August 1st to December 20th, both inclusive—Wild Ducks and Bustards (or Native Turkeys).

All other birds, native or imported, except those mentioned in the first and last lists, are protected from the 1st day of July to the 20th day of December, both inclusive.

THIRD LIST.

Birds not Protected.

1. Cormorants
2. Crows
3. English Chaffinches
4. English House Sparrows
5. English Starlings
6. Hawks
7. Rosella Parrots
8. Silver Eyes
9. Snipe
10. Sulphur-crested Cockatoos
11. Wattle-birds

Perhaps it is not generally understood how little trouble is necessary sometimes to sheet home an offence; people are apt to suppose that they must lay an information and appear at the Police Court, but this is a mistake. If they see protected birds exposed for sale, or being carried through the streets, or witness any breach of the law by shooting, catching, etc, they need only inform the nearest constable, and the work of prosecution passes at once into his hands; even if it be necessary to follow an offender till a constable can be met with, surely this is a labour no real bird lover would shirk when the benefit of making an object lesson of some unscrupulous law-breaker is considered; one or two examples of heavy fines being inflicted would have a most salutary effect.

1918.

TREE AND BIRD DAY COMPETITION.

Each competitor must draw from real life *one bird* and *one tree.* The bird may be sketched in more than one characteristic posture.

In one corner of the paper, either at the top or the bottom, there should be drawn in detail a leaf, blossom, and fruit of the tree.

Drawings from photographs and pictures will be disqualified. Entrance forms may be secured by the secretary from Mr A. G. Edquist, Adelaide High School. Rules governing the competition have appeared in the *Education Gazette* for February, 1918.

June 1918.

THE BIRDS OF THE MALLEE.

F. J. Butler
Parilla.

That part of South Australia lying south of the Murray, and extending eastwards from Tailem Bend to Pinnaroo, is generally known as the Mallee. A few years ago it was a blank portion on our maps, but now it is crossed by several lines of railway.

Hundreds of busy farmers are engaged in clearing the scrub, and in growing wheat for the people of the cities, who, in return, send back

1925.
Nest of Native Pheasant or Mallee Hen.

to the farmers implements, jams, soaps, and other goods which are made in the city factories. Before the farmers came there were but few birds in the mallee, because there were not many watering places; but now, on every farm there is a bore, which yields a supply of water sufficient for man, bird, and beast.

The most interesting member of the feathered tribe in this district, or, perhaps, in the whole world, is the mallee hen, or native pheasant. It lives almost entirely on the ground, and seldom uses its wings. Its nest is a great mound of earth, leaves, and twigs, which are raked together by the birds and placed over a hole, which is first scratched in the ground. The eggs, which are placed in the mound, are hatched by the heat, which is generated by the dampness and decaying leaves. The little mallee chickens are quite able to look after themselves as soon as hatched, and to hop from twig to twig to roost in a tree the first night they are out of the egg. The nest shown in the photograph is really a small one, and has been used for two seasons only. Some of the nests are used many times, and are often 12 ft in diameter. These birds are becoming scarce now, because so many are killed by that enemy of our native birds, the fox.

Although trees were not studied in the *Hour* with quite the same intensity as birds, articles explaining their importance, value, and beauty, and the care of them, appeared fairly regularly.

In 1904 a clear and helpful lesson on tree planting, printed in the *Hour*, carried an accompanying photograph of children (it seems to be only of boys) planting a tree in the Richmond School grounds:

Tree and Bird Day—What is it? The celebration of Tree and Bird Day originated in America, but it has been introduced with great success into several British colonies, including South Australia, Canada, New Zealand and Cape Colony.

It was suggested that South Australia should have a tree-planting day, marked by a school holiday, in early July each year. This soon happened. The name Arbor Day came to be generally used and the *Hour* gave the event great prominence, always including photographs

March 1914.

TREE (ARBOR) AND BIRD DAY COMPETITION.

THE fourth Tree and Bird Competition for the Challenge Cup shown in the accompanying illustration will take place in May 1914. It is anticipated that a hard tussle will take place between the members of the 355 bird clubs now established in South Australia, for each club is anxious to secure the coveted cup for twelve months. If your club wins the trophy, a silver shield telling of your success will be added to those already shown on the plinth.

Brave old soldiers say that a fight is not worth while, unless it is with a strong and determined enemy. Remember this true saying, and show what stuff you are made of by entering this competition, where you have over 2000 good fighters against you.

Do not listen to the boy who is afraid of being beaten, and who tries to hide his fear by saying that he *would* try, only he wants to give some other fellow a chance. Take no notice of the lazy person, who says in a tired voice, 'O! you won't have a chance against fellows in big schools.' This person does not know that each year in the past the little schools have beaten the big ones, and that boys in large schools often say, 'It's no good trying, the boys in the little country schools have the best chance because they see most birds and trees.' The truth is, those people with excuses are scared to try, and attempt to disguise their fear.

The writers of the 1st and 2nd prize essays will receive valuable books.

1914.
The Challenge Cup.
The small silver shields at the base show that the Cup has been won by each of the following Bird Clubs: Narridy, 1911; Wilkawatt, 1912; Lower Light, 1913.

taken at various schools, sometimes distant country ones. The cover bore the heading, 'Bird and Tree (Arbor) Day Number'.

Families joined in the ceremony and an essay competition for schoolchildren was held by the Royal Society for the Protection of Birds.

October 13th, 1893.

OUR ARBOR DAY.

by M. C.

We read in the papers accounts of Arbor Day at many another school, perhaps with a brief, 'That was nice'; but when the gentlemen on our Board of Advice fixed the eleventh of August as 'our' Arbor Day what a change there was! 'Grown-ups' looked at their barometers daily and children anxiously studied their great barometer—the sky, for we had had gloomy weather and showery days for so many weeks that we grew fearful lest the eleventh should be like its neighbours. The trustees of the school met a week or two previous to the great day and arranged to have a new fence of six wires round the playground, likewise the plough up of one triangular corner, fence it in, and have a little plantation there. The Booleroo Township provisional school children were to come up to our school (White Cliffs) on the eleventh and help us to plant the trees. Parents on all sides began to make their preparations for the day, and many a crackling fire was made expressly to cook goodies for the occasion. The day arrived! Surely the weather prophet knew it was the children's day, else that sparkling sunshine, that blue sky, that crisp air would never have been granted. 'Queen's weather', said the teacher, and hurried to school, meeting the children already assembled there with faces just as bright as the morning. A quick march into school. 'All present', a little chat about wonderful plants and trees in other lands, then we saw a wagon loaded with the Booleroo children coming down the road. So out the children marched again, and stood in ranks waiting the new arrivals, whose glad hurrahs were borne to us on the wings of the morning breeze. Silence in our ranks till the waggon rolled up, and then we too raised our voices and gave the newcomers hearty cheers by way of greeting. After being formed into ranks all marched back into school again when a few songs were sung, after which the children were dismissed to have games and a scramble for lollies till all was ready for them. By this time Mr McMartin, the member of the School Board allotted to us for the day, had arrived and with two of the school trustees was busily engaged measuring and pegging out the ground for the reception of the trees. Traps were rolling up every few minutes and the place began to look lively. The ladies, meanwhile, had been getting dinner ready, and anyone glancing at our big school shed which is nicely boarded, would have seen two long tables laden with good things. At about one o'clock the children were marshalled into the school room, while their elders took places around the tables, and soon all were busy emptying plates and cups and mugs. After dinner the children were formed into ranks in the yard—Mr McMartin addressed them; then they marched into the plantation, each taking his or her place at the side of a peg, and soon all the trees were planted. There were sixty children in all, and the teachers went round and named each tree after the child who had planted it. Mr McMartin then kindly gave each child an orange, and after another short speech on the care of trees and cheers for the trustees had been given they were dismissed to play. Each teacher planted a tree, and about twenty-four other ladies did likewise, and after all had partaken of tea, a general departure took place, each one agreeing with his neighbours that a very pleasant day had been spent.

October 1893.

ARBOR DAY AT WISANGER, KANGAROO ISLAND.

In the afternoon the parents and friends of the children assembled at the school, and found the children engaged in writing, drawing and various kinds of kindergarten work, which was much appreciated. Then a number of songs and recitations were given by the children and addresses bearing on trees. Mrs Strawbridge said in her address: 'The healthiness of this island is probably due to the eucalypti with which it abounds, for where belts of trees have been planted in the vicinity of even pestilential marshes these places have become salubrious and therefore habitable. It has been noticed that trees, like human beings, are social in their nature and will grow better in masses or in rows than when alone. This may give us a hint of the benefit of friendly intercourse and neighbourly kindness. This planting today, requiring as it has much preparation will also call for continued care; the infant trees must be protected in their feebleness and watched that insects do not check their growth, or idle fingers injure their tender bark. Tree planting may teach us unselfishness. You plant for others to give pleasure to persons whom you may never see, and so you work for the world of which you form a part. I hope our first Arbor Day will be remembered by us all as a pleasant occasion of friendly gathering and a prelude to many more.'

August 2nd, 1895.

ARBOR DAY.

(Address given by the Head Teacher, Glenelg School.)

WE are met to celebrate 'Arbor Day,' and it will be well to ask first of all what that expression means. Well, the word 'arbor' is from the Latin, and means a tree; and the name 'Arbor Day' has been given to a day set apart for the purpose of planting trees, especially forest trees.

So far as I know, the custom originated in the United States of America, and was the result of the wholesale destruction of the magnificent forests with which that country was covered through much of its extent when the white men took possession of it. The early settlers, taking no thought for the future, had only one aim—to clear the land of timber, so as to make room for corn planting. For many years their successors followed in their destructive course, so that a time arrived when the scarcity of timber began to press hardly upon the inhabitants, and the happy expedient was suggested, and warmly taken up by the people generally, that one day in the year should be set apart as a national holiday, and devoted to tree planting. This was done, and I believe the practice is still continued.

1913.
Arbor Day at Hundred of Macgillivray School.
Teacher—Miss M. B. Fisher.

1916.
Children of Burdett School on Arbor Day.
Teacher—Miss Bradly.

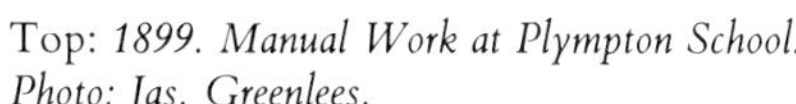

Top: *1899. Manual Work at Plympton School. Photo: Jas. Greenlees.*

Middle: *1915. Tickera School Garden. Teacher—Mr E. H. Hodges.*

Right: *1917. Garden Plot, Eudunda School. Teacher—Mr E. D. Nicholas.*

The love of the English for their gardens came with the first settlers to Australia. Throughout the colony, despite the long dry summers, the settlers instinctively began cultivating their plots of ground, whether large or small. Instinctively, too, they planted the familiar plants from 'home'—roses and honeysuckle grew around the door, violets and verbenas lined the paths, and the scent of lilacs brought a wave of nostalgia in the October air. Cottage gardens were thus a normal feature of Adelaide life, while the 'well-to-do' planned large and interesting gardens to complement their elegant mansions.

Early plans for Adelaide show a Botanic Garden on several different sites. The North Terrace garden was opened in 1856. It was developed with great care and soon formed an oasis of calm, beauty, and botanic expertise close to the heart of the city. *The Children's Hour* published photographs of the Garden to advertise its charm, and family visits there were very popular.

School gardens were started soon after the schools were set up, in many places. Some schools placed great emphasis on learning about plants and gardening methods. The photographs in the *Hour* show the results, which were often very successful, but occasionally touching and pathetic, when the efforts were frustrated by an impossibly dry climate.

There were job opportunities for boys in gardening, and no doubt this was one reason for giving some training at school. As early as 1897 the *Hour* carried an article by Lloyd Higginbottom of the Agricultural School, giving instructions on vine pruning, and another in 1898, entitled 'Weeds', explained the way in which such weeds as thistles, dandelions, Bathurst burr and clover 'are carried to different parts of the colony':

> Those countries with which we carry on our trade, supply us with the greatest number of foreign plants . . . Although we may say a great deal in favour of weeds, we must conclude that if they occupy the ground to the detriment of growing crops it is necessary to destroy them. In the next article we will deal with 'Extermination of Weeds'.

September 1897.

SCHOLARS' CORNER.

VINE PRUNING.

THE authorities of the North Terrace Lunatic Asylum left fifty unpruned vines for us to prune. On Wednesday, August 4th, the boys of the Agricultural School went to finish pruning these vines. The reason for going there was that we have no fruit-bearing vines of our own. Professor J. A. Perkins, from Roseworthy College, instructed us in the way of pruning. He said that fruit would be on yearly shoots growing from two-year old wood, and that this wood grew on three-year old wood. All yearly shoots not coming from two-year old wood are water shoots. The shape of the vine should resemble a wine-cup, with a stem about six or nine inches high. The first thing to do then is to cut off the water shoots as close as you can to the old wood. The great point is to keep the arms of a vine as short as possible, so as to lessen the dead wood; because as dead wood goes through the vine the sap has hard work to get through it. In order then to take the arms back, a water shoot may be used by cutting it just below the third bud, and then in two years time it will bear fruit. The arm may then be cut back. In choosing which shoot you will keep for a spur, take those which run in opposite directions. On the arm of a hardy vine, two spurs are generally left, the others are then cut off close to the stem, and dead wood should be cut square across. A shoot which is kept for a spur should be cut just below the third bud, so that a hard piece of wood is exposed to the air. The pruning shears (or secateurs), have one cutting blade and a blade that holds the vine. The cutting blade should be kept nearest to the vine, because the holding blade bruises the part of the vine which it holds. After giving three hearty cheers (in which the dogs of the Asylum took part by barking) for Professor J. A. Perkins, we were dismissed. Some of our boys took cuttings home to plant.

Lloyd Higginbottom
Agricultural School.

1913.
Hahndorf School Garden.
Spraying trees to kill insect and other pests.
Teacher—Mr O. A. Witt.

February 1912.

SEED WHEAT SELECTION.

Dear Girls and Boys—You will, I am sure, be pleased to know that, in spite of the short notice given, a number of very fine wheat plants have already been sent in for the competition that closes on the 29th February. I wonder who will be the prizewinners? If you have just been promoted from the Third to the Fourth Class, and do not know of this competition, you should read the November number of *The Children's Hour*, 1911.

Those who are competing this year will be delighted to know that Professor Lowrie, MA, BSc, Director of Agriculture in South Australia, has promised to act as a judge in the competition. But that is not all the good news. When the gentlemen who arrange and control the important Royal Agricultural and Horticultural Show of South Australia were told of the competition they very kindly offered to allow the exhibits to be displayed at the next Autumn Show, in order that everybody who came might see what some girls and boys are doing towards improving the wheat yield and thereby increasing the wealth of South Australia, and maybe of the whole Commonwealth. In years to come how happy will any man or woman feel who lives to see a field of fine quality wheat produced from the seed of the plant with which he or she won a prize when at school.

In schools, too, floral societies flourished and exhibitions were held which later coincided with the school's annual choral concert, known as the 'Decoration Society Concert'.

From time to time in the *Hour* lists of plants were published to help children with their planting programmes. Comparing the information for 1909 with the piece published in 1914, one finds that the introductory paragraphs are identical, and the list of plants in 1914 only slightly altered here and there, with one or two omitted and a few new ones added. It would seem that there was no problem of monetary inflation in those days—the seeds cost one penny a packet in 1909 and were still the same price in 1914! Both editions advised that, 'a small quantity of pansy seed has been procured from Germany and may be had at threepence per packet'. (Was the 'small quantity' continually being replenished from the other side of the world, or was it simply not a 'popular line'? Whatever the answer, the supply must surely have stopped with the outbreak of the First World War and the pansies may have become quite a collectors' item.)

February 1914.

SEEDS FOR SCHOOLS.

The Floral Society has imported another excellent assortment of seeds, which are sold at 1d. per packet, and your teacher will get them for you if you wish it. Since last year the seed list has been carefully revised and enlarged. Some unpopular kinds have been dropped, and their places filled by varieties with which you will certainly be pleased, if you give them a proper trial. Orders are to be sent only through teachers, and the sooner you send, the more likely you are to get what you want.

(Teachers are specially requested to note carefully the instructions in the February *Gazette*, 1914.)

SEEDS.

To sow at Once in Pots or Boxes, or in the Open Ground when the Rains come.
Seeds to Sow in Autumn.

1. Antirrhinum, mixed dwarf—Perennial, various colours; 1 ft; sow in boxes or nursery beds, and transplant.
2. Calliopsis, mixed, all varieties—Yellow and maroon; 1 ft; boxes.
3. Candytuft, mixed—White and lilac; boxes or ground; good edging.
4. Canterbury Bell, mixed—Perennial white, blue rose; 2 ft; boxes and transplant.
5. Carnation, mixed—White, pink; 18 in; boxes.
6. Columbine, mixed—Hardy perennial, various colours; 3 ft; sow in boxes and transplant.
7. Cornflower—Blue and white; boxes or ground; 1 ft.
8. Dianthus Heddewigi, mixed—Japan pink, very beautiful; 1 ft; boxes and ground.
9. Double Daisy—4 in; boxes; edgings.
10. Everlasting Pea—Various; ground; 6 ft.
11. Forget-me-not, mixed—Blue, 9 in; ground, in rings or borders.
12. Foxglove.
13. Gaillardia, mixed—Sulphur-yellow to purple; 1 ft; boxes or ground.
14. Godetia, mixed—Profuse bloomer; large showy flowers; 1 ft; boxes.
15. Hibiscus—Cream, purple centre.
16. Hollyhock.
17. Indian Pink—Hardy biennial, mixed; very varied beautiful colours; 9 in; sow in boxes or open ground.
18. Larkspur, dwarf, stock-flowered, mixed—All colours; 1 ft; ground.
19. Lavender—Well known for the fragrance of its flowers and leaves.
20. Lobelia, mixed—Blue; 4 in; beautiful edging plants; names and designs may be planted with it; boxes.
21. Love in a Mist—Dense foliage; blossom half hidden, half revealed; 1 ft; ground.
22. Leptosyne—Large, bright, golden; excellent for cutting.
23. Marguerite—White.
24. Mignonette, mixed—Ground; 6 in.
25. Mimulus, mixed—Various colours; 1 ft; boxes; good for pot culture.
26. Nasturtium, dwarf, mixed—All colours; 1 ft; ground.
27. Nicotiana—White; long tube-shaped fragrant flowers.
28. Pansy, mixed—All colours; sow in boxes at once, and transplant into rich soil in a shady place.
29. Pentstemon—Richly-coloured flowers on tall spikes.
30. Petunia 'Emperor'—Various colours; 2 ft; sow in boxes; cover with a pane of glass till the seed germinates, and water with the greatest care.
31. Phlox Drummondi, Grandiflora—Beautiful annuals that may be sown every week in the year; boxes.
32. Polyanthus—Splendid plants for pot culture; 6 in.
33. Poppy, single, mixed—Annuals; 1 ft; exceedingly beautiful for cutting for table decoration; open ground; difficult to transplant.
34. Ranunculus—Various colours; very showy.
35. Salpiglossis—Large funnel-shaped blossoms, with deeply-sunken veins. Very beautiful.
36. Schizanthus—Of great beauty and gracefulness.
37. Stocks, German, ten weeks; large flowered—Various colours; 1 ft; boxes.
38. Sweet Peas, mixed—All colours, climbers; 5 ft; ground.
39. Sweet Sultan—Free flowering, showy; excellent for cutting.
40. Sweet William, mixed, choice, auricular-eyed—Free flowering, having large heads of various colours; 9 in; boxes or ground.

41. Venue Looking Glass—Bell-like flower; fine bloomer; good either for pots, beds, or baskets; 9 in.
42. Verbena, choice seedlings—Sow in boxes and transplant.
43. Violet—The well-known garden variety, mixed; boxes, but better in shady ground; 6 in.
44. Virginian Stock, mixed—Blue and white; 6 in; ground, rings, edgings.
45. Wallflower—Various; 18 in; boxes or ground.

(Mr Edquist suggests that as the plant Nicotiana [No. 27] is easily injured by frosts, its seeds should be sown after the winter has passed, say in the months of September or October.)

To Sow in Spring.

46. Armeria—Rose-coloured flowers; hardy perennial; height, 1 ft.
47. Chrysanthemum, annual, mixed—Various colours; 18 in; boxes or ground.
48. Asters, mixed—Beautiful plants of various colours; will do well either in the garden in cool place or in pots; sow in boxes.
49. Balsam, mixed—Sow in boxes and transplant into cool places; should have plenty of water.
50. Celosia—Yellow, scarlet, and crimson; suitable for pots or the garden.
51. Cockscomb—Very singular, attractive, and showy.
52. Convolvulus Major—Climber; 10 ft; sow in ground against fence, trellis, or verandah.
53. Cosmos, Klondyke—Brilliant orange.
54. Cosmos, mixed, like single Dahlias—3 ft; ground.
55. Dahlia, Cactus.
56. Globe Amaranthus, mixed—Handsome everlasting; 1 ft; boxes or ground.
57. Golden-rod.
58. Marigold, African.
59. Miniature Sunflower—3 ft; ground.
60. Portulacca—All colours; 3 in; boxes or sandy soil or ground.
61. Salvia—Beautiful, free-blooming.
62. Zinnia, double—All colours; 1 ft to 2 ft; boxes and ground; water well.

A small quantity of special fine *pansy* seed has been procured from Germany, and may be had at 3d. per packet.

With few exceptions, the first settlers looked to little beyond their survival, and later their prosperity, in relation to the land and its flora and fauna. It is obvious to us, years later, that mistakes were made.

For example, it is alarming to us to read in the *Hour* of the seals in the Adelaide Zoo in 1916:

> They had a large pool of water to swim in, but, as the water was fresh, the seals did not do well in it. They had to be fed on fresh fish, which is an expensive food in Adelaide. The seals all died, and no others have since been kept at the Zoo.

On the other hand, the kangaroo, perhaps because it is Australia's national symbol, has often been the subject of conservation arguments, as an article in the *Hour* in 1921 shows:

> There are still living a few people who can recollect, years ago, seeing kangaroos moving over land now covered with huge buildings in Adelaide.

Nowadays, however, to see mobs of wild kangaroos one must travel far into the back blocks of South Australia. Even in these remote places the hunters have followed the poor creatures, and they are shot for their skins, which can be made into soft and useful leather.

It is well to know that the law of this State forbids the shooting of kangaroos between the first of July and the thirty-first of December of any year.

There are several areas in South Australia where the kangaroo is protected all the year round. No one may shoot kangaroos on land privately owned, unless the owner has given permission.

Those who enjoy eating oysters will read with a pang the last lines written in a *Children's Hour* article about Port Lincoln oysters in 1911: 'But Adelaide and other places asked too often for a helping from the oyster beds, which at last were raked clean and the oyster boats had to search elsewhere'. Perhaps the forerunner of the conservation movement was, in a way, the Society for the Prevention of Cruelty to Animals. The SPCA was continually working, and widening its influence, through the pages of the *Hour*. Essay competitions encouraged children to learn how to care for their pets and for domestic animals generally. People relied heavily on horses for many years—even in the city of Adelaide the baker's horse was dispensed with only in the 1970s. An article in April 1910 on caring for horses ended:

God has said of animals, 'Into your hands are they delivered', and this means that we must be very kind to them; that we must be careful that they have everything which can tend to their welfare; that we must never tease them; and that we must only kill them when their life is dangerous or their death useful to us.

September 1914.

SPCA EXAMINATION.

(See March *Children's Hour*).

Classes IV and V.

Mrs O'Leary writes—In Class V both the girls and boys reached a higher standard than last year, and great numbers show a real interest in the subject. Many good papers were spoilt by one or two bad mistakes in regard to watering and shoeing horses, and some indifferent papers contained one or more very good answers. We should have liked to give double the number of prizes in Class V. It is to be hoped the competitors will try again—previous efforts will be taken into consideration.

The following are excellent answers taken from various papers:

For the sake of the horses doing such splendid work in the war, let us look after ours at home well. Think how they serve the British Empire.

General Baden Powell is a great lover of horses so let the boy scouts do all they can to help them.

I would shoot it in the forehead four inches above level of the eyes. Father uses Greener's cattle-killer, it is the best for destroying animals.

If I had to shoot a horse which had met with an accident I would shoot it in the forehead, on a spot where a line drawn from the right ear to the left eye would cross a line from the left ear to the right eye, since a bullet in this spot kills a horse instantly without any pain. Always hold the revolver or gun close to the horse's head.

I have often interfered in cases of cruelty, and all last summer I watered a horse that had been turned on a waterless road to starve to death. The same horse, I am pleased to say, has since changed owners and is the well-cared-for military mount of its new owner. I have never reported a case to the SPCA or the police, but if any deliberate cruelty came under my notice I would most certainly do so.

I have one of my own. I know horses should always be watered before they are fed, because they digest their food better. If they are thirsty when they are eating their food they do not eat so well. Working horses should have three good meals a day and one the last thing at night, and a little lump of rock salt will not hurt them sometimes. Clean fresh water always should be where the horses can reach it, so that they can get a drink when they like. It won't hurt horses to drink when very hot if they are not allowed too much.

The harness should be kept clean and soft with a good harness polish. It needs oiling occasionally to keep the leather soft and pliable. The sweat and dirt should all be washed off before cleaning it, and the harness should be hung up in a sheltered place. The buckles and bit should be cleaned with a polish.

Great kindness, patience, and care should be taken while breaking in young horses, because then they will let you pat and catch them. You want to speak to young horses, because they seem to know what you say, and they do as you tell them. The man who loves horses can do ever so much more with them than one who has no regard for them. Rough handling when they are young is the cause of their so-called viciousness. The young horses are very nervous animals, and to frighten them is very cruel indeed when they are trying to do their best for their master's sake.

Nearly always young horses are hard to break in, because when they are foals they do not treat them so kindly as if they were older. By nature nearly all horses are kind and gentle if they are treated kindly. A horse continually ill-treated loses heart, and then he is like a man who is low-spirited. They know quickly when their master is not sympathetic with them. If you talk to young and old horses they work and pull for you better.

If a person sees an animal which is too sick or injured to recover, the law allows him to go to a Justice of the Peace and get a paper signed by him stating that the animal may be mercifully destroyed.

The principal thing in slaughtering an animal is to do it as quickly and as painlessly as possible. 'Good hands' in riding or driving means that you should have a steady, light, and gentle hand, and not tug or jerk at the reins. The reins should be held lightly and firmly.

When poultry is being forwarded to market they should be put in a box with room enough to stand upright in and not be overcrowded. They should have vessels fixed in the box for feed and water.

When a cow is being brought in to milk it should not be made to run. Cows want milking at the same time each day. They should not be ill-used, and should be fed at milking-time to make them used to coming in regularly, and to keep them in milk should be milked quite dry each time.

November 1920.

SOCIETY FOR THE PREVENTION OF CRUELTY TO ANIMALS

(JUNIOR BRANCH).

Dear Boys and Girls,
Some of you are not quite sure why horses should be shod about every six weeks. Well in six weeks' time a horse's hoofs have grown too big for its shoes, so that the shoes are uncomfortable, and even if the horse has not done much work and the shoes are very little worn, it should be taken to the blacksmith to have them removed, its hoofs cut back, and the shoes put on again.

If everyone was careful about this point we should not see so many horses running lame because their shoes pinch them, or lame from corns, and we should not see so many horses with broken knees, for it would make a horse likely to stumble if its shoes were hurting it. Horses working on hard roads often need shoeing sooner than six weeks, for their shoes wear out, and also some horses are much harder than others on shoes, just as some boys and girls are much rougher than others on their boots.

Most of you say that if a horse is not brushed down every day, and if its collar is not clean it will be likely to get sore shoulders. This is quite right. Sore shoulders are generally caused from neglect, carelessness, and indifference on the part of the owner. He neglects to keep his horse in good condition, clean, and healthy; he does not brush the sweat and loose hairs off every day; he does not see that the collar is clean, and he puts it on hard with dirt; he is careless, for he does not look to see if both traces are the same length, and however well a collar may fit, if a horse is pulling with uneven traces hard, or on a long trip, the shoulder might be rubbed sore; he is careless if he does not see that the collar is a good fit, it may be too big or too small; he does not have the collars mended when they begin to wear out, and if he has several horses he does not see that each horse always has its own collar.

This last-named point is very important, for each horse pulls differently, moves differently, and has different shaped shoulders, and so each horse would work the padding of its own collar into its own shape. If its collar was put on to another horse with differently shaped shoulders, and a different way of pulling, it would very likely mean sore shoulders. Some drivers are indifferent to the sufferings of their horses, and even when they know that the collar is rubbing a sore they do not trouble to alter it, and so ease the horse. You can tell by animals' eyes if they are kindly and fairly treated; if so, the eyes will be clear and trustful, with a soft expression; if the animal is treated roughly, overworked, and underfed the eyes will look scared and strained, and will have a tired expression.

Now, boys and girls, if you always do what you know to be right and fair to animals, if you are always kind and thoughtful, remembering how dependent they are on you for their daily wants and happiness, you will grow up much nicer, gentler men and women, much kinder to each other, and the future animals will have a much easier and a less suffering time, for you will have learnt to be kind and thoughtful for them, and you will all try to teach others round you by your kind action and words to be kind to them as well.

(Miss) E. C. Rischbieth, Hon. Sec.,
Rose Cottage, Blackwood.

March 1918.

SOCIETY FOR THE PREVENTION OF CRUELTY TO ANIMALS (JUNIOR BRANCH).

DEAR Boys and Girls—In last month's *Children's Hour* I told you that a Junior Branch had been started, and asked you all to join. I gave particulars about membership, and told you that an Essay Competition would be held.

Children of any age or Grade may compete. Members of the Society will be awarded prizes, three for boys and three for girls in each Grade; and non-members will receive a certificate.

Particulars as to membership were published in February *Children's Hour.*

Name, age, and address of each competitor must be stated. Each paper must be signed by teacher certifying that the work is the unaided effort of the competitor.

SPCA COMPETITION, 1918.

Grades IV, V, VI.

1. Describe how to treat and manage the following domestic animals and birds: The horse, donkey, cow, calf, sheep, pig, dog, cat, fowl, and any caged bird.
2. Give an instance of how you would have been able to help one or more of these animals or birds.
3. Why should we be kind to dumb animals?

Grades VII and VIII.

Children in Grades VII and VIII must write on above subjects, and also on the following: 'What effects on your own character result from your showing kindness to dumb animals?'

NB—All children in South Australia may try in this essay competition.

All papers must reach the following address by June 30th:

(Miss) E. C. Rischbieth, Hon. Sec.,
Rose Cottage, Blackwood.

SOCIETY FOR PREVENTION OF CRUELTY TO ANIMALS.

Below we print an examination paper forwarded to us by the above society. We trust that a large number of our readers will try to answer the questions, and that they will observe carefully the following conditions:

1. Name, age, and class at school of competitor should be written at the beginning of the paper.

2. Teacher or parent should sign below the foregoing information, thereby certifying that it is correct, and also that the answers given are the unaided work of the competitor.

3. To Fifth Class pupils six prizes will be given—three for boys and three for girls. The first prize for boys will be a Boys' Own Annual, and an equally valuable book will be selected as the first prize for girls; the second and third prizes will also please the hearts of those that win them.

4. Similar prizes will be awarded to the Fourth Class; that is, three for boys and three for girls.

5. All papers must reach the following address before April 13th, 1914:

The Secretary,
Society for Prevention of
Cruelty to Animals,
23 Waymouth Street, Adelaide.

Classes IV and V.

1. If you have to shoot a horse that has met with an accident how and where would you shoot it?

2. How often should a horse's shoes be removed?

3. Do you interfere in any cases of cruelty that you see? Do you ever report the same to the Society or to the police? If you have done so, give details of case.

4. What do you know of dogs and their management?

5. What do you know of horses and their management? In answering the foregoing question state all you know and think on the subject of—(a) Watering; (b) feeding; (c) shoeing; (d) driving; (e) riding; (f) grooming, and harness cleaning.

6. In what ways are sheep cruelly treated? Have you ever seen sheep-shearing?

7. Why should such great kindness, patience, and care be shown while breaking in young horses, and what is meant by 'good hands' in riding or, driving?

8. How should poultry be forwarded to market?

9. What do you know of the management and milking of cows?

10. If you see any animal which is too sick or injured to recover, what does the law allow you to do?

(Information that will help in answering question 10 may be found in the PCA Act for 1908, and also in the SPCA report for 1912, a copy of which has been forwarded to every school in South Australia.)

Native animals were studied, while not exclusively, at least predominantly, over the years. Articles were presented for children of all ages in numerous styles, and most children who read the *Hour* could not fail to have some idea of the behaviour and habits of kangaroos, wallabies, wombats, platypuses, possums and dingoes. However, we now know more about them than was known when this piece was published in April 1921:

> The female kangaroo, or doe, is not so large as the male. As soon as a young kangaroo is born, the mother places it in her pouch, with its mouth fastened firmly to the nipple of a teat. At first the tiny creature looks very unlike a kangaroo. If the doe is chased by dogs, and is very hard pressed, she will lift little 'joey' out of her pouch and throw him into a bush or a tuft of grass. Then, without her burden, she is able to increase her speed and perhaps escape from the dogs.
>
> Many writers have blamed the doe for thus forsaking her offspring, which they think is a very unmotherly act; for most wild animals, especially the mothers, will fight until death to protect their young ones. Maybe the mother kangaroo does not throw 'joey' away to save herself, but because she thinks that, although the cruel dogs may catch her, her baby, hidden in the bush, will escape their notice.

The progress of scientific thought was echoed slowly and spasmodically in the pages of *The Children's Hour.* Despite the influence of professional naturalists, the articles on the lives of people such as Pasteur and Lister, and the introduction of simple scientific experiments for the readers to try out, the general understanding of living things remained unsophisticated. They were God-given. The *Hour* allowed no questioning of a divine principle at work in the universe. If any of the contributors held a different view it certainly did not surface in those pages.

For many people there was no need to look for an explanation beyond the verses which appeared year after year in the *Hour*, and which were sung by children throughout their school lives:

All things bright and beautiful
All creatures great and small,
All things wise and wonderful,
The Lord God made them all.

He gave us eyes to see them
And lips that we might tell
How great is God Almighty
Who hath made all things well!

1924.

AN ANIMAL SANCTUARY.

SUPPOSE you lived in a land where you were very happy. Then suppose a big powerful enemy came and either killed you and yours, or drove you away from your country to starve. Further, suppose that a kind person (call him Mr Greatheart, if you like) made a place where you might find shelter from your enemies and where food and drink were plentiful. Would you not feel grateful to Mr Greatheart?

Now, years and years ago, near the place where these lines have been written, and probably where they are being read, there were thousands of creatures living happy lives. Can you guess some of their names? They were kangaroos, wallabies, wombats, opossums, and large flocks of parrots, cockatoos, and other birds.

But then came big ships to our shores bringing white folk—some were the grandparents of people now living in South Australia. Soon they began cutting down the trees, which meant destroying the homes of birds. The dogs and cats brought from overseas began to kill the native animals and birds; and the guns of the white men shot many and frightened more. In a few years the wild creatures had left the settled parts of South Australia.

Many years ago Mr T. P. Bellchambers came to South Australia and spent many years wandering about the unsettled parts studying the ways of wild animals. He learnt to love them and longed for the time when he would be able to save some from destruction by keeping them in a place of shelter. At last his wish was granted. Some years ago he was able to secure the lease of some rough country in the Barossa Ranges.

In this out-of-the-way country Mr Bellchambers lives and has made it a sheltering place for native animals and birds. Here they may come and be welcomed without fear of cruel guns, fierce dogs, sly cats, or other enemies of wild creatures.

1903.
Christmas Morning.

CHAPTER FIVE

LANDS OF HOPE AND GLORY

South Australia, in common with the other States of Australia, gives a strong clue to its origins in the proliferation of names belonging to British royalty. South Australia's capital city was named Adelaide in honour of the wife of King William IV who was the reigning King of England at the time the State was founded. The main street of the city is named King William Street and a sculptural figure of Queen Victoria stands in the centre of the city, in the centre of Victoria Square.

Many years later, in 1953, a satellite town was established and named Elizabeth, honouring the newly crowned British Queen. *The Children's Hour* was a paper of general readership and reflected common attitudes of the times, and so it provides insight into the importance of the monarchy in the lives of everyday South Australians, from the 1890s onwards. But there is evidence of republican views too, for thoughts of independence and nationhood exist in most colonies whether they are openly expressed or lying beneath the surface. In Australia the issue has surfaced and resurfaced occasionally, over many years, sometimes with ardour but seldom with violence. Reading *The Children's Hour*, however, one is mostly aware of the royal presence in the early decades of its publication, when the monarchy was set secure in the centre of South Australian life. (It is not until about the 1920s that one notices a lessening of ties with Britain in the pages of the *Hour*.)

The first settlers built their initial security and their future confidence on the heritage of centuries of European civilisation incorporated in the British way of life. From its beginning, South Australia was a British colony by temperament, and it remained so for many years.

In the June issue of the *Hour* in 1894, 'News of the Month' referred to the Birthday Honours:

> It is pleasant to know that our colony has not been forgotten in the awarding of titles of honour which usually mark the Queen's birthday. This year the South Australians thus honoured are Mr Charles Todd CMG, our highly esteemed Postmaster-General, who has been Knighted

1910.

AN AUSTRALIAN BOY'S THOUGHT.

I say with pride, I say with joy,
I am a free Australian boy.
I think my land the best on earth;
I love it, for it gave me birth.
Yet, though I dwell in this far clime,
I am a Briton all the time.

August 1894.

SCHOLARS' CORNER.

THE UNVEILING OF THE QUEEN'S STATUE.

IT is now some time since I first wrote to *The Children's Hour* and I am sending an account of the unveiling of the Queen's Statue, which took place on Saturday, August 11th in the square which bears Her Majesty's name. The statue is of bronze and the pedestal is made of granite; total cost was £1000, and it is a very imposing structure. It was presented to the Mayor and Corporation of Adelaide, by Sir Edwin Thomas Smith, who is well known in the colony for his generosity and kindness of heart. The ceremony took place at about four o'clock in the afternoon and was witnessed by crowds of men, women and children, as well as the sailors from the Protector and the militiamen. One hundred children from each of the five chief schools were invited to attend the ceremony, and these formed a procession from the Grote St School, the North Adelaide children leading with their band. The school children were arranged on the left hand side of the statue. The third regiment of soldiers and the police and drum and fife bands were behind them. At about 3.45 pm the Governor and Major Seabright arrived in a carriage and after them came Sir Edwin and Lady Smith. The Governor opened the proceedings by a well delivered speech, and then asked Lady Smith to unveil the statue. Directly the veil which covered the statue was removed the children began to sing 'God Save the Queen' with the bands accompanying them, and at the same moment the guns were fired on the Parade Grounds and the Town Hall bells struck up a merry peal. The performance was brought to a close by the children and bands playing and singing the national song of Australia. Cheers were then given for the Queen, the Governor and Sir Edwin and Lady Smith, the latter had kindly provided oranges and sweets for the children, which were distributed in the Grote St playground.

Alice Nash
North Adelaide School.

and Dr E. C. Stirling who, as an enthusiast in natural science, is well known, and on whom Her Majesty has been pleased to confer the distinction of CMG.

Despite strong ties and allegiances to Britain, fresh challenges and achievements and the enthusiasm of the colonists created a new devotion and loyalty—to the land itself.

This dual allegiance produced no conflict—the two strands ran together and seemed natural and unremarkable.

In 1907 a page of the *Hour* held a trio of ennobling hymns. These were: 'God Save the Queen' (despite the fact that she had died six years earlier); 'The Old Hundredth' (the name given to the hymn, 'All people that on earth do dwell'); 'The Song of Australia' (without the first verse which is the most familiar). The latter was made up of music composed by Carl Linger to the words written by Mrs C. J. Carleton, and it enjoyed great popularity in the early part of this century. It was included with 'God Save the Queen' on many public, as well as school, occasions, and it was still well known to those who went to school in the 1930s and 1940s. It was printed in the *Hour* with monotonous regularity and had many verses—every new or special occasion would prompt another!

At the turn of the century, a feeling for the Australian landscape showed in the songs and verses which were appearing more frequently in the *Hour*. This was both a part of, and a result of, an emerging national awareness on a larger scale. A good example is the first page of the December issue in 1904, which was devoted to 'Christmas: In England and Australia', by the late J. C. F. Johnson.

PRESENT TIME ADDITIONS TO THE SONG OF AUSTRALIA.

Bertha Limbert.

There is a land, where hand clasps hand
To join in one united band
And strong among the nations stand,
Whose sons are fired with steadfast zeal,
And work together true as steel,
For Federation and its weal—
Australia!

And now we see with joy sublime
A vision in the coming time
Of gladness for our sunny clime;
The land new-born, with strength endowed,
Shall flourish, federated, proud,
And vaunt the name that ne'er was cowed—
Australia!

A way of life was developing in response to the nature of the land, which was in obvious contrast to life in the 'Old Country'. In July 1898 the *Hour* had published 'An Australian Anthem' by the Revd William Allen of Petersham, New South Wales. It makes a reference to Federation which had been an ideal and an aim of many colonists from as early as 1850, and which was finally realised in 1901.

CHRISTMAS: IN ENGLAND AND AUSTRALIA.

The late J. C. F. Johnson.

ENGLAND.

A sky of mist, with cloud-wrack from the sea,
Sodden with sleet, and laden all with snow,
A biting wind that sweeps o'er lawn and lea,
And whirls the drifts in mad chase to and fro.
The hoar frost sparkles on each leafless bough,
The ice sets thick on all the streams and ponds;
Wild Winter rules; his potent touch hath now
The landscape bound in hard and glittering bonds.
Holly and mistletoe in hall are hung,
The yule log crackles in the chimney wide,
The Christmas joybells gleefully are rung,
And happy homes will welcome Christmastide.
Within, warmth, merriment, and dancing feet—
Without, want, misery that seems past cure;
God help the homeless starving in the street!
Now, Christlike Christians, see ye aid His poor.
Think mid your glee of those in hunger's thrall
Walking through weary ways in hopeless gloom.
On them no beams of bright red firelight fall,
For them small joy from cradle to the tomb.
Kind Father Christmas, cheery, bright, and old,
To-day through many lands thy praises ring;
Mark these wan children crouching in the cold.
What gifts for them doth this thy season bring?
Lord, let Thy little ones be borne in mind,
Let kindness govern, pity lend a tear.
Grant on Thy birthday each a friend may find;
Soften all hearts this one day in the year.

Hark! the bells' music falling, swelling higher,
Wafting glad tidings over field and fen,
Wake a faint echo of the heavenly choir,
Breathes peace on earth and good will still to men.

AUSTRALIA.

A cloudless sky of tender turquoise blue
Smiles o'er the warm, glad, sun-kissed southern land.
A sapphire sea, dreamlike in distant view,
Marged by a belt of glittering silver sand.
The rich, red sun rays quiver as they fall
On golden grasses, and on amber wheat;
While shrill cicadas from the branches call,
Droning and clanging in the drowsy heat.
The gum trees' balm, and perfume of the pine,
Steal faintly forth, as when in sacred fane
The censer wafts dim sweetness, and combine
Their myrrh and frankincense in scented rain.
A crystal creek is murm'ring rhythmic rhymes,
And soft, low music makes mid mossy stones.
The bell bird's note rings out in mellow chimes,
And magpies carol yule in flute-like tones.
Fair Austral Christmas, mid thy ferns and flowers
And outdoor joyance, thou art welcome now;
Summer thy advent with rich beauty dowers;
No grey old wintry blooded man art thou
We see a bright-haired youth with sun-tanned face,
Radiant with youth's high hopes, frank fearless eyes,
Slender, lithe limbed, Apollo like in grace,
And checks aglow with thoughts of high emprise.
No note of anguish clouds his glorious smile,
No cry of starving brothers in their pain.
O'er our great Island, stretching mile on mile,
Joy holds her sway, and peace and plenty reign.
Keep thus our Christmas, free from care and crime,
Lord, in our Elder Brother's name we pray,
And grant each year as dawns the holy time,
A prosperous land may greet His natal day.

AN AUSTRALIAN ANTHEM.

GOD SAVE OUR AUSTRAL LAND.

Rev. Wm Allen, Petersham, NSW.

God save our Austral land,
Close knit the federal band
That makes us one.
For treasures manifold,
Rich store of gems and gold
Increase of field and fold
Be homage done.

But richer gifts, O Lord,
Than all thy works afford
We gain would find
Give kindly spirits free
Give hearts that yearn to see
A true fraternity
Of all mankind.

Be home of equal laws
And freedom's holy cause
This Austral land.
Justice and liberty
And godlike charity
Our guardian angels be.
God save our land!

March 2nd, 1897.

TOPICS OF TO-DAY.

MY Dear Boys and Girls—For this month's letter it seems that there are only two topics to write about, so full have the papers been of Federation and the troubles in Crete.

Before you read this, the election for representatives in the Federal Convention will have been held, and the fortunate ten selected who shall represent our province of South Australia.

More than forty years ago, the idea of a Federation of the Australian Colonies was spoken of. But it has been left to recent times to make a real advance. Conventions have been held in Melbourne and Sydney, and now comes the most important of all to be held in our own city. There are a great many details to be arranged, and many difficulties to be overcome, but it promises to be now but a matter of a short time, when we shall be able to speak of ourselves as *Australians*, and not merely as South Australians, Victorians, Queenslanders, or New South Welshmen.

My readers will grow up to be citizens of the great Commonwealth of Australia, and all Australians be brothers from Point Danger to Shark Bay, from Cape York to South Cape.

As Kipling sings:

Our fathers held by purchase,
But we by the right of birth:

Our hearts where they rocked our cradle,
Our love where we spend our toil,
And our faith and our hope and our honour
We pledge to our native soil.

UNION PRIZE
COMMONWEALTH ODE.

Awake! Arise! The wings of dawn
Are beating at the Gates of Day!
The morning star hath been withdrawn,
The silver vapours melt away.
Rise royally, O sun, and crown
The shoreward billow, streaming white,
The forelands and the mountain's brown
with crested light;
Flood with soft beams the valleys wide,
The mighty plains, the desert sand,
Till the New Day hath won for bride
This Austral land.
Come too, thou Sun Maid, in whose veins
Forever burns the tropic fire;
Whose cattle roam a thousand plains
Come, with gold and pearls for tire;
And that Sweet Harvester who twines
The tender vine and binds the sheaf,
And she, the Western Queen, who mines
The desert reef;
And thou, against whose flowery throne
And orchards green the wave is hurled
Australia claims you — ye are one
Before the world!

MY LAND.

T. O. Davis.

(The poet who wrote the following lines was an Irishman, and he intended them to refer to his native land. The poem, however, tells what all good Australians think of their own land.)

She is a rich and rare land;
O, she's a fresh and fair land;
She is a dear and rare land—
This native land of mine.

No men than hers are braver;
Her women's hearts ne'er waver;
I'd freely die to save her,
And think my lot divine.

She's not a dull or cold land;
No, she's a warm and bold land;
O, she's a true and old land—
This native land of mine.

Could beauty ever guard her,
And virtue still reward her,
No foe would cross her border,
No friend within it pine.

O, she's a fresh and fair land;
O, she's a true and rare land;
Yes, she's a rare and fair land—
This native land of mine.

Considering the momentous nature of the decision for all Australians, it received surprisingly little comment in the *Hour* beforehand. But when a poem by Mr George Essex Evans won the prize of fifty pounds, offered by the Government of New South Wales for a poem to celebrate the event, it was published in the newspapers of every State and was later included in the *Hour*, accompanied by one or two explanatory notes to help the reader.

The lofty phrases so characteristic of many such odes would have been very difficult for most children, and many adults, to understand without some explanation:

'Sun Maid'—Queensland
'Sweet Harvester'—South Australia
'Western Queen'—Western Australia

When Federation Day arrived the *Hour* published a facsimile of the Proclamation, and photographs of the new Governor-General, Lord Hopetoun.

The report of this historic event was framed by a black line. This was not a gloomy prediction on Australia's future unity, but a mark of respect for the dead, for Queen Victoria died on 22 January 1901, only three weeks after Federation, and both occasions had to be given due honour in the February issue!

February 1901.

OUR GOOD AND GREAT QUEEN IS DEAD.

Just as *The Children's Hours* are to be printed the sorrowful news has reached us that our beloved Queen is dead. Only a little more than a week ago she received Lord Roberts and attended to other state duties, and now we are told that the noblest and greatest Queen the world has yet known passed peacefully to her well earned rest on the evening of January 22nd. We cannot do more than announce the sorrowful fact now; but in a future issue we shall deal more fully with the life and

work of one who has during her long reign endeared herself to the whole civilised world, and become enshrined in the hearts of her own three hundred and sixty millions of loyal and devoted subjects.

Queen Victoria came to the throne in 1837, the year after South Australia was proclaimed, so that its formative years were much influenced by her reign, as indeed was the entire British Empire. The Queen became the personification of British power, wealth, and

Top: *1 January 1901. The Governor-General Escorted to the Swearing-in Pavilion, Sydney.*
(Kindly lent by Sir Langdon Bonython.)
Photo: Henry King, Sydney.

Bottom: *1 January 1901.*
The Imperial Troops, Sydney.
(Kindly lent by Sir Langdon Bonython.)
Photo: Henry King, Sydney.

moral influence. As the mother figure, she was looked up to with respect close to religious reverence, and, despite her seemingly unbending demeanour, people referred to her as 'Our dear Queen' and 'the beloved Queen', so she may have inspired affection too:

> May 1899.
>
> Our beloved Queen will be eighty years of age on the twenty-fourth of this month, and on the twentieth of June she will have reigned for sixty-two years. When enjoying your holiday on Monday, May 29th, I want you all to think of her, and lovingly say 'God bless our Queen'.

Cymro's letter gave this piece of information about Her Majesty:

> When she was three months old she was vaccinated and it is very interesting to note that she was the first member of the Royal family of England to receive the benefit of Dr Jenner's discovery.

As in matters moral, so in matters medical, the monarch set the right example.

Her continuing presence as ruler gave a great sense of permanence to the British way of life, and a feeling of confidence and security, especially to remote colonies like South Australia. To be British may not have guaranteed comfort, but it did guarantee safety.

Queen Victoria.
Born, 24 May 1819.
Died, 22 January 1901.

In 1896 'Topics of To-day' drew attention to the fact that:

> Queen Victoria has now reigned over the greatest empire the world has ever seen for fifty-nine years, making her reign the second longest in history. Long may she reign! As a part of the British Empire we share the great blessings of freedom. Looking away from our own land of Australia we may see great cause to be thankful that we are not living in such a country, for example, as Turkey.

The Queen's authority as 'head of the family' was not stifling, and being part of the British Empire aroused sentiments of pride in South Australians. Not only did they belong to the Empire but the Empire also belonged to them!

In 1897 the Empire proudly shared in celebrating the Queen's sixty-year reign with the Diamond Jubilee. There were references to the event in the *Hour* months beforehand, and lengthy accounts of the occasion continued to dazzle and excite the readers for months afterwards.

Schoolchildren were granted a week's holiday, which seems surprisingly generous in an age when the work ethic held sway and minutes had to be well accounted for! Such was the immense importance of the Queen's reign.

When in June the Jubilee day arrived, excitement was intense, and *The Children's Hour* used the heightened loyalty of the time to bring out a ten-page résumé of British achievements during the Queen's reign. No one reading it then, or now, could fail to be impressed by such a success story. No wonder people responded so joyously to the Jubilee. In July 'Topics of To-day' devoted several pages to the celebrations in both London and Adelaide which captured the atmosphere brilliantly. Photographs brought the excitement closer to those who had not been able to join in the Adelaide festivities.

A surprising number of Australians had travelled to England for the occasion. In September Cymro commented:

> The people who were lucky enough to go to England for the Jubilee are returning to Australia in hundreds by each steamer. Some I suppose will be sorry to leave London but many will be glad to get back to this sunny country.

It is interesting that Cymro on this occasion did not refer to either Britain or Australia as 'home' although England was always regarded as the mother country, the homeland, for many years. *The Children's Hour* reprinted the following lines in 1914:

> Britain is like a mother with many children who have gone from her into other countries to earn their own living. She still loves them, she sends them many kind messages, and helps them in every way she can. And the children, the people far away from her, love her in return.
>
> *Adapted from the* Commonwealth School Paper, 1914.

June 25th, 1897.

TOPICS OF TO-DAY.

Dear Boys and Girls—Our Jubilee holiday, looked for with so much anxiety, has come and gone. I hope you all had a real good time, and thoroughly enjoyed yourselves.

May 19th, 1897.

CYMRO'S LETTER.

MY Dear Boys and Girls.—My letter this month will contain no local news, as I have been asked to write purely on matters connected with our famous Queen. On June 20th her reign will have extended for more than sixty years, and in honour of this event there will be great rejoicings in England, particularly in London, and in all lands throughout the world wherever the English language is spoken.

Our Queen's grandfather, George III, had fifteen children, and her father, the Duke of Kent, was the fifth child. Her mother, the Duchess of Kent, was a German lady. A number of sad deaths happened among the brothers and sisters of the Duke of Kent and their children, so that when William IV died his niece, Princess Victoria, had the best claim to the crown, and she accordingly became Queen.

Her Majesty was born at Kensington Palace, London, at 4 am on the 24th day of May, 1819, so that in five days more she will be seventy-eight years old. Only one ruler of England since the time of the Normans has reached an age beyond that which the Queen is, and that was her grandfather, George III, who reached the grand age of eighty-two years. The length of her reign, however, has not been beaten by any English ruler. She was christened on the 24th of June, in the house where she was born, just when she was one month old, and the name she received was Alexandrina Victoria. It is said that her father wished her to be called Elizabeth, but the Duke's brother, who was then really ruler of England, had his own way, and called her Alexandrina, and then added Victoria, which was the name of her mother.

22 June 1897.
No. 2—North Park Lands, Jubilee Day.
(From a copyright photograph by Ernest Gall.)

Almost, if not quite, all of you took part in the demonstrations, either in your own towns, or in the city. But, as many of you were not in Adelaide, my letter will contain a little about the celebrations there.

The Diamond Jubilee celebrations in the city began with the feasting of the poor at the Exhibition Building, over 1200 families being supplied with provisions for three days.

Then on Sunday came the thanksgiving services, when, not in Adelaide only, but throughout the whole Empire, the people thronged the churches to join in the services which expressed their thanks to the Almighty for the great blessings we as a people enjoy under the rule of Queen Victoria.

On Monday our military and naval forces paraded to the number of just over a thousand, when the various branches of our little army were reviewed by His Excellency the Governor at Montefiore Hill. The varied uniforms of the mounted rifles, artillery, blue-jackets, infantry, &c., made up a very interesting sight. On Monday evening there were fireworks, and the streets were gaily decorated and rendered almost as bright as day by the brilliant electric, gas, and other illuminations, the Queen's statue in Victoria Square being especially brilliant, while the whole width of road and paths was fully occupied by the crowds of orderly sightseers, on pleasure bent.

Tuesday morning brought the greatest day of all for my readers, when the schools paraded, nearly 20 000 strong. Assembling early round the Queen's statue in Victoria Square, the different schools, to the number of over eighty, fell in at their appointed stations. Music was supplied by the Military, Police Fire Brigade, Eastern Suburban, and Locomotive Brass Bands, the Scotch Piper Band, and numerous drum and fife bands belonging to different schools. The uniforms of the bands, and especially of the firemen with their bright brass helmets and long boots, and the kilts of the Scotch pipers, with the thousands of flags and banners, backed by the greenery of the square's plantations (looking so fresh after the recent rains), made up a most brilliant and beautiful picture. I should not forget to mention the Mounted Infantry men who very kindly volunteered to help the troopers in keeping the ground clear of the general public, who thronged around. At the foot of the Queen's statue, so handsomely decorated with beautiful flowers by the skilful hands of the girls, the Governor was presented with two addresses, one from the corporation representing the citizens of Adelaide, and the other from the Local Government Association, representing the corporations and district councils throughout the colony.

Then the 20 000 children, arranged eight abreast, marched off from their respective stations and joined in the great procession. With bands playing and banners and flags waving, they marched through the dense masses of spectators crowding King William Street, and filling every window-ledge, balcony, or other place where a footing could be obtained to get a sight of the procession.

By half-past 12 the scholars (covering much over an acre of ground) had reached Montefiore Hill, and taken their places facing the platform, on which stood the Governor and other gentlemen connected with the celebrations. Then the whole body of children, under the conductorship of Inspector Clark, sang the 'Old Hundredth.' Speeches followed from Mr Bonython, the presentation of an address to His Excellency, and of an address to be forwarded to the Queen. His Excellency the Governor, Sir Edwin Smith, and the Hon. Minister of Education (Dr Cockburn) also addressed the children in noble words, which I am sorry want of space will not allow me to reproduce here, but which I hope you have all read in the papers.

After the singing of the National Anthem and 'The Song of Australia' the children were marched to their stations for refreshments, afterwards being allowed some time for play, and were then marched off, very tired, but happy. The scene from Montefiore Hill, looking down upon the mass of moving figures with the bright colours of the flags and dresses, was one never to be forgotten.

In the evening immense crowds again filled the streets to admire the illuminations and decorations. At 9 o'clock the whole of the vast crowd near the Town Hall joined in singing 'God Save the Queen,' which at that moment was being sung all the world over in the British dominions. It was then 12 o'clock, midday (Tuesday), in London, and the great procession had just halted before St Paul's and were singing 'God Save the Queen' there. So ended the demonstration in the city of Adelaide.

The British governors of colonies, or States, as they later became, maintained the links with Britain and the Crown. Being representatives of the King or the Queen, they were held in almost the same high regard as the monarch. They were looked up to for their dignity, eminence and integrity; looked to for example, leadership and support; and in return given respect, loyalty and affection.

In the *Hour* of April 1896, Scholars' Corner published 'A Memorable Picnic', written by Annie Anderson of the Montacute School. It described a visit to the vice-regal residence at Marble Hill, Norton Summit:

One hundred little guests marched from nearby schools. After 'lining up' with military precision—God Save the Queen floated from our many

1909.

THE GOVERNOR'S MESSAGE TO THE CHILDREN OF SOUTH AUSTRALIA.

ON the day previous to the departure of Sir Geo. Le Hunte from South Australia the Director of Education asked His Excellency for a message of farewell to the children of this State. Sir George at once wrote the following, and requested Mr Williams to have it brought under the notice of the children in the public schools.

To the Children of South Australia—In leaving South Australia for my new work in Trinidad, I wish to tell my special friends, the children of South Australia, how much I have felt all your loyalty and love to me, not only as the Governor of your State and the King's representative for the time being, but also as a real personal friend of your own. That is what I wanted you to feel: that you are the children of the King just as much as those in the Old Country, and that your Governor belonged to you. Keep your flag flying for the Empire, and make your life your help to it. Thank you, too, for your kind affection to my dear wife, Lady Le Hunte. Many of your own mothers know how true a friend she is to you. We will not forget each other. We wish you all a very happy New Year, and God's blessing to all in this happy land, which your grandfathers and fathers and mothers have made for you. Good-bye. Work well; play well.

Your true and
affectionate Governor,
George R. Le Hunte.

voices. Sir Fowell Buxton [the Governor] bade us welcome and we were soon seated at a good tea, which we enjoyed as only children can. After our hearty meal we received a great surprise, viz., tug-of-war for the boys, races for both boys and girls' games and swings and such like.

Lady Victoria presented suitable and pretty prizes to the winners of the various races. The Song of Australia was then sung, bags of lollies were distributed; lusty cheers were given for the Governor, Lady Victoria and family, and each child, with a happy heart, started off for home at 6.30 pm.

Bearing in mind that many of the children then faced a walk of miles, trailing home through the hills in the gathering April darkness, one realises that to enjoy such hospitality was considered to be an immense privilege. It is typical of the relationship which then existed and which was never seen as patronising. On the contrary, class differences were expected, respected and accepted. The vice-regal influence carried far and was deeply felt in colonial life. In the *Hour* there was a steady flow of reports of school visits and messages of goodwill from 'Their Excellencies', and sometimes photographs of them formally addressing, or informally mingling, and always giving an impression of kindliness and loving concern:

January 1908
Message from His Excellency the Governor
Marble Hill, Adelaide
New Year's Day, 1908
Dear Mr Williams—will you kindly convey to all in your Department and to the schools my very best wishes for a very happy and successful year.
Yours very sincerely,
George R. LeHunte.

The arrival of a new governor with his family was happily noted in 1899:

Through the kindness of Sir Langdon Bonython, the proprietor of *The Chronicle* and the proprietors of *The Adelaide Observer* we are enabled to present to our readers this month a set of interesting pictures connected with our new Governor, Lord Tennyson, and his family.

Nor were the affectionate ties broken, it seems, when a governor's term ended and he went elsewhere. In 1907 there was a report of the visit, while in England, by Mr Williams, 'our Director of Education', to Lord and Lady Tennyson, whose term at Government House had ended in 1902. The following was published in January 1908, when Mr Williams returned:

Lady Tennyson gave to Mr Williams the following message, in which she shows how she admires the brave men who did so much for our land and how she loves the children of Australia.

Aldworth,
October 29th, 1907.

To the Children of Australia—I have been reading with great pleasure and interest some copies of your *Children's Hour*, which Mr Williams kindly sent me, containing accounts of the great English discoverers of Australia and the famous explorers of the continent.

When I think of you, children of Australia, my heart goes out to you in love.

18 August 1921.
His Excellency Sir Archibald, Lady Weigall, and Their Little daughter, Miss Priscilla, on Their Visit to Greenock School.

May you try to grow up like those old heroes, 'Strong with the strength of the race to command, to obey, to endure'.

Your affectionate friend,
Audrey F. Tennyson.

It was the death of the Governor, the Earl of Kintore, which inspired a lengthy ode by Claud C. Wilson: 'It is here printed by order of the Hon Minister of Education—Editor, *Children's Hour*, February 1906'. The last of its many stanzas makes an interesting and appropriate reference to the Mediterranean climate shared by South Australia and much of the Middle East:

Heirs of this beauteous isle beyond the sea,
We now, Thy suppliant creatures, bend the knee,
And ask that in Thy own good time and way
Thou'lt grant us all we need from day to day.
May we, like ancient Israel, safe recline
Beneath the fig tree's shade and sheltering vine;

Our garners full and yielding plenteous store,
Our wine and oil pressed down and running o'er;
May harvests prosper, may our flocks increase,
And every home be filled with joy and peace.
O lead us onward, till this land shall rise
A greater Britain 'neath these southern skies!

Claud C. Wilson.

Children of the Governor and his wife [Lord and Lady Tennyson].
(Kindly lent by Proprietors Adelaide Observer.*)*
Photo: S. G. Spink.

27 February 1901.
The Governor, Lord Tennyson, Proclaiming King Edward VII.

The early decades of the 1900s brought a cluster of royal events which gave added strength to the ties with Britain, and crowded the pages of the *Hour*. Following the death of Queen Victoria, Edward VII was proclaimed King and subsequently his coronation took place.

The thousands of umbrellas shown in this photograph were a protection, not from rain but from the scorching heat of a day late in February 1901.

King Edward reigned for only nine years. In May 1910 *The Children's Hour* edition came out once more outlined in black, with the King's portrait on the front cover. The issue was given over to a great number of verses dwelling on the theme of the Empire. Many of these now seem embarrassingly self-congratulatory and smug. Children reading such sentiments could have been forgiven for assuming that God was an Englishman!

May 1910.

THE DEATH OF OUR KING,
EDWARD VII.

OUR Empire number has been held back for us briefly to refer to the mournful news that has been flashed over the whole world, telling that King Edward is dead. He, but for a few hours ago the ruler of the mightiest Empire the world has ever known, now lies still and cold at Buckingham Palace, London. But yesterday hundreds of millions of his people, living on every continent of the world, willingly obeyed and felt proud of their King, who was so cheerful, so manly, and so skilful as a ruler; to-day those people are flying their flags half-mast and tolling their bells to show their grief for the loss of their beloved Sovereign. The death of no other man in the whole world would have caused so many hearts to sorrow as has the passing of King Edward.

May 1910 (Edward VII's death).

BRITAIN.

Oliver Wendell Holmes.

Hugged in the clinging billow's clasp
From seaweed fringe to mountain heather
The British oak with rooted grasp,
Her slender handfuls holds together
With cliffs of white and bowers of green,
And ocean narrowing to caress her
And hills and threaded streams between—
Our little Mother Isle—God bless her!

King Edward VII.
Born, 9 November 1841.
Died, 6 May 1910.

WHERE IS THE BRITON'S HOME?
Bulwer Lytton.

Where is the Briton's home?
Where the free step can roam,
Where the free sun can glow,
Where a free air can blow,
Where a free ship can bear
Hope and strength—everywhere
Wave upon wave can roll,
East and west, pole to pole,
Where a free step can roam—
There is the Briton's home!

Where is the Briton's home?
Where the brave heart can come,
Where labour wins a soil,
Where a stout heart can toil—
Wherever by rough winds blown,
Any fair seed is sown—
Where gold or fame is won,
Where never sets the sun,
Where a brave heart can come—
There is the Briton's home!

Where is the Briton's home?
Where the mind's light can come—
Where our God's holy word
Breaks on the savage herd;
Where a new flock is won
To the bright Shepherd. One,
Where the church bell can toll,
Where the soul can comfort soul,
Where holy faith can come—
There is the Briton's home!

Where is the Briton's home?
Where man's great law can come,
Where the great truth can speak,
Where the slave's chain can break,
Where the white's scourge can cease,
Where the black dwells in peace,
Where, from his angel-hall,
God sees us brothers all—
Where light and freedom come—
There is the Briton's home!

The article announcing the forthcoming visit of the Duke and Duchess of York in 1927 sounds a prophetic note:

April 1927.

THE DUKE AND DUCHESS OF YORK.

The Duke of York is the second son of King George and Queen Mary. On next December 14th the Duke will be thirty-two years of age. His eldest brother is the Prince of Wales, who, if he lives, will be our next King. Should, however, the Prince of Wales die before his father, King George, the Duke of York will next wear the Crown of England. The Duke, then, is second from the throne.

The little Princess Elizabeth was too young to come with her parents to Australia. She is now living with her grandfather and grandmother, King George and Queen Mary. She is a very precious little baby, because she is the third in order who can come to the throne. Some day she may be Queen of England.

Royal visits to the colonies became the custom, and the *Hour* gave them very thorough coverage—they made popular family reading. But as early as 1881, before the *Hour* existed, there had been a visit

June 1920.

THE KING'S FIRST VISIT TO SOUTH AUSTRALIA.

THE two boys were midshipmen on board a large man-of-war. For three years they sailed in this ship, visiting every important part of the British Empire. It was a grand lesson to teach the boys how vast was the British Empire, over which, some day, one of them was to rule.

They had with them their tutor, Mr Dalton. Every day on board ship he gave lessons to his pupils, and when they went ashore he went with them to see the sights of the country.

The first part of the Commonwealth in which they landed was Western Australia. There they spent some days in sight-seeing and then they sailed for our State. It was Sunday evening, June 12th, 1881, when the three—the two princes and Mr Dalton—landed on the Glenelg jetty and took train for Adelaide.

They were driven from the railway station to Government House, where they stayed whilst in Adelaide. Next morning they played a game of tennis in Government House grounds, and later they were taken to the top of the high tower of the Adelaide Post Office, and saw beneath them the straight streets, the five squares and the parklands around the city.

1901.
Doris Fern Booker Waiting with Flowers for the Duchess.

to Adelaide by Prince Albert, who was seventeen, and Prince George, aged sixteen.

Prince George revisited Australia years later with his wife, as the Duke and Duchess of Cornwall and York. Later they became King George V and Queen Mary.

August 1901.

OUR PICTURES.

As some thousands of our readers were not able to come to Adelaide during the week's festivities recently held in honour of the visit of their Royal Highnesses the Duke and Duchess of Cornwall and York, we print in the present numbers of *The Children's Hour* a varied lot of pictures, which, added to those in our July issues, will afford some idea of what passed in Adelaide during the Royal visit.

While the Royal party were kept 'on the go' early and late from the hour they landed at Port Adelaide on Tuesday, July 9th, to the time when they embarked on the *Ophir* on Monday, July 15th, the scenes and events most interesting to our young folks were the beautiful illuminations each night, the march through the city on the Tuesday, the schools' demonstration at the Adelaide Oval on the Thursday, and the laying of the foundation stone of the Queen Victoria Mothers' Home at Rose Park on Saturday.

Of course, many of you are aware that this is not the first visit of the Duke to our shores. He was here twenty years ago when he and his elder brother, the late Prince Edward, were happy sailor boys on a British man-of-war. But it is the first time he has come to us as the next heir to the Throne of England and the Empire, and it is also the first time that a Princess of the Royal family of England has set foot on Australian soil.

To do honour to Prince George and his beautiful Royal Consort the Princess May, who will in due time we trust succeed to the Crown and Throne of England, Adelaide was beautifully decorated by day and splendidly illuminated by night.

On Tuesday 12 000 school children lined the two sides of Wakefield Street from Victoria Square to Pulteney Street, and as the Royal procession passed between these lines the children must all have had a good view of the Duke and Duchess and their party.

At East Terrace 1200 children from over thirty country schools were provided with seats on a large gallery, and as the Royal carriage stopped for a few minutes these children, accompanied by a good brass band, sang 'God Save the King'. At this point the Duke received an address from the Market Gardeners, and the Duchess, a lovely basket of flowers. The address was handed to the Duke by young Claude Charlick, and the flowers to the Duchess by little Agnes Nelson from Scott's Creek school. These two were supported by sixteen other children, all very prettily dressed in white, and each holding a bunch of pink and white roses. This modest display of loyalty on the part of Mr Charlick and his East End friends and the gardeners and their children will, I am sure, be long remembered by the Duchess.

It was in 1920 that Edward Prince of Wales embarked on the glamorous world tour which surpassed all others in splendour and spectacle despite the fact that the country had barely recovered from the 1914–1918 Great War.

May 1920.

THE TOUR OF THE PRINCE OF WALES.

At the end of last March the Prince of Wales, in the battle cruiser *Repulse*, left England to visit several outlying parts of the British Empire. If all goes well the tour will last six months, and will conclude with a visit to the Argentine Republic. The Prince will gain much knowledge that will be of use to him when he becomes the ruler of the British Empire; and millions of British subjects, white or black in colour, speaking many languages, and with different ways of worshipping God will all be drawn to a Prince who has a wonderful power of charming his future subjects.

The early ties with Britain had been centred on the Crown, but later more emphasis was placed on the Empire as the uniting force. So persuasive and captivating was the notion of the Empire that it almost assumed the proportions of a cult or a religion. In 1901 the League of the British Commonwealth and Empire came into existence, sometimes simply called the Empire League. Its purpose was to develop and promote contact between Britain and her colonies through educational means. Inter-empire conferences took place, but gradually the emphasis shifted and an interchange of teachers became its chief concern.

1920.

THE PRINCE AT TEROWIE.

THERE is a story about the Prince which should interest our readers. On the evening of the day after the Prince had left Hughes, the out-back station on the East-West line, his train drew up at the platform of the Terowie Station. Here the royal party had to change trains, because of the break of gauge on the railway line.

The Head Teacher of the Terowie School (Mr O. A. Witt) had his pupils lined up on the railway platform ready to pay their respects to their future King. The fife-and-drum band, clad in neat uniforms, looked smart and capable.

As soon as the train drew up at the station the band played a few bars of the National Anthem. The Prince stepped out of his carriage and first inspected a squad of returned soldiers, for the Prince himself is proud to be numbered among the 'diggers'. After making some remarks to his comrades in arms, he turned his attention to the school children.

They first sang a verse from 'Motherland', and, the Prince complimented them on their musical skill, both as singers and players; he also added that they deserved a long holiday. This remark seemed to please the members of the band, for they struck up the well-known tune, 'For He's a Jolly Good Fellow'. The Prince laughed heartily, and clapped his hands in applause.

Top: *1920. King William Street, Adelaide, Illuminations. The General Post Office is on the left, the Town Hall on the right. The dark statue in the foreground is Colonel Light's.*

Left: *1920. The Exhibition Building on North Terrace, Illuminated in Honour of HRH The Prince of Wales. From a photograph kindly supplied by Private Edward O'Halloran (Queensland).*

Top: *1920. The Children's Demonstration at the Adelaide Oval—the 'Prince of Wales' Feathers.*
Photo: Kodak Limited.

Right: *1920. Adelaide Town Hall and Treasury Buildings Illuminated.*
From a photograph kindly supplied by Private Edward O'Halloran (Queensland), a wounded soldier.

1928.

EMPIRE DAY.

DO you wonder why such little children as you are asked to keep Empire Day? Well, I will tell you. None of you are too young to be grateful for the kind things that grown-up people do for you every hour that you live. You are very pleased to smile at Mother or big Sister, and to thank them for their care. You love to meet Father as he comes in from his day's work. You hang up his coat and get out his slippers, and draw his chair up to the table, or run down the garden to bring his evening paper, and many other duties besides. All these things help to make home a sweet home.

Now, our Empire is a great home of many nations in many lands, and many great men and women won those lands for us all in the days gone by. They were the fathers and mothers, the big sisters and brothers, of us all. They left their homes in England, Ireland, Scotland, or Wales, and went out to find new lands. They journeyed over great and almost unknown oceans, and they left their bones on many shores, but they planted the flag of Empire. Then others followed in their tracks. Over desert and forest, through fire and flood, they came. They began to build the towns in which you live to-day in peace and plenty. They were the pioneers of Empire. It is partly in their honour that you keep Empire Day.

In 1907 *The Children's Hour* announced:

> The Lord Meath Empire Day Prize for 1907. A Silver Challenge Cup, value ten guineas, presented by the Right Hon. Lord Meath KP and a personal prize of three guineas given by the League of the Empire, is offered for competition, inter-elementary schools of the Empire, for an Empire Day essay *not exceeding* 1000 words. Age limit 14 years. Subject 'The History of British India'.

The organisation of this League, and of the prize in particular, was an astonishing achievement. Essays had first to be judged worthy of inclusion by schools, then sent to local league representatives, of whom there must have been hundreds dotted throughout the Empire. They ultimately reached headquarters in London, by 1 February each year, so as to be judged in time for the announcement of the winner on Empire Day. This was celebrated every year on 4 May, Queen Victoria's birthday. The report of the League in June 1906 informed the *Hour*'s readers that the winner that year was:

> Andrew Phillips of the Millchester State School, Queensland. Other essays considered by the judges to have merit were sent in by the Kensel Rise Girls' School, London, the Perth Girls' School, Western Australia and the Victoria School, Hong Kong. The cup and prize offered for competition between all schools of the Empire have been won by Eton College.

The affairs of the League were circulated to South Australian schools through the pages of the *Hour*. The secretary was Miss Marion Rees George. The League had a vast membership. The list of new members in 1906 recorded 21 from Forest Range alone, and the total had reached 2042! A letter from Miss Rees George was published in the *Hour* every month. Her enthusiasm and devotion shone out, 'My dear Comrades—We *are* an Empire and this we should never forget' (August 1911). Essay competitions went on month by month, but it seems the interest sometimes flagged and the tireless secretary would comment reproachfully, 'So far very few have been sent in this year, and they are open to you all'. The essay subjects were predictable—'Empire Day' and 'Winter in Australia' being typical examples.

Everyone took part in Empire Day celebrations which could range from a stirring gathering in the Victoria Hall, in Gawler Place, Adelaide, which the Governor and several hundred citizens attended, to the simple ceremony of unfurling the flag, enacted by a handful of children and their parents at a remote country school.

For such occasions songs like this were specially written:

Dedicated to the Right Hon. The Earl of Meath in recognition of his efforts to cherish patriotism in hearts of the Children of Great Britain, Ireland and The Colonies.

THE FLAG OF BRITAIN.

Flag of Britain, proudly waving
Over many distant seas,
Flag of Britain, boldly braving
Blinding fog and adverse breeze,
We salute thee, and we pray
God to bless our land to-day.

Flag of Britain! wheresoever
Thy bright colours are outspread,
Slavery must cease for ever,
Light and freedom reign instead.
We salute thee, and we pray
God to bless our land to-day.

Flag of Britain! 'mid the nations
May it ever speak of peace,
And proclaim to farthest stations,
All unworthy strife must cease.
We salute it, and we pray
God to bless our land to-day.

But if duty sternly need it,
Freely let it be unfurl'd.
Winds of Heaven then may speed it
To each quarter of the world.
We salute it, and we pray
God to bless our land to-day.

The Union Jack was nearly always on view and, despite the fact that an Australian flag had been born with Federation, 'The Jack' seems to have been too well established in people's minds to be easily replaced.

April 1905.

LEAGUE OF EMPIRE.

IN Adelaide one of the most interesting features of the celebration of the League of the Empire to the number of over 900 in the Victoria Hall, Gawler Place, under the direction of His Excellency the Lieutenant Governor Sir Samuel James Way, Bart, the President of the South Australian branch of the League, Lady Le Hunte and party, Lady Way and many other adult members of the League were present, and joined in the general enthusiasm of the meeting. Uncle Harry recited in splendid style, with bag pipe accompaniment, the 'Defence of Lucknow'. Patriotic songs and choruses were sung, and stirring addresses were given on 'Empire Day' by the Chief Justice; 'Australia' by the Rev. W. Potts; and on 'Windsor Castle, the Home of our King' illustrated with beautiful lantern pictures by H. P. Gill Esq. The Flinders St School band played a musical selection.

Soon after Federation a song about the 'new' flag was published in the *Hour*:

November 1901.

THE FEDERAL FLAG.

A National Song of Australia.

Air—'The Red, White and Blue'.

Australians now o'er our nation
The sign of our unity waves!
With joy let us hail Federation
And vow that we ne'er will be slaves;
May the God of our fathers guard ever
And prosper the deed we have done,
And bless every future endeavour
'Neath the flag that in peace we have won.

Refrain
'Neath the flag that in peace we have won,
'Neath the flag that in peace we have won
And bless every future endeavour
'Neath the flag that in peace we have won.

The subject of flags appealed to the editors of the *Hour*, and the 'Empire Numbers' in the editions of 1908 and 1914 had exactly the same covers—the flag displayed there was the Australian flag, even though the endless stream of verses and songs that swamped the pages referred almost exclusively to the Union Jack! For example:

BRITANNIA'S FLAG.

We love the old flag with the crosses three
'Tis honoured alike over land and sea . . .
Our fearless Union Jack.

In 1907 'The Story of the Union Jack' began with these lines:

It is only a small bit of bunting
It is only an old coloured rag
Yet thousands have died for its honour
And shed their best for the flag.

Still later, in 1915, South Australian children, happily confused as to their national emblem, were heartily singing:

But the Union Jack, the Union Jack,
This is the flag for me!

For many years children in South Australian schools went through a daily ritual of honouring the flag. There have been many versions; this is one of them:

I am an Australian [added later]
I love my country the British Empire
I salute her flag the Union Jack
I honour her King.
I promise cheerfully to obey his laws.

From the time of proclamation until after the Second World War, South Australian life contained a very obvious military presence. In

May 1911.

OUR FLAG.

M. E. Miethke.

We are only little people
Who love our flag so well,
And we've learned its simple meaning
And this is what we'll tell.

Red is for the hardy soldiers
Who bore the flag so brave
The white is stands for purity,
Oh, may it ever wave.

Last this bright and lovely colour
Shows the good and true
What can we find any better
Than the dear old blue?

So we have in our dear flag
The brave, the pure and true,
The Union Jack, the Union Jack
The red, the white, the blue.

And now with flags in hand we turn
And then we stand just so
Ready now to march in line,
Just as our soldiers do.

All the boys and girls are marching
Up and down we go,
Holding firm our little flagstaffs,
Waving to and fro.

Watch our little flags a flutter—
Brave and pure and true—
Oh we love our Union Jack,
The red, the white, the blue.

(To the tune of 'Coming Through the Rye' children march up and down the room, shouldering flags, fluttering and finishing by two rows of them making an archway of flags for the other children to march under.)

Top: *1914. Empire Day at Pyap West School. Teacher—Mr E. H. Polkinghorne.*

Middle: *Empire Day, 1915. 'Unfurling the Flag' at Mount Muirhead School. Teacher—Miss Margaret M. Smith.*

Left: *1914. Young Cadets. Photo: Miss Longman.*

August 1905.
The Band of the Red, White and Blue.

the early days, every public occasion, every festive event, was given an air of formality, of style and pageantry, by the presence of soldiers, and sometimes sailors, who marched to the accompaniment of brass bands or bagpipes. In addition to the regular permanent servicemen, many of these men belonged to volunteer military regiments, for the British tradition of giving service to one's country was not just honoured, but also expected. In this environment, training children to march, to drill, to salute the flag seemed perfectly natural.

In 1898 the 'Topics of To-day' for November referred to 'a most destructive war against the slave-holding Arabs of the Soudan' which 'the British troops have had to wage, and our cousins in the United States have had, in the interests of humanity, to inflict terrible punishment upon the Spaniards'. After lamenting the futility of war, the writer described the compulsory military service implemented in many European countries, pointing out that:

> . . . the expense of keeping these millions of men with the cost of the vast numbers of cannon, rifles, horses, etc amounts to millions of pounds every year, all of which has to be made up by taxes upon the earnings of the people who do the useful work of the state—the farmers, the manufacturers, the traders and others.

Then in 1900 Australian soldiers went to fight with the British against the Boers in South Africa. Adelaide's best-known monument is probably the equestrian statue erected as a memorial to the South African war veterans, which rises dramatically at the intersection of King William Street and North Terrace. Something of the glory of soldiering was promoted in the *Hour* at this time, but more often sentimentality surrounded the accounts of the grim tragedies of war. An example comes from the *Hour* in April 1900:

> There is a wee cottage by the bonnie burnside, the bereaved mother bows her aged head and says, 'Thy will be done'. There also the heart-broken-once wife, newly made widow, pours out the anguish of her soul as she clasps her fatherless bairn to her warm bosom. Her man comes no more. For the Highland Brigade has buried its dead. (*South Australian Register*, 16 January 1900.)

In August 1900 children read:

> We are all now hoping soon to hear that the Boers have seen the wisdom of giving up their useless attempts to oppose the advance of the British. As you know, great preparations have been made, not only in our province, but all through the British Empire, to celebrate the conclusion of the war when that joyful news is proclaimed.

But despite the 'joyful news' the war was not quickly forgotten, as the touching list of donations to the 'Soldiers' Graves Fund' shows in the issue of August 1902. Little towns, with little schools now long since lost, sent in their collections, along with those from places which became flourishing country centres—Laura donated £1 2s, the highest amount on this list, while Wistow and Richmans Valley each raised 1 shilling.

But it was the Great War of 1914–1918 which dominated the pages of the *Hour* as nothing else did, changing its character as surely as the war was changing the entire world:

ADDRESS TO SCHOOL CHILDREN.

(Delivered by the Right Rev Gilbert White, Bishop of Willochra, to Gladstone schoolchildren, July 1917.)

Dear Children—You are living at the greatest moment in the history of the world. In fifty years' time those of you who are then alive will be able to say, 'I remember the great war, which, for better or for worse, changed the whole world'. Nothing in your history books is nearly so important as what is now going on day by day. No one knows what the end is going to be, but the happiness of your lives depends upon it. It matters much more to you than it does to me, who has so many fewer years to live on this earth.

I have said that no one knows the end, but we do know what the end depends on. Under God, it depends on the patience, perseverance, courage, resolution, and self-control of the people of allied races that are fighting for the safety and liberty of the world, and in a few years' time the safety and happiness of the world will largely depend on you children, who will then be the young men and women of the world.

At present the greater part of the nations of the world are fighting for their life and their liberty against the greatest military Power that the world has ever known.

August 1902.

SOLDIERS' GRAVES FUND.

THE following amounts have been duly received from the schools named: Victor Harbor 12s; Rockleigh 3s 6d; Clements' Gap 4s; Balaklava 15s; Clinton North 5s 6d; Koolunga 12s 6d; Inman Valley 3s 6d; Tailem Bend 4s 6d; Crafers 10s; Manoora 10s; Corny Point 6s; Minlaton 5s; Wandearah East 10s 3d; Tarpeena 7s 3d; Le Fevre's Peninsula—Infant Room 11s; First Boys 25s 7d; Second Boys 25s 11½d; Second Girls 5s 4½d; Third Boys A, 4s 5d; B, 6s 6d; Girls 5s 4½d; Fifth Class 7s 1½d; Sixth Class 2s 8d; Total £3.15.8d; Goolwa 6s; Port Germein 11s 6d; Kingston 8s 6d; Penfield 3s; Mallala 10s; Dollings Corner 3s 8d; Laura £1.2s; Wistow 1s; Richman's Valley 1s; Poonindie 4s; Morn Hill 7s; Naracoorte 17s; White's River 2s 4d; Millicent 8s 6d; Buckingham 1s 6d; Frankton 2s.

Now, it is very important to know what liberty means, because a great many people do not know. They think that liberty means everyone doing what they like, which really means that no one can do what he wants to do. In politics, liberty means the government of the people by the people for the good of the people. Some foolish people think that liberty means no government at all, which really means confusion and ruin, and no one being able to do anything. Just think what would happen in school if there were no government in it, if every boy and girl could shout and sing and run about and play just as they liked. No one would be able to get anything done, no one could learn any lessons, and you would grow up ignorant and useless in the world, to say nothing of the quarrelling that would take place between those who wanted to do their work and those who were preventing them from doing anything.

We see this in Russia to-day. We were all very glad when the Russian people got rid of autocracy, and we thought that they were going to show the world what great things a free people could do; but, unhappily, a great number of them thought that freedom meant doing as you like, and obeying nobody, and they have thrown all their country into confusion, and given a great victory to the enemy, and perhaps added years to the war. I am sure all you children want to help to save your country and to bring peace and liberty to the world. What can you do?

1. You can make up your minds that you will try to grow up as true citizens, loving true freedom, but always remembering that people can never be really free unless they are well and wisely governed, and that if everyone is determined to have everything his own way, the result will be the utter ruin of our country. You must not think only of your own self, or of your own friends, or your own class only. You must think of the whole people, and love and work for your country as a whole.

2. Some of you can help by working for the Red Cross, and in other ways, to make things for the sick and wounded, and for the soldiers in the trenches, who are fighting so bravely for you and for Australia.

3. You can all help by buying war savings stamps instead of spending your money on lollies or on picture shows, or wasting it in any other way. You can buy a stamp at the post office for six-pence, and paste it into a little book, which will be given you, and when you have got thirty-five stamps in the book you can change it for a war certificate for one pound, which means that in three years you can get one pound for it, and that in the meantime your money will be used for getting food and clothes for our men at the front, and for sending other men out to help them, and for doctors and nurses to look after them when they are sick or wounded, and for rifles and cannon to defend them against the enemy. If we do not send these things, they will be defeated and killed, and it will be our fault.

4. You can all of you help most of all by praying God to help the Allies to win the victory, and to protect and keep our soldiers, and to give us a just and lasting peace.

I sum up all I have to say to you as good citizens in three words—Work, pay, and pray.

The tension, mounting up to the climax of declared war, could be sensed in the photographs in the *Hour* in 1913.

1913.
Sword Drill, Streaky Bay School.
Teacher—Mr J. S. R. Oborn.
1913.
Gun Squad at Streaky Bay School.

Then war was declared and children were caught in the wave of fervent patriotism which swept into every aspect and every corner of South Australian life. *The Children's Hour* reflected it all—the excitement, the loyalty and pride, the honour and glory, the brave, the glorious, the tragic, and the pathetic! Many verses such as 'The Bugle Call', by Florence Hoare, flooded the pages of the *Hour*, many providing distorted and romantic ideas of war:

Our father's spirit leads us
To fight when our country needs us
But the voice that we love, ev'ry voice above,
Is the strain that we greet
When the foe are there to beat
The music of the bugle
The call that never sounds retreat.

Social life throughout the war years was largely devoted to fund-raising for the 'war effort'. The part children played in collecting and raising money was encouraged and promoted by *The Children's Hour*, their efforts praised and their financial successes published. Page after page of photographs displayed little girls dressed up as Red Cross 'nurses', collecting donations and selling posies on Australia Day or similar occasions. Boys donned army hats and jackets—much of the time they looked not inspiring, but simply funny! But the figure of 'Harry Stopp (8 years, 4 months), who by his singing at recent Australia Day entertainments has collected £7 4s for Australian

Above: *1916. Swan Reach School.*
Harry Stopp (8 years 4 months), who by his Singing at Recent Australia Day Entertainments has Collected £7 4s. for Australian Wounded Soldiers' Fund.

Top left: *1916. Australia Day at Paskeville.*
Schoolgirl flower sellers.

Top right: *1915. Red Cross Helpers.*
Inman Valley Public School.
Teacher—Miss Emily H. Frost.
Photo: Miss Peacock.

Middle: *1917. Hog Bay School.*
Girls and boys knitting for the soldiers.
Head Teacher—Mr Jos. P. O'Loughlin.

Right: *1916. Boys of Quorn School Knitting for our Soldiers.*

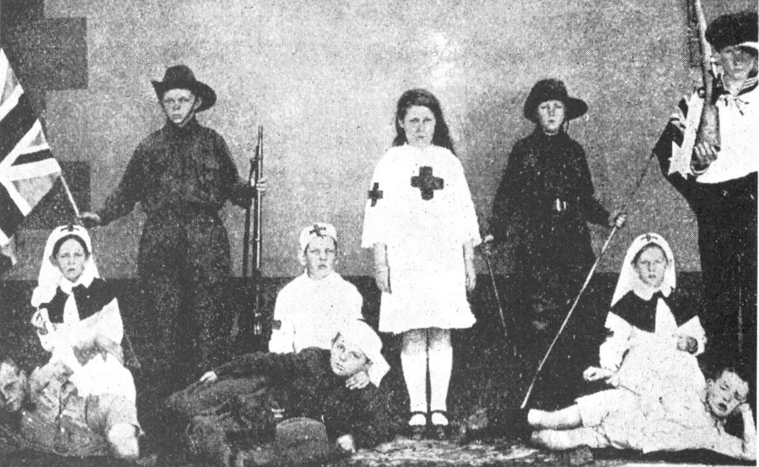

Above: *1916. 'Young Australia'.*
Luna South, of the Auburn Primary School, collected £15 for the wounded soldiers on Australia Day.

Top: *1915. 'The Handy Men Behind the Gun'.*
Paskeville School.
Teacher—Mr A. Canning.
Photo: A. C.

Middle: *1917. Greenock School Concert—Red Cross Tableau.*
Head Teacher—Mr Wm Innes.

Left: *1915. The League of the Empire Stall at the Recent Fête at Government House.*

1916.
SANDBAGS FROM HEATHFIELD SCHOOL.

LIEUTENANT-COLONEL Lorenzo, who left South Australia in 1914, as adjutant of the 10th Battalion, has written to the Director of Education asking him to thank the children of Heathfield Public School for the sandbags they made and sent to the front. The Colonel's men used the bags and, as they were filling them, noticed the names of the makers. The soldiers were not only satisfied with the good work put into the bags, but were cheered with the thought that the children were helping them to defeat the enemy. The Colonel photographed the bags in position, and asked the Director to send the photograph to Heathfield School.

Wounded Soldiers' Fund', seems to tell the whole tragic story. He stands, miserably bundled into his too-big army jacket, photographed for the *Hour* in December 1916. In other illustrations intended to be emotionally appealing, little girl 'nurses' surround the prostrate figures of small boys temporarily confined to stretchers, with telling bandages wrapped about their foreheads.

Photographs show tableaux entitled 'Red Cross' and 'Children of the Empire' which had dragged in all manner of costumes and flags (Union Jacks!), and many school groups were photographed patriotically knitting for soldiers—boys knitted as enthusiastically as girls! Even gardening reflected patriotism—the Athelstone School garden was laid out in the shape of a Union Jack.

The staggering financial burdens of war were kept well to the fore, and the Children's Patriotic Fund that was organised in schools had its affairs published in the pages of the *Hour*. A system of War Service Medals and Bars was introduced and this competitive element boosted the cause and gave the necessary incentive to children to raise money. In September 1917 the organisers reported:

> At the time of writing there are quite 500 of you who have received this decoration of honour to mark your splendid service to the fund. Some children have already sent the patriotic page containing *their* names to brothers and fathers at the front, and right glad they will be at seeing the names of those dear to them, figuring proudly amongst the home people who are helping to win the war on this side of the water.

1916.
Sandbags Filled and in the Trenches.
Photo: Lieut.-Colonel Francis Lorenzo, DSO.

Money too was required for prisoners of war:

Supposing your own father or brother were a prisoner of war, half-starved, half-clothed, perhaps sick and wounded, longing for help from his own dear people, shut off from all his chums and mates, waiting, waiting, for parcels—that didn't come!

The Red Cross Fund needed continual support, and yet another, the Children's Belgian Relief Fund, raised 'a substantial sum' and this brought a congratulatory letter in the *Hour*, from Marie Carola Galway—the wife of the Governor:

Both the teachers and the children are to be thanked, and also to be congratulated, for these offerings are the best proof that the great lesson of kind heartedness and solidarity has been well taught by the one and really appreciated by the other. I would feel much obliged if you could convey to the children of the state schools my warmest thanks in the name of these children across the seas, who will benefit by their generous action.

For many people 'The Anzac Story' seems to epitomise the Australian spirit more than anything else. As myth and legend, pivotal pieces on which to found a national identity, 'Gallipoli' grows in significance as the years go by. It has inspired some of Australia's finest artistic expressions through painting, sculpture, poetry, prose, and, more recently, film. The story of Gallipoli, told shortly after it had happened, was by circumstance a different one. The *Hour* published excerpts from *A Child's History of Anzac* by E. C. Buley in May 1917. It was not so much a history as a personal recollection.

May 1917.

SOME HEROES OF ANZAC.

From *A Child's History of Anzac*
E. C. Buley.

(This interesting book, price 3s 6d, is most suitable for school libraries. The three pictures below are reproduced from photographs taken by Pte A. O. Thiele, of the AIF, while he was fighting at the Dardenelles.—Ed.)

The landing on Gallipoli, with the battle which followed, was the first trial of the Anzacs in war. History will say that their first real ordeal by battle took place on April 25th, 1915. They had gone to face the enemy, meaning to do credit to their country and their Empire. Only very brave men could have done what they did; and already that fight for the cliffside is set down as one of the most glorious feats of arms in the whole history of war.

The men who were wounded in the first day's fighting showed what spirit was in them when they were taken back to the warships in boats. The sailors crowded to the side of their ships to see them pass, and to their astonishment these wounded men were singing and cheering. The doctors who tended them found that no suffering could make them groan or complain; they endured in silence, and even tried to smile in their agony. For five days and nights they had to fight without any interval; gradually making their trenches deeper and their positions more secure.

Each day saw their numbers growing smaller, while they became more and more weary from fatigue and lack of food and sleep. In those five days they learned to know their officers and themselves, and, to use

1917.

FOR ENGLAND.

THE writer of the following beautiful lines was Corporal J. D. Burns, who fell at Gallipoli, killed by a Turkish bullet, on September 18th, 1915. He was then in his twenty-first year. Corporal Burns was the eldest son of the Rev. H. M. Burns, Presbyterian Minister, of Lilydale, Victoria. The young soldier's mother is a South Australian lady, she being the daughter of the late Rev. Jas. Lyall, for 40 years the honoured minister of the Presbyterian Church, Flinders Street, Adelaide.

Corporal Burns gave every promise of being a distinguished man, but the high hopes of his future formed by his friends now lie in one of the many graves on that lonely peninsula where so much that was noble and good and gifted of Australia was buried. We are indebted to the late soldier's father for kindly giving permission to publish the poem.

Corporal J. D. Burns.

The bugles of England were blowing o'er the sea,
As they had called a thousand years, calling now to me;
They woke me from dreaming in the dawning of the day,
The bugles of England—and how could I stay?

The banners of England, unfurled across the sea,
Floating out upon the wind, beckoning to me;
Storm-rent and battle-torn, smoke stained and grey,
The banners of England—and how could I stay?

O, England, I heard the cry of those who died for thee,
Sounding like an organ-voice above the winter sea;
They lived and died for England, and gladly went their way,
England, O, England—how could I stay?

July 1915.

THE DARDANELLES.

THE following interesting letter was written by a South Australian officer to his little daughter. The officer, who has high rank, is known, at least by name, to most people in South Australia. He is now at the Dardanelles fighting with Australian soldiers against the Turks. May his work and that of his brave men be crowned with victory, and may they all soon return to hear from our lips how proud we are of their noble deeds.

Gallipoli Peninsula, May 12th, 1915.

My Dear Beryl—You would laugh if you saw the place I am living in. We are at the top of a steep hill, a bit like the steep hills at Uncle Ben's, at Forreston. Here we have dug a hole like a cellar, with an opening down the hill. Over the top of the cellar we have put thick pieces of wood across, and on the top of them bags filled with dirt, and on top of them again branches of trees. The wood and the dirt are to keep the bullets from hitting us whilst we are sleeping or writing.

Major H——, Captain L——, Dr N——, and I sleep in this hole. We certainly quite fill it up when we are all in there. The men—there are thousands of them here—sleep in a trench like the one masons dig for a foundation before they start building a house. The soldiers make their trench 6 ft deep, then they make a sort of opening in the wall about a foot from the bottom into which they coil themselves like cats having a rest.

They cut smaller holes on the other wall at the back of them, and here they boil water for tea and fry bacon and potatoes for their dinner. They do not have any bread, neither do I, but we get very hard biscuits instead, which take a long time to eat and break our teeth off unless we are very careful.

You would laugh to see hundreds of men, who are not in the trenches, in their little homes—just a big hole dug out of the side of the hill—only big enough to crawl into. Sometimes the dirt falls down on top of them; they do not like that.

The Turks fire at our trenches all night long and all day too. Last night it rained a little and, of course, every one got a bit wet, and the paths are very muddy. This morning I was going through the trenches at 4 a.m. We are all very happy. We snap our fingers and bear our troubles like men—or try to.

I would not like you to be here, and I would sooner sleep in a nice warm, soft bed than on the hard, cold ground; but Kaiser 'Bill' has to be brought to his knees before I can think of coming home.

I think I love you and mother more than ever now, and I hope to see you before Christmas.

I remain,
Your affectionate father.

a phrase employed by one of their leaders, 'found themselves' as a fighting force.

The tales of the heroic deeds they performed in those days, if collected, would make a great book, and then all would not be told.

A year after the landing I was present at a great gathering of Anzacs in London, when General Birdwood rose to say a few words to them. They had not seen him for many months, and rose as one man, some of them with moist eyes, and cheered as I have never heard men cheer before. He was a hero to every one of them.

The officers were so brave that very many of them lost their lives in the first week. There was no help for it. The leaders had to be where the men were, and at their head set them an example of cool courage which had its effect in the splendid behaviour of the men.

July 1915.

A SOLDIER'S LETTERS
TO HIS LITTLE
DAUGHTER.

The following three letters were written by an officer (Dadboy) to his little daughter. At the time of writing the last letter he was fighting with the Australians against the Turks.

Somewhere, 14/4/15.

My dear little Daughter—The men here wear such funny clothes, just made out of sheep skin with the wool turned inwards. They must be warm, and their boots are made out of the same stuff. The donkeys are queer little things, and make a noise like a rusty old pump. All the sheep have little bells, which tinkle as they move. The grass is so green, Gwen, and covered with wild flowers; but if you want sand, you must go to Egypt for it. Give Mummy a big kiss and a love for me, dear.

Lots of love, dearie, from
DADBOY.

In the Trenches,
In Turkey, 9/5/15.

My dear little Gwen—It is such a lovely Sunday morning, and Dadboy has been fighting Turks for two weeks now. Somehow we seem to have been here for years, and it's hard to remember anything else. We get a wash only in a mouthful of water every other day or so, so your Dadboy is such a dirty, grimy fellow in a dirty, torn, old uniform, and has no shine worth mentioning on his boots.

But, after all, we are pretty happy, and the 'Turkeys' are very frightened of the Australians. They make a big noise and blow their trumpets, but somehow they do not come very close to us, and when we charge them, don't they run!

I'm glad you like your bangle, Gwen. When the war is over and Dadboy has a lot of money he'll bring some lovely presents home for you and Mummy, so you must be a brave girl, and tell Mummy not to worry, as Dadboy is coming home to her without fail.

With fond love and kisses from your old.

DADBOY.

Trenchland, 16/5/15.

My own darling Gwen—Trenchland is such a queer place; in it are miles and miles of deep passages winding about, and places for men to shoot 'Turkeys' from, and always men making more trenches night and day, just like a lot of rabbits. When the 'Turkeys' fire their big guns at us we all take cover, except our men who keep watch both night and day, and then hardly anyone gets hurt, and when Mr Turkey stops his jokes, out all of us, like rabbits, come again.

Shall I tell you what we have to eat? At 6.30 in the morning we get hot tea with, if it has been raining, some rum in it. At 8 o'clock some more tea with no milk and very little sugar. We have also fried bacon and army biscuits fried in fat, and very nice they are, too. For lunch we have stew made of bully beef, potatoes, and onions. At tea we have jam and cheese with biscuits.

But always at meal times the Turks send us shells, the men call them 'iron rations'. One shell upset a man's tea and set his stew flying; but it didn't hurt him. Another shell filled old Dadboy's tea with dirt, but it was quite nice to drink when it settled.

I haven't had a wash for three days, as water isn't too plentiful for that purpose, still one doesn't mind being grimy, it seems so natural somehow.

You must keep on growing, Gwen, and taking your malt, and then won't you be a big girl when Dadboy comes home, and what times we'll have. Somehow I don't think it will be so very long before I come home.

Fondest love, dear little daughter, and many kisses, from

DADBOY.

Schools set up honour rolls and in some cases the names were inscribed on elaborately designed marble tablets which frequently contrasted markedly with their simple surroundings, as even very small country schools felt bound to remember their patriotic scholars in this way. Violet Day, 26 June, was recognised each year:

> Everyone at school will, if practicable, wear a spray of these fragrant flowers in memory of the noble men who have given their lives for us on distant battle fields. There they lie in their silent graves—the young, the strong, and the brave, and we, living in peace and comfort, should on that day at least give to their memory some of our thoughts. If there is a Roll of Honour in the school perhaps the girls might decorate it with violets.

The Great War, and the Anzac experience in particular, had brought suffering to the Australian nation as a whole for the first time. Just as some people are reshaped and refined by adversity, so Australia as a country had developed a deeper dimension. The shared experience of hardship and loss had brought a new unity to the nation. By the late 1920s, hardship, suffering and, for some, financial ruin, were shared again when Australia felt the crushing weight of the World Depression. For Australia, the strong arm of mother England was no longer able to guarantee prosperity. Self-reliance, rather than loyal dependence, was increasingly emphasised in *The Children's Hour*, and in March 1930 the Premier, Mr (later Sir) Richard Butler, sent a message to the children of South Australia which is an interesting

1929.

THE KING.

ON the front page is a picture of King George seated in a bath chair, and, standing by his side, is Queen Mary. They are in a garden in the south of England. The picture is reproduced from a photograph taken on March 11th last, which was the first day for sixteen weeks since the King was allowed to be brought out in the sunshine.

The King has passed through a severe illness. During last November he caught cold, for weeks it was uncertain whether he would recover. The skill of several great London doctors and the care of nurses helped much to save King George, and perhaps the good life he has lived helped more than even the doctors and the careful nurses.

The King is becoming an old man. On the third of this month he was sixty-four years of age. He has been King for nineteen years. During that time his country passed through the biggest war known in history, and during that awful time King George acted so wisely that his people learned to love and to trust him.

mixture of respect for their intelligence and patronising condescension:

Be Australian. Buy Australian.
AN APPEAL BY THE PREMIER OF SOUTH AUSTRALIA.

Dear Children—

I think you realise, even at your young age, that if we are to hold this country, our happy home land, we must fill it with people to make it secure. To do this we must have many factories making all kinds of goods for our use. This will provide work for many people under conditions better than those anywhere else in the world. So we must all be loyal and help our industries.

We can best do this by buying South Australian-made goods whenever we can.

Be true, little Australians, and help your home state. Ask mother and father to buy clothes, food, and other things that are made in South Australia whenever they can do so.

If you can get them to do this it will help in these times, which even you young children must have realised are difficult for the grown-ups.

Do not worry yourself about things which must be left to your elders, but tell your parents that by buying South Australian-made goods they can help to provide other children's fathers and brothers with employment, and give those little friends of yours more happiness in life.

With kind regard to all,
I am, Yours very truly,
Richard Butler.

1929.
The King and Queen in the Garden.

CHAPTER SIX

MORALS AND MANNERS

In the beginning was the Word, and the Word was with God, and the Word was God.

St John 1:1.

The first British settlers, setting out to start a new life in South Australia, left their homeland when it was experiencing a wave of renewed spiritual awareness and religious life. This mood had been generated largely by the 'Wesleyan Revival' of the mid-nineteenth century. Church and chapel attendance, Sunday school, family prayers and daily Bible reading were customary in many families at that time.

The British settlers were predominantly members of the Church of England, and church attendance offered social contact as well as the opportunity to worship. Most of the Cornish and Welsh miners who hastened to South Australia when copper was discovered at Kapunda, Burra and Moonta, during the first decade of settlement, were members of the non-conformist faiths, and the many denominations all had their ardent followers. Religion was central to colonial life.

'Freedom of religious worship' was a feature of South Australian colonisation. It was one of a number of reasons which persuaded the German settlers to come here. The Lutheran churches, particularly in the Barossa Valley, stand as a permanent reminder of their influence.

A Bible accompanied most of the first-comers, tucked among personal belongings, for as well as being the corner-stone of their religion, the Bible provided many of them with their only reading material. Books were a rarity in the colony, so that, for those who knew and longed for the solace of reading, the beautiful language of the Bible was a 'God-send' in more than one sense.

Although formal religious teaching was forbidden in State schools for many years, early South Australian life was naturally and inevitably built around Christian principles. In addition to being the basis of family life, the Christian ethic also formed the basis of training. In schools too, although it could not be openly acknowledged, Christian

1904.

COLUMN FOR GIRLS.

THE Minda home is at present at Fullarton, and because there is not sufficient room for all the children there, the committee are anxious to build a new Home in the hills, which will cost about £4000. About £2000 is already collected, so you see there is a great deal more wanted yet, and the committee will be very grateful for any help you can give them. There is to be another fete this year in aid of the Home, and I should like to tell you how you may help. Last year the large boxes of goods which were sent by country children to *The Children's Hour* stall cost so much money for carriage to Adelaide that the editor felt quite sad about it, and he thinks it would be much better if the children who contributed so generously to the Central Stall last time would hold fetes of their own in their own schools. You could decide on any time that would suit the convenience of the school—after your examination, for instance—as long as you had your money ready to send to the committee about, say, the end of October next. In this way, I feel sure, very much more money could be raised, and with less trouble, than by sending your goods to town. I shall be glad to hear from anyone who is willing to help in this way, and feel sure that your teachers will be only too pleased to give you all the advice and assistance you need. I had intended offering some suggestions, but, after all, your teachers will be better able to tell you how to set about getting up a little fete of your own than I can.

The Editor suggests the following places where fetes might be held:—Mount Gambier, Naracoorte, Millicent, Murray Bridge, Bordertown, Strathalbyn, Mount Barker, Mount Pleasant, Oakbank, Aldgate, Yankalilla, Clarendon, Angaston, Gawler, Clare, Burra, Petersburg, Port Pirie, Quorn, Port Wakefield, Balaklava, Kadina, Moonta, Walkerville, East Adelaide, Glenelg, Unley, Port Adelaide, Marryatville.

I should not be at all surprised if some *quite small* schools in country places were able to help very considerably. Perhaps some of them could give school concerts. When you have decided what you are going to do, please let me know. You see, I take it for granted that many of you will be as glad to help this time as you have been on other occasions.

morality was both implied and applied, and *The Children's Hour* adopted the same approach.

For example, in 1902 the *Hour* included the well-known passage from St Paul's epistle to the Corinthians concerning faith, hope and charity. The piece is headed 'Love', and the word 'charity' is replaced by the word 'love' which is sensible and surprisingly modern. The lines are attributed simply to 'Paul' and there is no further clue to their origin. This may have been sufficiently vague for it not to be identified by children reading it, but it would not have fooled their Bible-bred parents.

Moral influences can be exerted on people's thoughts and behaviour in many ways, and *The Children's Hour* editors were aware of the responsibility their publication carried.

At the time of colonisation, Australia was a country of vast riches waiting to be discovered, developed and enjoyed. It offered a great opportunity for those of sufficient strength, tenacity, courage, and even shrewdness. For the colony to develop, and its people to prosper, the main thing required was hard work!

1913.

DO YOUR BEST.

Do your best, your very best,
And do it every day—
Little boys and little girls
That is the wisest way.

What if your lessons should be hard,
Do not give up to sorrow;
For if you bravely work today,
You'll surely win tomorrow.

Sometimes social conditions influence moral attitudes, and sometimes they support them or, conversely, change them. It is easy to see how the 'work ethic', for instance, fitted so well into the social environment of the early days. The 'Protestant', or 'Christian', or 'Puritan' work ethic, as it is variously referred to, promised reward for effort, built on a number of convictions. In *The Children's Hour* these emerge very clearly and very frequently: hard work leads to independence, financial success, respectability and social status, power and authority, physical well-being.

Knowledge and strength of character also came from hard work and the additional quality, discipline, a running-mate of the work ethic: 'Never say it's good enough till it can be no better'. The clear message was that hard work would lead eventually to any desirable reward, provided one was patient enough, industrious enough, and lived long enough! For the Christian, the reward could be less tangible, less material, but no less sweet. Toiling uncomplainingly, and living a virtuous life, might be hard at the time, but one was assured of unfailing 'treasures in heaven'. Their faith in the promise of better times in the hereafter inspired and sustained many through lives of gruelling labour and meagre comforts.

By emphasising the virtue of hard work, the sin of 'wasting time' came into sharp focus. *The Children's Hour* was preoccupied with 'time-wasting' to an almost obsessive degree. Perhaps the awareness of a great land inviting development aroused a heightened sense of urgency. In the publication of February 1913 it was summed up in this way:

There are four ways of wasting time:
1. Doing nothing. 2. Not doing what we ought to do. 3. Doing a thing badly. 4. Doing a thing at the wrong time.

Children were made to feel guilty if they slowed down or took things easily. Simply working, although important, was not enough: the expectation of *high standards* was ever present. 'Doing a good job' was a common phrase in the frequent lectures which urged children to be continually 'busy'.

1907.

THE 'NO-TIMERS' AND THE 'NEAR ENOUGHS'.

Busy, industrious people have time for everything; it is only the idlers who have 'no time'. The 'No-timers' form a very large body, and it is a pity any more should join them. Whatever you do, do not become one of them, when you begin to find yourself saying, 'I haven't time', pull yourself up, and do not say it; turn the sentence another way, and say 'I will make time'. It is quite possible to do so.

The reason why industrious people can find time for everything is that they plan out their work for the day or week; they face what they have to do, and they do it in a steady, orderly manner. They do not waste half an hour thinking about it, and another half-hour looking for their tools, then ten minutes settling down to work. They have their tools, or books or work in good order, they begin punctually, and work steadily.

One of the first things you must realise is odd minutes. Some persons belong to an 'Odd-Minute Society', and keep a piece of knitting, or work of some kind, to take up when they have two or three spare minutes, and it is astonishing how many scarfs and pair of socks they make in a year in this way.

A man once kept five friends waiting an hour for him. 'You need not be annoyed', he said, 'I didn't waste so very much of your day'.

'You have wasted five hours of it', answered one of them.

Every one of you must learn to be thrifty in the matter of time, to make the most of it and the best of it, to be tidy and orderly, and thorough in all you do.

There is another large body of people that I shall call the 'Near-enoughs', for those words, or 'O, that will do', or 'That is good enough', are for ever on their lips.

Now, whatever you do, do not belong to the 'Near-enoughs'; they are worse than the 'No-timers', for they do more harm. They do nothing thoroughly; they think it does not matter, or they do not know how, or they do not care. But it does matter, and very greatly, too. 'Whatever is worth doing is worth doing well.'

The 'Near-enoughs' are the men who make the flawed axles that cause trains to be wrecked and men, women and children to be killed or injured. They make the imperfect boilers that explode. They lay drains so carelessly that fever and diphtheria are able to spread in streets and towns, and gas pipes so faultily that houses are wrecked, and people are killed through explosions.

January 1910.

ACRES OF YOUR OWN.

Alexander McLachlan.

Here's the road to independence!
Who would bow and dance attendance?
Who with e'er a spark of pride,
While the bush is wild and wide,
Would be but a hanger-on.
Begging favours from a throne,
While beneath yon smiling sun
Farms by labour can be won?
Up! be stirring, be alive,
Get upon a farm and thrive!
He's a king upon a throne
Who has acres of his own!

Tho' the cabin's walls are bare,
What of that if love be there?
What, although your back is bent,
There are none to hound for rent;
What tho' you must chip and plough,
None dare ask, 'What doest thou?'
What though homespun is your coat,
Kings might envy you your lot!
Up! be stirring, be alive;
Get upon a farm and thrive!
He's a king upon a throne
Who has acres of his own!

Would'st thou honest labour shirk?
Thou art far too good to work?
Such gentility's a fudge;
True men all must toil and drudge.
Nature's true nobility
Scorns such mock gentility;
Fools but talk of blood and birth,
Every man must prove his worth!
Up! be stirring, be alive,
Get upon a farm and thrive!
He's a king upon a throne
Who has acres of his own.

1898.

COLUMN FOR GIRLS.

Little maiden, time is precious;
Work well done brings joy for aye.

THE motto chosen for this year was sent by Effie Watson, Gumbowie school. I hope you will all like it. It is certainly simple and easy to remember—two things every motto ought to be; and it also reminds us of two very important things: *time* and *work*.

1907.

SELF-CULTURE.

A WELL-KNOWN author and publisher, the late Dr William Chambers, of Edinburgh, speaking before an assemblage of young men in that city, thus briefly described to them, for their encouragement, his humble beginnings:

'I stand before you', he said, 'a self-educated man. My education was that which is supplied at the humble parish schools of Scotland, and it was only when I went to Edinburgh, a poor boy, that I devoted my evenings, after the labours of the day, to the cultivation of that intellect which God has given me.

'From seven or eight in the morning till nine or ten at night was I at my business as a bookseller's apprentice, and it was only during hours after these, stolen from sleep, that I could devote myself to study. I did not read novels. My attention was directed to physical science and other useful matters. I also taught myself French. I look back to these times with great pleasure, and am almost sorry I have not to go through the same experience again; for I reaped more pleasure when I had not a sixpence in my pocket, studying in a garret in Edinburgh, than I now find when sitting amidst all the elegancies and comforts of a parlour.'

June 1906.

KEEP GOING.

WHEN one task is finished, jump into another.
Don't hesitate. Don't falter. Don't waver. Don't wait. Keep going. Keep going. Doing something is always better than doing nothing.
For activity breed ambition, energy, progress, power.
And inactivity breeds idleness, laziness, shiftlessness, sloth.
Don't dawdle in the hope that inspiration will strike you. Inspiration is more likely to strike a busy man than an idle one.
Save the half hours that are wasted in waiting.
That is the secret of system. Keep going.

They are the unthrifty, who do little but waste and destroy wherever they go, who do no good to anyone, only harm. We have far too many 'Near-enoughs' in the world. You can see them loafing in every town. It is high time we made up our minds to get rid of them altogether.

Mabel Quiller-Couch.
(A Little Book on Thrift.)

The work ethic, potently linked to education, ensured that children could not avoid a deep sense of obligation to acquire knowledge, to use their brains and ability, and to develop the discipline essential to learning. Judging by the examples in the early copies of *The Children's Hour*, this approach seems to have produced a surprisingly literate and articulate society. Parents were ambitious and eager for their children to be better educated than they themselves were, and most gave their children encouragement, and sometimes strict supervision.

An address to the young men of Edinburgh, reprinted in the *Hour* in 1907, is a good example of the value and importance attached to education. It is redolent with the staunch discipline for which Scottish education was renowned, and it would have been in accord with the stern Protestantism of the colony's early days.

The high expectations placed on children at that time must have been daunting and suggest that pressures to achieve are no new phenomenon. Many children must surely have despaired of reaching the high standards held up to them.

Children must have read with a sense of relief and some comfort an article published in 1900 entitled 'Dull Boys':

Some minds are like trees that are slow in growth, but they strike their roots deep. Some of the greatest men have been dull boys. So was Goldsmith. So was Gibbon. So was Sir Walter Scott. Napoleon at school had so much difficulty in learning letters that the master said it would need a gimlet to get a word into 'the dull pupil's head'. Douglas Jerrold was so backward in his boyhood that at nine he was scarcely able to read. Isaac Barrow, (one of the greatest preachers the Church of England ever produced) was so stupid in his early years that his father more than once said that if God took away any of his children he hoped it would be Isaac, as he feared he would never be fit for anything in this world.

By 1930 there was, apparently, a better understanding of an individual's ability and worth:

1930.

SLOW MINDS AND QUICK.

One of the speakers at a school Speech Day had been stating that the great prizes of life seldom go to the boys who have taken prizes at school.

That is scarcely encouraging to those who do work and win honours. Perhaps it would be more just to say that a boy who is slow and unsuccessful in his early studies may yet attain honour and eminence, developing gradually but surely, till he eventually outstrips those who had distanced him at the beginning of his career.

Our own history affords many such examples. The Duke of Wellington's mother said of her slow-witted boy, 'I vow I do not know what to do with my awkward son Arthur'; and a close observer, studying him in his youth remarked, 'Let who will get on in the world, you certainly will not'. Yet the slow boy became the saviour of Europe.

'Why trouble to tell him a thing twenty times?' said the father of John Wesley to the boy's mother. 'Because the other nineteen would be wasted', was her reply. We owe much to minds which have ripened slowly; Laurence Sterne, Sir Walter Scott, and Oliver Goldsmith came to maturity with oaklike deliberation, but what fruit their ripening yielded!

Great things have been done and will yet be done for the world by brains which have taken long to work.

Although the slow boy may become a genius in time, it does not follow that the boy of high talent is doomed to burn out prematurely, as is so often said.

Edison began his career as a boy of twelve, and is still at it at eighty-one. James Watt, father of the steam-engine, was active from childhood to a green old age. Lord Kelvin's fertile genus, flowering in his early boyhood, was still unexhausted when he died at eighty-four; and Victor Hugo, the most astounding boy prodigy France has produced since Pascal, lived eighty-two years, busy from his early to his last years in a career of unexcelled accomplishment.

Dunces may become dons, doctors, and dictators, wonderful fellows all, and they are not to be despaired of, but genius too, can run its race and maintain a long course.

(*Children's Newspaper.*)

One of the most effective ways of influencing young minds is by emphasising the desirable qualities in characters whom they admire and may emulate. The *Hour* made great use of 'heroic models'. (In the chapter 'Exploration' there are many examples.)

Starting in 1904 a series of articles appeared entitled 'Good Women'. They were, of course, expressly, and probably exclusively, 'For Girls'. Florence Nightingale headed the list. There was an account of her work which presents a more idealistic picture of her than more recent biographies have done.

September 1910.

FLORENCE NIGHTINGALE.

Last month the whole of the English-speaking world sorrowed because of the death of Miss Florence Nightingale. She had lived a very long life—last May she passed her ninetieth birthday—but for many years she was an invalid. King Edward conferred on her the Order of Merit, which is not only the highest of such honours, but Florence Nightingale is the only woman who has received it. Her life was a truly noble one, for she did much—perhaps more than any other woman—to decrease pain and suffering, and she left the world better than she found it.

Similar accounts were given of the work of Elizabeth Fry, Grace Darling, Elizabeth Barrett Browning (despite her being associated with drugs!) and Hannah More. The following story of the contribution to education by Hannah More, who began the first Sunday School,

1906.

BE SOMETHING.

Be something in this living age
And prove your right to be
A light upon some darkened page
A pilot on some sea.
Find out the place where you may stand,
Beneath some burden bow;
Take up the task with willing hand
Be something, somewhere, now.

January 1905.

A GOOD MOTTO.

Dear Boys, I want to give to you
A motto safe and good;
Twill make your lives successful,
If you heed it as you should
Obey it in the spirit,
Obey it in the letter—
Don't say a thing is 'good enough'
Till it can be no better.

And whether at your lessons
Or at your daily work,
Don't be a halfway dabbler—
Don't slip and chide and shirk,
And think it doesn't matter
That such talk is 'trash' and 'stuff',
For until your task is perfect
It is never 'good enough'.

If your work is in the schoolroom
Make every lesson tell;
No matter what you mean to be,
Build your foundation well.
Every knotty point and problem
That you bravely master now
Will increase your skill in labour
With the pen or with the plough.

If you sweep a store or stable
Be sure you go behind
Every box and bale and counter;
It will pay, you'll always find,
To be careful, patient, thorough,
Though the work be hard and rough;
Make your task complete and perfect;
Twill then be 'good enough'.

So you'd better take my motto,
If you ever mean to work
To any station higher
Than a stable boy or clerk.
It will make you independent,
It will make you no man's debtor;
Then never say 'it's good enough'
Till it can be no better.

Florence Nightingale.
Born, 12 May 1820.
Died, 14 August 1910.

1904.

FLORENCE NIGHTINGALE.

BY transposing the letters of the above name the following pretty anagram may be made: 'Flit on, Cheering Angel'.

The Lady of the Lamp was indeed a cheering angel to the sick and wounded and dying soldiers of the Crimean War fifty years ago.

was considered suitably inspiring reading for little girls living in Australia in 1904:

Some of the richer farmers (in England) on whose land the parents of the poor children, and often the children themselves, were employed as labourers, thought that if people were educated they would become lazy. But Hannah More was wiser. She knew that education made people better, that it made them have more respect for life and property of other people, and that it helped them to live better and purer as well as happier lives. So, to make a long story short, she and her sister made up their minds to start a school in one of the villages near.

May 1904.

GOOD WOMEN.

ELIZABETH FRY.

By Talsie.

Until the early part of the eighteenth century the criminal laws of England were very different from what they are now. Men and women were put

1904.
Elizabeth Fry and Anna Buxton Visit Newgate Prison.

to death for crimes which to-day are looked upon as only slight offences. For instance, some boys—and, I am afraid, girls too—have been known to break down and injure trees and shrubs in the park lands and squares—trees planted to beautify and improve our city. If these thoughtless ones had lived a hundred years ago they would have laid themselves open to a death sentence. Again, a man who killed a sheep or deer belonging to his neighbour received the same punishment that would be given to the vilest murderer to-day. Making or passing false coin, forging, smuggling, shop-lifting, were all punishable by death.

To make matters worse, all prisoners—old and young, those who were criminals and those who were perhaps quite innocent of crime—were crowded together without sufficient air, food or clothing. Indeed, a farmer now would not be allowed to keep his pigs and cattle in such a state of dirt and misery as was the common lot of prisoners until well on in the nineteenth century.

This dreadful state of affairs came to the ears of a great and good man named John Howard, and also touched the pitiful heart of a gentle Quaker lady, Elizabeth Fry, and I want to tell you how much good was wrought by one delicate woman to bring about a better state of things.

Many passages in the *Hour* were reprinted from addresses to schools, or were articles specially written by well-known people in the Australian community, in England, and sometimes in America. They were quite clearly selected for their moral influence and the writers themselves were regarded as models of good character. Famous soldiers were considered particularly appropriate as examples of manliness and discipline and, as is evident in the chapter 'Lands of Hope and Glory', royalty appeared to rank next to godliness! *The Children's Hour* did not overlook those in their midst, the living examples of moral uprightness in the persons of the Governor, the Premier, the Minister of Education, the Director of Education and others in dignified positions.

It was assumed in *The Children's Hour* that the lives of those in high positions were as dignified as their callings, and virtuous beyond reproach. In most of the articles contributed by such 'notables' the word 'character' is dominant:

1909.

MR PRICE'S LAST MESSAGE TO THE BOYS AND GIRLS OF SOUTH AUSTRALIA.

Character is best of all.

BOYS, grow up to be manly men. Develop a backbone; don't be blown about, like men of straw, from one side to the other. Get clear opinions on things, and stick to them—fight for them, if need be. Above all, try to grow up morally pure.

GIRLS, your mission in life is to be modest, to be pure, and to make the boys and men better because they have known you. Learn to be good housewives, and take a pride in your home.

Often I used to wish that some of my own children would turn out to be geniuses—in music or in science. But all such thoughts were changed by my visit to the Old Country. Now my only wish is that they may become good, upright, conscientious men and women. Character is best after all.

1898.

COLUMN FOR GIRLS.

GOOD MANNERS.

Manners are the most potent weapon for good or ill which a woman holds, and happy is she who knows how to use them with sweetness and effect.

GOOD MANNERS AT HOME.

IT is a much more important thing than many people believe that good manners should have their starting point in the home. The other day I found the following excellent rules gummed on the flyleaf of a little book which a very careful and loving mother gave to her little son thirty years ago, and I am anxious to pass them on to the boys of our schools. I should like to remind you all at the same time of the old proverb which says, 'Manners make the man'. Manners are, or should be, the outward expression of the internal life; therefore all outward graces are most real when they spring from an inward loving heart, a heart which never likes to cause pain or inconvenience to others. Blessed is that boy, and all who have to do with him, who will take these rules into his heart and carry them out in his daily life.

Some Excellent Rules.

1. Shut every door after you without slamming it.
2. Never stamp, jump or run in the house.
3. Never call to persons upstairs or in the next room; if you wish to speak to them, go quietly to where they are.
4. Always speak kindly and politely to the servants if you would have them do the same to you.
5. When told to do or not to do a thing, by either parent, never ask why you should or should not do it.
6. Tell of your own faults, not of those of your brothers and sisters.
7. Carefully clean the mud from your shoes before entering the house.
8. Be prompt at every meal.
9. Never sit down at the table or in the parlour with dirty hands or tumbled hair.
10. Never interrupt any conversation, but wait patiently for your turn to speak.
11. Never reserve your good manners for strangers, but be equally polite at home or abroad.
12. Let your first, last, and best confidant be your mother.

1906.

EDUCATIONAL LADDER.

THERE are few (if any) children in the upper classes of our schools who have not been interested by the story of Jack and the Beanstalk. Probably many of these readers now doubt that there ever was such a daring boy as Jack, who climbed from the lowly position in which he was born high up into a kingdom where he had such stirring adventures and won such high renown.

It may come as a surprise to such doubters to be told that at the door of every school under the Education Department of South Australia, if there is not a beanstalk, there is a ladder which leads up to the University of Adelaide.

To climb the ladder boys (or girls) require to have a strong will, the power of working hard, and a clever mind; and so with perseverance, industry, and ability they may gain an entry into the highest positions in the State.

Perhaps some boy will enquire whether anyone has climbed such a ladder. The reply is that the names of many could be given who have succeeded in doing so; and are now among the doctors, lawyers, engineers, and other important positions in South Australia.

It may also be said that during the last few years several rungs have been placed in the ladder, by which the ascent is made easier to children who attend the small schools.

It is the wish of the Director of Education that every pupil in the public and provisional schools shall know fully the steps of this ladder, so that at the beginning of each year there will be many bold climbers, both girls and boys, who will do credit to their schools and to South Australia.

1906.

THE DEVELOPMENT OF CHARACTER.

C. A. Uhrlaub.

Character and reputation are like the substance and its shadow. Character is what you are in yourself; reputation is what people think of you. The shadow may be sometimes a little longer and at other times a little shorter; but in the main, among unprejudiced people, the substance and the shadow will answer to each other. Reputation is important, but, however valuable reputation may be, character is still more valuable. But what is character? It is made up of habits, and habits spring from acts. When you have done a thing once it is easier to do it a second time, and easier still to do it a third time; and so on until use becomes a kind of second nature. Therefore, in whatsoever affects your moral character, if it is not right to do a thing, beware how you suffer yourself to do it once.

Since habits are made up of acts as a chain is made up of links, every action we perform has an influence on our character. The habits we should cultivate in early youth are habits of honesty, habits of kindness, habits of patience, and habits of temperance. These habits, after all, constitute our moral character; but the least understood of these habits is the habit of temperance. Temperance means moderation. It is especially opposed to drunkenness and gluttony, because these vices invariably result in the moral and physical ruin of all who become their slaves.

Another strong aspect of moral training was 'Duty'. A sense of duty was instilled hand-in-hand with discipline. So intensely was duty promoted that sometimes it seems to have taken the place of kindness. There is little to suggest in the *Hour* that kindliness was a simple response of love and concern. One gains the impression that being helpful and considerate was a duty, carrying with it appropriate rewards, according to a moral scale. Being dutiful won approval.

1913.

DON'T AND DO.

Don't be rude. Never forget to say 'please' and 'thank you'.
Don't be unkind. Speak gently. Help the little ones, the old and the weak.
Don't quarrel. The Bible says 'Blessed are the peacemakers'.
Don't throw stones. You may break a window and hurt some person.
Don't be selfish. Think of others and share your good things with them.
Don't be untidy. Keep your hands and face and dress clean and neat.
Don't be careless. Careless people break and spoil many things.
Don't be late. Late scholars lose their own time, and hinder those who are early.
Don't tell tales. A tell-tale does great harm and causes much pain to others.
Don't copy. If you copy an answer, you cheat your teacher and also yourself.
Don't tell a lie. If you do, no one will believe you when you speak the truth.
Don't use bad words. Never take God's name in vain.

Do.

Do to others as you would have others do to you. This is the golden rule.
Do as your parents tell you. The Bible says 'Children, obey your parents'.
Do as your teachers tell you. They wish to make you good and useful men and women.

Do everything at the right time. Work put off comes in the way of work and play.
Do your best. No one will expect you to do more.

Do your best, your very best,
And do it every day;
Little boys and little girls,
That is the wisest way.

Do the least thing in the best way. What is worth doing is worth doing well.
Do what is right *because* it is right. Do not expect praise for doing right.
Do your duty. The path of duty is the path of safety.
Do good and be good. Be kind and gentle to all. Return good for evil.

March 1918.

WHAT NOT TO DO

Throw paper and fruit skins about the school ground or streets.
Mark walls of buildings with chalk or pencil.
Injure shade trees or flower beds.
Throw stones at birds for they destroy worms and insects and cheer us with their songs.

1929.

RIGHT CHILDHOOD.

The first character of right childhood is that it is modest. A well-bred child does not think it can teach its parents, or that it knows everything. It may think its father and mother know everything—perhaps that all grown-up people know everything; very certainly it is sure that it does not. And it is always asking questions and wanting to know more.

Then the second character of right childhood is to be faithful. Perceiving that its father knows best what is good for it, and having found always, when it has tried its own way against his, that he was right and it was wrong, a noble child trusts him at last wholly, gives him its hand, and will walk blindfold with him if he bids it.

Then the third character of right childhood is to be loving and caring. Give a little love to a child, and you get a great deal back. It loves everything near it, when it is a right kind of child—would hurt nothing, would give the best it has always, if you need it—does not lay plans for getting everything in the house for itself, and delights in helping people; you cannot please it so much by giving it a chance of being useful, in ever so little a way.

And because of all these characters lastly, it is cheerful. Putting its trust in its father, it is careful for nothing—being full of love to every creature, it is happy always, whether in its play or its duty.

John Ruskin.

1925.

GET OUT OF THE RUT.

(During last October, when 'Boy Week' was held in Adelaide, the Director of Education, Mr W. T. McCoy, delivered the following address. It contains much that may be laid to heart by our readers.)

Mr McCoy said that, speaking generally, they were all moving in ruts. They did the same thing day in and day out, and gave little thought to self-improvement. If they wanted to get out of the rut the first thing they had to get into their heads was that success was not a matter of

July 1909.

ADVICE TO BOYS.

HORACE Mann, a great American teacher, once gave this bit of advice:
Boys, you are made to be kind, generous—and magnanimous. If there is a boy in school who has a club foot, don't let him know you even saw it. If there is a boy in ragged clothes, don't talk about rags in his hearing. If there is a lame boy, allow him to take part in some game. If there is a hungry one, give him part of your dinner. If there is a dull one, help him to learn his lessons. If there is a bright one, be not envious of him; for if one boy is proud of his talents and another envious of them, there are two great wrongs and no more talent than before. If a bigger or stronger boy has injured you, and is sorry for it forgive him. All the school will show you in some way how much better it is to forgive than to have a great fuss.

1903.

Three things to govern—tongue, temper and conduct.
Three things to love—courage, gentleness and affection.
Three things to hate—cruelty, arrogance, ingratitude.
Three things to delight in—frankness, freedom and beauty.
Three things to wish for—health, friends and a cheerful spirit.
Three things to avoid—idleness, loquacity, and flippant jesting.
Three things to fight for—honour, country and home.
Three things to admire—intellectual power, dignity and gracefulness.
Three things to think about—life, death and eternity.

June 1903.

He lives longest who thinks most, feels most, and acts the best.

No life is commonplace to him who lives with uncommon aims.

1919.

IMPORTANT RULES FOR YOUNG AUSTRALIANS.

(Adapted from *American Magazine*, April 1918.)

BOYS, and girls who wish to be good Australians will try to become healthy, strong, and useful, so that our country may become ever greater and better. Therefore we obey the ten laws of right living which the best Australians have always followed. Only the best was good enough for the Anzacs. We shall publish several of these laws in this and others in subsequent issues. Read them carefully, again and again, and train yourself to carry them out.

1. The Law of Health.

1. I will keep my mind clean. I will not listen to impure stories, see bad pictures, nor read impure books. My language shall be clean.
2. I will keep my body, my clothes, and everything about me clean.
3. I will avoid those habits which would harm me, and will make and keep those habits which will help me.
4. I will try to take such food, exercise, and sleep as will keep me in perfect health.

2. The Law of Self Control.

1. I will control my tongue, and will not allow it to speak mean, course, or profane words.
2. I will control my temper, and will not get unjustly angry when people or things displease me.
3. I will control my thoughts, and will not allow a foolish wish to spoil a wise purpose.

3. The Law of Self Reliance.

Self conceit is silly, but self reliance is necessary if I am to be strong and useful. Therefore—

1. I will gladly listen to the advice of older and wiser people; but I will learn to think for myself, choose for myself, and act for myself.
2. I will not be afraid of being laughed at.
3. I will always try to do right, even when the crowd does wrong.

4. The Law of Reliability.

Our country grows great and good as her citizens are able to fully trust each other. Therefore—

1. I will be honest in word and in act. I will not lie, sneak, or pretend.
2. I cannot hide the truth from myself, and will not try to hide it from others; therefore I will try not to do wrong of any kind.
3. I will not take without permission what does not belong to me.
4. I will do promptly what I have promised to do. If I have made a foolish promise, I will at once admit my mistake, and will try to make good any harm my mistake may have caused. I will so speak and act that people will find they can always trust me.

luck, but of long and careful preparation. It never happened that a man who was careless, half-hearted, unpunctual, and haphazard in his work became a successful boss.

The first essential, if a boy was to make a success of his life, was a good education. They had to remember that they did not leave school educated. Their schooling was merely given them as a foundation upon which to educate themselves as they went through life. They should read the thoughts of great men, make use of the libraries, attend lectures, and so on. Life was their big school, and their education went on as long as they lived.

He advised them not to spend too much time upon sport. In its place, sport was a great thing, and a most important part of their education. At the same time, looking on at a game being played was no good. They should play the game themselves, learn the rules, and they would thereby be helped in playing the game of life. They should not give too much time to sport, however, or their education would be one-sided. Pictures were another thing at which they should not spend more of their time than was wise. Some pictures were a good educative medium, but there was a limit to their use.

Another important point was that a boy needed a strong and good character. A boy who did not have those attributes was a failure. In building up a character, a great deal depended upon the boy, and a great deal upon his home life. They should make a choice of good companions. They should not choose a companion who was untidy in his dress, careless in speech, unpunctual at his work, irresponsible in his actions, and who gave no heed to the morrow. These would be of no help to a boy. Rather they should select a companion possessed of high ideals, and clean in mind and tongue. That was the type of boy who would help another on the road to success.

A boy should also be quick, clean, punctual, and zealous in his work. Those were attributes that caught the eye of the boss. A boy should learn to love his work for his own sake, and should take pains with his duties. He would counsel them, if they wanted to make a success of life, to show ability, have a good character, and secure a suitable education. If they possessed those three things, they would soon lift themselves out of the rut.

1913.

YOU WILL NEVER BE SORRY!

For using gentle words.
For doing your level best.
For being kind to the poor.
For looking before leaping.
For learning before judging.
For thinking before speaking.
For harbouring clean thoughts.
For standing by your principles.
For asking pardon when in error.
For being generous to an enemy.
For showing courtesy to your seniors.
For helping an unfortunate person.
For doing what you can to make others happy.
For refusing to take an unfair advantage of a schoolfellow.

1925.

BOYS AND BUSINESS.

Sir Henry Braddon.

(Several years ago the following lecture was delivered to school boys in Sydney. The lecturer was the Hon. Sir Henry Braddon, a well-known businessman connected with the firm of Dalgety and Co. He was the first Trade Commissioner appointed to represent Australia in the United States.)

Now the business world is so tremendous, so wide and varied—from the huge banking concerns to the petty grocery on the corner—that it would be quite impossible to bring it all in detail within the scope of a short address. Yet, throughout the whole, there are certain guiding principles.

Many of you will presently be in the business world. You need not be discouraged by its tremendous scale, for you will be entering a very modest little part of it. You will not at the outset find anything very difficult. You will be quite up to anything that you are asked to do, as long as you carefully observe certain rules of conduct, accuracy, neatness, obedience, and some reasonable measure of speed.

If there is any one thing I would stress more than another it is courtesy. Always be courteous—that is the one factor which makes the whole business world easy, and you cannot start too soon to acquire a habit of courtesy. There will be times when little troubles and frictions will unavoidably arise between you and those whom you have to meet in business, but they will vanish like breath from a mirror with a little tactful courtesy. It is always quite enough to settle the difficulty in hand, without introducing needless difficulties arising out of impatience or anger. Courtesy is the lubricant that makes the wheels of business run smoothly.

Later on—but perhaps that is looking rather a long way ahead—you will rise to positions of command. You won't be concerned so much with books and letters and other routine details, but you will have assumed something needing a bigger mind. You will have great responsibilities. You will require organising capacity, and power to face difficulties with a balanced mind. The difficulties will increase with your responsibilities, and, mind you, in the business world you must meet these successfully or pay the penalty. In the professional world these penalties are not so apparent. The lawyer or the doctor usually gets his fee whether he makes a success of his case or not, but in the business world there is no escaping from the results of a mistake; these will show inevitably in the balance sheet. It is not always a mere matter of mathematical calculation.

You will be called upon to come to a decision, and, if you make a mistake, you are going to pay for it. The responsibilities of the business world are great, because so often you have to leap these traps by using your own judgement. Nevertheless never dodge responsibilities, always face them bravely.

The particular point I would stress with you boys is that even today, at your school work you can begin to prepare yourselves for those graver responsibilities you will all encounter later on. Learn to do everything well, no matter how trivial it may appear, the habit will grow upon you. The making of your characters is necessarily in your own hands. In a sense, fate is cruel to youngsters. If you are slovenly or careless now-a-days you will certainly have to 'foot the bill' sooner or later; there is no escape. Men differ as to the age when it will no longer be possible for you to modify your characters—some say twenty-one,

5. The Law of Clean Play.

1. I will not cheat, nor will I play for "keeps" or for money. A game is not worth playing except for its own sake.
2. I will treat my opponent with kindness and fairness.
3. In a group game (football, cricket, etc) I will play for the success of my team, and for the fun of the game, but not for my own glory.
4. I will be a good loser or a generous winner.

6. The Law of Duty.

The shirker or the idler lives upon the labor of others, and burdens others with the work he ought to do himself. He is a nuisance, therefore.

1. I will try to find out what my duty is, and do it, whether it is easy or difficult. What I ought to do I can do.
2. I will make the best use of my time. My country needs it. My conscience demands it.

7. The Law of Good Workmanship.

1. I will get the best education I can, and learn to do the right thing in the best way.
2. I will take an interest in my work, and will not be satisfied with merely passable work. Only the best is good enough for me.
3. Anything I start I will finish.

8. The Law of Team Work.

We must work with others. One man alone cannot build his own house, make his clothes, grow and prepare his food, and educate his children. One man may begin a thing, another carry on, and a third finish it. So we must learn to work together, and each do what others require. Therefore:

1. Whatever work I have to do, I will do my part, mind my own business, and help my neighbour to do his part.
2. I will learn to be tidy, orderly, and methodical. Disorder makes confusion and wastes time.
3. In all my work with others, I will be cheerful and try to make others cheerful.
4. When I receive money for my work, I will be neither a miser nor a waster. I will save when I can, so that I may not be a drag on others in bad times. I will spend as one of the friendly workers of Australia.

9. The Law of Loyalty.

If our Australia is to become ever greater and better, her citizens must be loyal and devotedly faithful in everything.

1. I will be loyal to my family. I will gladly obey my parents or guardians. I will help each member of the family to be good and useful.
2. I will be loyal to my school. I will obey, and help others to obey, those rules which are made for the good of all.

1906.

LIARS.

A. G. Grenfell.

ONE of the hardest things for any boy to be is truthful: for that very reason, and because the earlier one begins to try the easier it becomes later on, he must be always trying.

We know that grown men, in their business, detest liars and have neither use nor pity for them; the first time, they say, that they catch a man lying to them is always the last. And it is. From the shame in our hearts when we have lied, even successfully, we know how loathsome lying is to God.

some rather more; but never forget that at the present moment every one of you boys is busy building up the man you are going to be. Nobody else can do it for you. Teachers, parents, friends may advise and encourage—but still the job is really your own, and you only have a year or two before you to complete it.

Always do your work in the best way you possibly can, not only because it is your duty, but because in that way you will attain your greatest efficiency and happiness.

Alcohol arrived in Australia with the First Fleet and quickly became the cause of one of its greatest social problems:

> In Adelaide there was little activity on social problems outside the churches. The Total Abstinence Society raised the banner for Temperance in 1840, but there were few restrictions on the sale of alcoholic liquors, and drunkenness was causing much unhappiness and misery among the people.

So wrote Mrs Willett Bevan in 1947, in *Torch-bearers*, a history of the Woman's Christian Temperance Union. This remarkable organisation had spread to Australia from the United States of America where it had been founded in 1874. Such was the warmth of response to its introduction into Australia that branches sprang up in all the colonies. In Adelaide a union was set up in April 1886 with fifty-seven members. (By 1927 it had grown to almost 4000 members!) The members of the WCTU were known as White Ribboners—they wore white ribbons. Their connections with religious organisations, and their participation in church activities—Bible study was a regular part of union life—cloaked their work with a mantle of respectability, and enabled them to embark on all kinds of projects normally regarded at that time as 'unsuitable' for them. It is astonishing to read in *Torch-bearers* of their involvement in so many political issues, as:

> . . . growing strong of soul, they were able to rise to the demands of an organisation which placed hurdle upon hurdle before them—the suffrage of women, the abolition of the powerfully entrenched liquor traffic, of commercialised vice, and of war and its causes. They even challenged the great Imperial Parliament on its right to force the opium trade upon the Chinese people.

Closer to home they initiated Public House Visits. Striding fearlessly in pairs into hotel bars on Saturday evenings, between 8 pm and 10 pm, they castigated husbands and fathers for spending, in alcoholic self-indulgence, the money which should have sustained their families, condemning their drunkenness which brought untold misery to women and children.

Of particular relevance to *The Children's Hour* was the successful attempt by the WCTU to have temperance literature introduced to schools in the form of tracts and leaflets. The *Temperance Wall Sheet* found its way into the classrooms, and Cassells published *A Temperance Reader*. Schoolchildren were encouraged, and in some cases expected, to 'sign the pledge'. *The Children's Hour* by 1900 was reiterating the evils of alcohol and the perils of drunkenness. The health risks were stressed, while the degradation and financial destitution accompanying drunkenness were heavily expounded. As in most matters of morality, exemplary models were presented to add weight to the message.

1906.

TEMPERANCE.

Drinks such as beer, wine and spirits are not foods as milk is a food; they do not help to make the body grow, they do not help to keep the body from wearing away, and they cannot increase the total amount of bodily strength and warmth.

They contain a dangerous substance—alcohol—which is harmful to the body. In small quantities, alcohol is a stimulant; but a healthy, vigorous person does not need a stimulant. The well-known comparison that stimulants are the whip and the spur, and not the corn and the grass, is strictly true.

Much alcohol lowers the power of the body to resist disease. An habitual drunkard may die from a disease which, in the case of other people, might mean only a short illness.

The more a person is given to heavy drinking, the more serious does a wound or an injury become.

Persons who drink to excess do not, as a rule, lead long or healthy lives. Many insurance companies offer more favourable terms to total abstainers than to others. No alcohol drinks quench thirst so well as water does; they are apt to make people more thirsty, and so cause a desire for more. There is always the danger that the desire may become irresistible.

Avoid forming the habit of drinking. A person's first glass of beer is no more pleasurable than his first pipe. People usually begin to drink through seeing others drink.

It has been proved that alcohol lowers the power to endure fatigue or undergo hardships. Total abstainers, or those who drink very little, have been shown to be the best soldiers on the march and the best men for hard physical work. A gang of navvies, composed of abstainers, working on the Great Northern Railway, England, did more work each day than other gangs, although they worked shorter hours. Polar explorers forbid the use of alcohol; it causes men to succumb quickly to the cold. Athletes, when in training, nearly always abstain from alcohol in any form.

Money spent on alcoholic drinks is money wasted. Beverages such as milk and cocoa, which generally speaking, cost less than alcoholic drinks, are heat-giving, and, at the same time, flesh-forming, whereas alcoholic drinks are of little real value as heat-givers and of no use as flesh-formers. For the money that a man spends on a glass of beer, he could buy bread containing about 15 oz. of heat-giving food and 2½ oz. of flesh-forming food.

Everybody admits that many crimes are caused through drink. Consumption, inflammation of the lungs, cancer and brain disease are among the diseases to which alcohol may render a person specially liable.

Children and young people ought not to take alcoholic liquor in any form, except by a doctor's express orders.

Sir Michael Foster says, 'If we could take away from the world all the ill health, all the poverty, all the wretchedness, all the cruelty, all the crime that have been brought about by drinking too much wine, beer, spirits, or the like, how much happier, wealthier and brighter the world would be'.

(*Temperance Wall Sheet*, No. 1, Education Department, New Zealand.)

1912.

ESSAY COMPETITION.

THE Woman's Christian Temperance Union of South Australia announce the following Essay Competition:

Subject: "The Value of Total Abstinence from Alcohol." Entries to be received between March 15th and May 15th, and essays to be sent in to W.C.T.U. Office, Wakefield Street, by June 15th.

Divisions: (1) All under 12 years; (2) from 12 to 14; (3) from 14 to 17; (4) all over 17.

Prizes: (1) 7s. 6d., 5s., 2s. 6d.; (2) 10s., 7s. 6d., 5s.; (3) 15s., 10s., 7s. 6d.; (4) 20s., 15s., 10s.

Number of words: (1) 300; (2) 500; (3) 1,000; (4) 1,500.

Essays to be signed by nom-de-plume and names to be sent in sealed envelopes *with nom-de-plume and date and age at last birthday on the outside.*

The following gentlemen have kindly consented to act as judges: — Dr. P. Bollen, Dr. Hone, Dr. F. J. Chapple, and Mr. M. Trüdinger.

1926.

PENN'S REMEDY FOR DRUNKENNESS.

William Penn, the Quaker, was once advising a man to leave off his habit of drinking.

'Can you tell me how to do it?' said the slave of the appetite.

'Yes', answered Penn; 'it is as easy as to open your hand, friend'.

'Convince me of that, and I will promise upon my honour to do as you tell me.'

'Well my friend', said the great Quaker, 'when thou findest a vessel of intoxicating liquid in thy hand, open the hand that grasps it before it reaches thy mouth, and thou will never be drunk again'.

The man was so struck by the quaint advice that he followed it.

January 1915.

LORD ROBERTS AND STRONG DRINK.

During the past sixty years of his (Lord Roberts) life he had been a soldier, eager to make the army victorious over our enemies. He always tried to abolish drunkenness among his soldiers, and spoke and wrote much to gain such a result. The day before he died the following letter, written by him, appeared in the *Times*, perhaps the best known paper in the whole world. It is plain that the grand old soldier understood that strong drink is often more dangerous to our soldiers than are the enemy's guns:

Temptations to Soldiers.

I feel it my duty to point out to the civil population that putting temptation in the way of soldiers by injudiciously treating them to drink is injurious to them and prejudicial to our chances of victory. Thousands of your recruits are now collected together in various places and are having their work interfered with and their constitutions undermined by being tempted to drink by a friendly but thoughtless public and also by the fact that public houses are kept open to a late hour of the night. I beg most earnestly that publicans in particular and the public generally will do their best to prevent our young soldiers being tempted to drink.

F. M. Roberts.

1908.

THE DRINK.

Come here, all ye who have learned to think,
And hear me speak of the drink, drink, drink!
Come, male and female; come, age and youth;
And list while I tell the simple truth.

It's bad for
the pocket,
it's bad for fame,
It's bad
when often
it bears no
blame;
It's bad for
friendship, it's worse
for strife; It's bad for the
husband; it's bad for the wife.
It's bad for the brain, it's bad for the
nerves, For the man that buys, and the
man that serves; It's bad for the eyes and
it's bad for the breath, It's bad for the life, it's
worse for death. It's bad when there's trades-
men's bills to pay; It's bad—oh, how bad—for a
rainy day; It's bad, for it leads from bad to worse,
Not only bad, but a giant curse. It's bad for the face,
when pimples come; It's bad for the children and
worse for the home; It's bad for the strong, it's
bad for the weak; for the sallow tinge that
it lends to the cheek. It's bad for the day
when you pay the rent, And bad for
the child with the bottle sent; It's
bad in the morning, it's bad at
night; Though the table is
laid and the fire burns bright.

The poor man's bane—destruction's gate;
The Church's shame—the blight of the State;
A poison-fly with a venomous sting,
That makes our glory a tainted thing.

(*Cassell's Temperance Reader.*)

1918.

ALCOHOL IN THE ANTARCTIC.

On his return from the Antarctic regions Professor David, one of the great men of Sydney University, said: 'Throughout the long journey extending over four months—that in search of the Magnetic Pole—not one drop of alcohol was taken by any of us. On one occasion, however, during the stay in the Antarctic we had a little wine, as it was the birthday of one of the party. We found that our resistance to cold dropped, and we therefore "dropped" alcohol.'

Just as intense as the fight against alcohol was the battle to abolish cigarette smoking among children—'Young men before the age of twenty-one'. Much was made of the stunting of growth, the impairment of faculties and the generally detrimental effects of smoking. Such results were, it was claimed, unavoidable and indisputable.

1910.

NOTE THE DIFFERENCES.

Young Ever-smoke has shaky hands,
He writes [example of poor writing]
Young Never-smoke knows truth's commands,
And writes 'like this you see'. [firm and clear]

It seems unlikely that boys found this convincing. One can all too easily picture a robust and bright-witted young lad (possessed of a good firm hand!) reading such warnings in *The Children's Hour* while enjoying an elicit cigarette behind the lunch shed! There were, however, some convincing names among the non-smoking leaders of the day which may have lent some weight to the argument:

The International Cigarette League had a branch in Adelaide and the Hon. Secretary, Miss A. M. Hussey, managed to have frequent references to the League's work included in *The Children's Hour*. Her trump card in the pack of heroic models was Major-General Baden-Powell, the founder of the Boy Scout Movement, who was of course also a sound supporter:

March 1907.

ANTI-CIGARETTE LEAGUE.

(We have been asked to publish the following which has already appeared in the daily press.)

Message from the hero of Mafeking:

Do you remember who the hero of Mafeking is? I feel sure if he were to visit South Australia all the schoolboys and girls would like to hear him speak; but failing that, they would like a message from this world-renowned soldier and with this thought in view I wrote asking him to send a few words to the boys of South Australia. Here it is:

Inverary, 12 October 1906.

Dear Miss Hussey,
I cordially sympathise with you in your work of preventing juvenile smoking in South Australia. If your boys are going to be the hardy men that their fathers have proved themselves in the war, they will not take to smoking, as it only spoils a lad's health. Here in England all the boys who are worth anything have made up their minds not to smoke till they are over 18 years, or 20 years of age. It is only the 'rotters' as they are called, who smoke. They do it in order to appear like grown up men, but they only succeed in looking silly and in spoiling their eyesight and digestion.

Yours truly,
R. S. S. Baden-Powell.

1911.

WHY BOYS SHOULD NOT USE TOBACCO.

PERHAPS some boy will say, 'Grown people are always telling us "This will do for men but it is not good for boys".'

Now, wise doctors have stated that the boy who uses tobacco while he is growing makes every part of his body less strong than it otherwise would be. Even his bones will not grow so well.

If you were going to build a house would it be wise of you to put into the stonework of the cellar something that would make it less strong, something into the brickwork or the mortar, the woodwork, the walls, or the chimneys that would make them weak and tottering instead of strong and steady?

It would be bad enough if you should repair your house with poor materials; but surely it must be built in the first place with the best you can get.

Children are building their bodies day after day, until at last they reach full size. Afterwards they must be repaired as fast as they wear out. It would be foolish to build any part in a way to make it weaker than need be.

Boys who smoke cannot become such big, fine-looking men as they would if they did not smoke.

Cigarettes are small, but they are very poisonous. Tobacco in any form is a great enemy to youth. It stunts the growth, hurts the mind, and cripples in every way the boy who uses it.

Not that it does all this to every youth who smokes; but it is always true that no boy can make a practice of smoking and have so fine a body and mind when he is twenty-one years old as he would have had if he had never used tobacco. It you want to be strong and able men, do not use tobacco in any form..

(*Child's Health Primer, Pathfinder Physiology*, No. 1.)

1906.

WHAT THE CIGARETTE CAN DO.

I SUPPOSE you have never heard of a cigarette working at arithmetic; but if a cigarette could speak you would hear it tell you the following:

I can *add* to a boy's nervous troubles, *subtract* from his physical strength, *multiply* his aches and pains, *divide* his mental powers, take *interest* from his work and discount his chances of success.

1910.

SMOKING.

A SCOUT does not smoke; it is not such a very wonderful thing to do. But a scout will not do it because he is not such a fool. He knows that when a lad smokes before he is fully grown up it is almost sure to make his heart feeble, and the heart is the most important organ in a lad's body. It pumps the blood all over him to form flesh, bone, and muscle. If the heart does not do its work the body cannot grow to be healthy. Any scout knows that smoking spoils his eyesight and also his sense of smell, which is of greatest importance to him for scouting or active service.

Sir William Broadbent, the great doctor, and Professor Sims Woodhead, have both told us what bad effects tobacco smoking has on the health of boys. Numerous well-known sportsmen and others in all kinds of professions have given up the use of tobacco as they find they can do better without it. Lord Roberts and Lord Wolseley as soldiers, Lord Charles Beresford as a sailor, the Archbishop of Canterbury, Judge Sir William Grantham all do not smoke, nor do Mr Grace the cricketer and Mr Noble and several of the chief Australian cricketers and Mr Eustice Miles, the champion tennis player.

1907.

INTERNATIONAL ANTI-CIGARETTE LEAGUE.

A. M. Hussey.

This league now numbers over 58 000, the members consisting chiefly of lads who have pledged themselves not to smoke till they are over twenty-one years of age. This league was founded in London in 1901. Major-General R. S. Baden-Powell is the chairman. One of the secretaries of the league recently wrote to the Major-General telling him how successfully his league was progressing. I am quite sure you would like to hear the reply which was received:

Dear Sir—I much regret the delay that has occurred in replying to your letter. I am very glad that you are reviving your Anti-Cigarette League, as I believe that smoking by fellows who are still growing does them an infinite amount of harm and those who are sensible don't take up smoking until they are twenty years of age or so.

Those who smoke before that age generally turn out 'rotters' afterwards. They only do it because they think it looks swagger and manly, but any man who has done any scouting or big game hunting &c. knows that they are fools. So I hope your league will have a good number of members and every success.

R. S. S. Baden-Powell.

(We have published the above letter, sent by Major-General Baden-Powell to Miss A. M. Hussey (the Hon. Secretary of the Anti-Cigarette League) at the lady's earnest request. We trust that, while the boys remember the good advice of the gallant soldier, they will forget the slang expressions contained in his letter.—Ed.)

The Boy Scout Movement, which he had begun in Great Britain in 1907, started in South Australia by a sort of spontaneous combustion. *Scouting for Boys* was circulated throughout the colonies by the Scout Movement, and it was as a direct result of reading this fortnightly paper that boys were prompted to form their own scout troops here. Once formed, boys enlisted adult support and linked themselves with the 'Imperial Society'; that is, directly to Britain. The aims of scouting are well known—self-reliance, honour, loyalty, comradeship, discipline and courage, to name some of them. By 1908 scouts' troops had sprung up in the country even before they had got started in Adelaide, so it is not surprising to discover that by 1910 the wide circulation of the *Hour* was promoting and supporting the movement all over the State.

Few things have changed more markedly during the last century than attitudes towards money. It is difficult for those who have had no experience of it, to understand the former deeply ingrained and universal respect for thrift. The word is so unfamiliar nowadays that some do not even understand it!

But the first generations of settlers were brought up to deplore waste, an attitude which was perpetuated by necessity in many families as they experienced the heavy financial burdens of the First World War, the Depression, and the Second World War. Even people who were well off were 'careful' in their daily lives. Food was not wasted, clothing was mended—as was linen. Produce from gardens was preserved, tools were cared for and subsequently repaired, as was

1910.
Sir Robert Baden-Powell, who was recently knighted by King Edward. Sir Robert is the head of the Boy Scouts.

furniture. Houses and gardens and personal belongings were all respected—as was ownership of them—and the purchase of replacements was permitted only when all manner of repairs had been exhausted! The observance of such standards, or neglect of them, was an indication of character, as was the management, or mismanagement, of personal and business affairs. Closely linked to this respect for possessions and the conduct of one's life was the accepted obligation to save money.

'Take care of the pence and the pounds will take care of themselves' was the catch-phrase of the State Savings Bank. A penny, trivial as it may seem today, did in fact buy something worth having in 1900. A good example is penny postage—it took a letter anywhere in the world! In 1904 the Governor of the day, Sir George Le Hunte, remarked that while he was living in the West Indies he had been associated with a savings bank which had a penny bank department

1910.

TO BOYS OF SENSE.

BOYS should carefully read and think about the following questions and answers:

1. Does any boy need to smoke? Not one.

2. Is smoking a habit conducive to health? No.

What does Dr Henry Gibbons say? He says that tobacco poisons the blood and weakens the heart.

What does Dr Hardwicke, coroner for Central Middlesex, say? He says: 'A large proportion of the deaths that occur between the ages of thirty and sixty result from diseases of the nervous system; and that these diseases are very much hastened by the prevalent habits of smoking and drinking'.

What does Mr Townson, MRCS, say? He says: 'Nearly everyone I have rejected, after examining them for life policies, has brought on an affection of the heart by smoking'.

What does Dr Jolly say? He says:

'The use of tobacco is a common cause of deafness, weak sight, and even paralysis'.

What does Professor Bonisson say? He says: 'Tobacco, which answers no natural want, has become the most common cause of cancer in the mouth'.

What said Whittier, the great American poet? Whittier said: 'I feel a great interest in any effort to check the bad habit of tobacco using. It is not only a nuisance, but a moral and physical evil, and a shame to our boasted refinement and civilization'.

Is smoking specially injurious to the young? 'Yes; this is everywhere admitted.'

What says the well-known medical journal, the *Lancet*? The *Lancet* says: 'To the young, tobacco is injurious in any form, in any quantity, and at all times'.

Why are so many boys now fond of smoking? Many of them are ignorant, not knowing the mischief they are doing to themselves; but many of them smoke because they like to imitate men.

1915.

CYMRO.

I OFTEN tell boys and girls that they should have a Savings Bank book. Some laugh, as if it were a joke, thinking that only rich men's sons and daughters have bank books. In most towns in South Australia a child can get a Savings Bank book. At any one of these, any boy or girl can start by handing in not less than one shilling to the agent. You will be asked to sign your name on a piece of paper, and in a few days a neat little book with your name, age, and name of town therein, will be sent from the big office in Adelaide.

As soon as you have saved another shilling, take it and your book to the agent, and he will take your shilling and write the amount down, putting two shillings as a total in the proper place.

Remember not *less* than one shilling is taken, but you may hand in as much as you like above that amount.

On July 1st of every year you will give your book to the agent, and he will send it to his head office, and in a few days you will get it back. When you open it you will notice that the banker at the head office has given you a little present in money, which he adds to your amount.

Since May 5th, 1908, the Director of Education has allowed any of our schools (if the teachers wish) to have Penny Banks, and these belong to the Savings Bank of South Australia. In the school penny bank you may begin with a penny, and put in a penny, or any amount up to five shillings, every bank-day at your school. At Gawler School we had bank days on the first and third Fridays of each month, and at Parkside we have them every Friday.

for children's savings. This remark probably led to the opening in 1907 of 'The Penny Bank Department', through which the State Savings Bank would receive deposits of not less than one penny, (halfpennies and farthings were still part of the currency). Schoolteachers were appointed as agents throughout the State, and week by week children would line up on 'bank day' to make their deposits. So popular was the scheme that in one year over 4600 children were salting away their savings, and by 1927 the State Savings Bank held 75 042 pennies saved by 50 000 depositors! By 1915 the minimum deposit was one shilling, which says something about the state of the economy.

The Savings Bank's concern with education extended far beyond encouraging children to save in the school bank. Scholarships were awarded to regular depositors on the marks obtained in the Qualifying Certificate of the State schools. To mark the State Saving's Bank's centenary its history was published, and the following paragraph from that book highlights the fact that thrift and financial prudence had become a continuing tradition:

> In assessing the degree of thrift education, the Education Department's Inspectors take cognizance not only of the saving of money, but of school thrift projects, such as the Schools Patriotic Fund, which rendered such signal service during the War, in the prevention of waste, and by the salvage and reclamation of material which otherwise would have been lost to the nation. This organisation has rightly been acclaimed as a classic example of thrift in its widest sense.
>
> As the children of today are the citizens of tomorrow, the Bank looks upon them as the most fertile field for that 'encouragement of frugality for which it was established one hundred years ago'.

1925.

WHY I PRACTISE THE SAVINGS BANK HABIT.

John Rolfe.

(The following essay was recently written by an American boy attending a High School near Chicago. The prize offered for the essay contest was $250 (about £50) and a one-year scholarship tenable at any College or University in the United States.)

Somewhere, I don't remember where just now, I heard a saying: 'The boy is father to the man'. It seems as though people were just awaking to the truth of that statement. Habits formed in the child never loose their hold.

I am at an age when I am forming habits, and since they are to be permanent, I am trying to form as many good ones as possible.

My reasons for practising this habit may be packed into a nutshell by the ninth Scout law. I am a member of the Boy Scouts of America, and the ninth of the twelve laws says: 'A Scout is thrifty, he never wantonly destroys property. He saves his money so that he may pay his own way'. I am going to save money in order to be able to 'pay my own way' through life.

In summer, if you look in the parks, or in winter, in hotel lobbies and waiting rooms, you will see shabby men standing despondently, hands in pockets. These men never have saved: some of them will tell of the time they had good positions which paid well. They have nothing to prove their statements now, because as fast as their money came it went; none of it was put away for a rainy day. Now it is raining, and they are penniless.

Sickness sometimes is a cause of poverty, but more often poverty is a result of wasted prosperity. I do not want to be poor through my own waste and carelessness. Poverty carries with it debt, and I want to go through life without being continually worried about debts. I can remember in my own life a time when there had been a hard winter, with bills to pay and no money coming in. I can remember the time when my father had trouble with his eyes and could not work. I am going to save for the day when my wage-earning powers will be nil.

I know that some day there will be no work for me. Some day, if God and the truck-drivers allow, I shall be infirm. Some day my diet will be milk. Some day I shall have to be careful to wear my rubbers. Some day, in a swimming suit, I shall look as full of angles as a geometry problem. In other words, some day I shall be old. I wish my old age to be spent in peace and comfort, and not in grumbling, cold, and misery.

'You can't teach an old dog new tricks', said some wise man years ago. Neither can you teach an old waster to save any more than you can teach an old man to drive an airplane. Everything you learn early you keep. That is why we go to school between the ages of six and twenty, instead of seventy and ninety.

Therefore, I am going to be a good father to myself and furnish myself with a well-stocked larder of good habits and prominent among them will be thrift.

The Children's Hour also supported the principle of community service, encouraging children to raise funds for charities. They were urged to allot a portion of their pocket-money to a worthy cause, and lists were regularly published reporting the contributions made by various schools, and the progress of various fund-raising efforts. This reached great heights during the First World War (see the Chapter 'Lands of Hope and Glory') and there was enthusiastic competition between schools. In peacetime the children were supporting the Queen Victoria Home (the hospital for women), the Children's Hospital, and Minda Home, among others.

October 1903.

COLUMN FOR GIRLS.

Give unto me, made lowly wise,
The spirit of self-sacrifice.

Last month we had ample evidence of the practical way in which many of those who read *The Children's Hour* live up to our motto. I wish very much that some of the country children could have seen their beautiful flowers and their delicious cakes, and their piles of fresh butter and boxes of eggs, on the lovely stall that we were able to have at the Minda *fête*. Of course, the town children helped too, most nobly, but they were able to come and admire their gifts, while the country children just had to put all their presents in a box and send them away where they would never see them again. Well, when I opened *your* boxes, I felt as if from out of each came spirits of love, and sympathy, and unselfishness, and true kindness. I cannot say all that I should like to say to those who helped so generously to make *The Children's Hour* stall such a pronounced

1910.

NOTHING SHOULD BE WASTED.

THERE are few common things which, when worn out, are entirely useless.

Old, worn-out boots would seem to be about as valueless things as could be imagined yet they are not regarded as refuse. Chopped into small pieces, treated with chemicals and ground to a fine powder, they are returned to the public in the forms of buttons, combs, and other small and useful articles, many of which are supposed to be made of rubber.

Old carpets are made up into cheap rugs. Old tin canisters and the like reappear as toy soldiers or metal roofing; broken gun barrels are made into flat-irons. Old photographic films and print paper are burnt to extract the gold and silver contained in them.

After some years of use the board floor of a manufacturing jeweller's workshop is taken up and burnt. The ashes are carefully preserved, and, when examined, are found to contain quantities of both gold and silver, which well repay the owner for the loss of the floor. These metals entered the boards as fine dust or shavings thrown out from the machines used in making the articles of jewellery.

Even broken window panes are not despised; remelted and mixed with colouring matter they are made into glass vases.

1915.

THRIFT.

Cymro.

MY dear girls and boys,—About fourteen years ago I wrote a letter to *The Children's Hour* on saving money, on how useful it would be if boys and girls would begin by putting their pennies in the Savings Bank, and I also wrote on the same subject to you about six years ago. Many did what I asked, and have kept up the good habit; and I thought I would write again, as I did to your big brothers, big sisters, and their chums.

I don't want you to think that saving money is the chief aim of life, but I do want you to feel that boys and girls who begin to save in their school days are learning one of the first lessons in making a great nation. Also you must all learn to save so as to be ready for the days when you will be too old or too ill to work.

We, who live in South Australia, are the most saving of all the people who dwell in the big island of Australia, and you must help to carry on the good name. Don't let us lose it. You all like your favourite cricketers, footballers, and runners to make records, and you and I must assist to keep the record we have in the savings banks.

Most of you get money every Saturday for helping mother in the house, or for doing such outside work as cleaning the yard, weeding the garden, sweeping the paths, chopping the wood, shining father's boots, lighting the morning fire, bathing the baby, washing up, nursing the baby, darning socks and stockings, feeding the fowls, milking the cow, and many other kinds of work that are a great help to your mother, who has so many dozens of things to do.

Suppose you earned a threepenny piece every Saturday for helping mother. What would you do with it? Would you spend it all on yourself? Would you put it away in your money-box? Or would you place it in the Children's Hospital box, or Minda box, or any other box to help others worse off than yourself?

If you spend it all on yourself for something not wanted, then you are training yourself to be greedy and selfish. If you *always* put it in your money-box you are perhaps taking the first step towards making yourself a miser; and in my eyes a miser is the saddest sight in this beautiful world. If you put all your threepence, or part of it, in the Children's Hospital box, or Minda box, or any other box for helping others, then you are training yourself to be kind, and assisting to give your face that lovely look which makes all kind faces shine like bright stars among many faces.

success. If a list of the children's names were printed it would be long enough to fill—well, I should not like to say how much of *The Children's Hour.* Truly, 'Kind hearts are more than coronets'.

Sir J. H. Symon wishes me to thank all who assisted in *any* way, and says that the committee of 'Minda' much appreciate the substantial help they have received. I must tell you that the Governor admired our stall, and thought it a great credit to you all, and was pleased to hear with what cheerful willingness every one of you worked.

After paying the expenses, which were not heavy, the editor had the pleasure of handing over to the committee the sum of £27 11s as a *Children's Hour first* donation to the new building fund. We were also able to send to 'Minda' a large box of cakes and sweets, and another large box of jam; and to the Carrington Street Orphan Home for Girls a parcel of cakes and fruit, for which the matron was very grateful; and to the babies at the Crêche a small box of sweets. Some girls were only too delighted to take a basket of beautiful violets and daffodils to the Adelaide Hospital, 'where', says one of the lady patients, 'they brightened the whole ward'.

In addition to the subtly persuasive teaching of moral values by example, *The Children's Hour* sometimes took the bull by the horns and simply printed lists of what to do and what not to do. They make an interesting indicator of social change. For example, few boys nowadays wear school caps, so few are aware of the convention of raising one's hat to a lady. Sometimes such moralising was way over the heads of the children for whom it was intended: 'Three things to avoid—idleness, loquacity and flippant jesting'!

1919.

WHAT TO DO.

1. Come to school in time, wearing as clean clothing as possible, with face and hands and neck and ears washed, teeth brushed, nails cleaned, shoes polished, and hair neatly brushed and combed.

2. Be cheerful. Say 'Good Morning' and 'Good Afternoon' to your teacher and your schoolmates.

3. Treat the school buildings and the school furniture with respect. They are for use, but not for abuse. Talk and move quietly in the school at all times. If you are a boy, take off your hat when you enter the door of the school building.

4. Use all books carefully, keeping them as clean and in as good condition as possible.

5. Treat the school ground with respect. Throw all pieces of paper, scraps of food, etc, into the dust bin. Help sometimes to put the school yard in good order. Take pride in the way it looks.

6. Be kind to the younger and weaker boys and girls, to those who are crippled, to strangers and foreigners, and to all others who need your help.

7. If you are a boy, be respectful to ladies and to girls. Raise your hat when you greet them. Stand aside to let them pass out of a doorway first. Carry heavy bundles for them.

8. If you are a girl, receive the attention of the boys courteously. Always

say 'Thank you' distinctly, so they can hear you, whenever boys have done favors for you, such as opening doors, carrying parcels, or handing you something you have dropped.

9. Stand and walk with head erect and shoulders thrown back.

10. Lift your feet in walking; have a spring in your step.

11. Look people straight in the eyes.

12. Always say 'Excuse me' or 'Pardon me' when you cannot avoid passing in front of a person.

13. Repeat to your friends the pleasant things you hear said of them, and try to forget the unpleasant ones.

14. Remember to offer your services from time to time. Do not wait until teacher asks a favor of you, but before she makes the request ask her if you can be of help.

15. Be thoughtful for your schoolmates who are ill and out of school. Write to them. If possible, send them flowers or other little gifts. Perhaps, unless ill with a disease which is catching, you can visit them sometimes; at least, ask how they are.

February 1919.

WHAT *NOT* TO DO.

1. Do not pout when asked to do something which seems unpleasant.

2. Do not tease those who are deformed or crippled, or any who are weaker than yourself.

3. Do not laugh at the mistakes or failures of others.

4. Do not boast when you win in a contest.

5. Do not whine when you are beaten in a contest.

6. Do not crowd or push through doorways.

7. Do not look over another's shoulder to see what he is reading or writing.

8. Do not interrupt a person speaking.

9. Do not flatly contradict anyone.

10. Do not listen at doors or windows to conversations which you are not expected to overhear.

11. Do not rudely stare at strangers, nor question them curiously about their private affairs.

12. Do not talk nor laugh noisily nor play roughly in the school building.

13. Do not spit on the floor or on any part of the school building or buildings.

14. Do not forget to have a clean handkerchief, nor to use it when necessary.

15. Do not handle books carelessly or with dirty hands.

16. Do not forget to say 'Good Morning' and 'Good Afternoon' to your teacher, nor to say it pleasantly and heartily. If you are a boy

1902.

COLUMN FOR GIRLS.

DO THE NEXT THING.

THOSE girls who wrote to me some time last year asking if I knew of any way in which they could help the funds of the Mothers' Hospital will, I am sure, be pleased to hear that they can all help very materially, and in such a delightfully easy way.

I have suggested to Lady Tennyson, who, I know, is so deeply interested in the hospital and who herself has worked so hard for this good cause, that every girl who is anxious to help should make *just one plain cover pillow-slip.* Every girl who reads *The Children's Hour* can sew well enough for that, and even tiny girls in the First Grades might make one. As a matter of fact I know some little ones who have started already, and are so pleased to be able to do something for the 'poor sick mothers'.

Lady Tennyson says in her letter, 'I am extremely grateful to all those who are so gladly willing to help in this way. Anything in the way of bed linen, &c., will be *most* helpful, and help to save the funds, which, alas, are not very large, though quite large enough to start on.' Now let us all make up our minds to set to work at once and 'do the next thing'. For my own part I am very hopeful indeed that through *The Children's Hour* the home will be stocked with a good supply of really well-made pillow-slips, which we shall be pleased and proud to hand over to Lady Tennyson by the time the building is complete and ready for opening.

Of course, everything sent to me will be acknowledged in *The Children's Hour.* So sure am I that many of you will wish to start at once that I must give you what I think will be about the proper size for a single-bed pillow. Get calico 36 in. wide, and let the pillow-slip be 28 in. long when finished.

A yard of calico will be a little more than enough for one, and it should cost about 6d or 7d a yard. Buttons and button holes will be better than tapes for fastenings. I hope no one will think this too simple a way of helping. Remember that the people who *do* the little things and help in little ways are much more useful in the world than those who only dream of doing something grand and big and end in doing nothing at all.

When you send a parcel be sure that your name is on the outside as well as the name of your school, or I shall not be able to acknowledge your gift. A single pillow-slip will come through the post for a penny. Should a larger parcel be sent from a school, it would be cheaper to send it by rail, as 7 lbs. weight will cost only 6d. Address all parcels—

Mrs Twiss, Marlborough Street,
College Park, Adelaide.

1899.

BERTIE'S THRASHING.

HAND up that book, sir, at once!' Bertie raised his head from his desk and looked at his master. Had he really caught him copying? Now Bertie had often done it before; many a time when the master had been explaining things to other boys at the end of the room he had 'cribbed', but never before had he been caught in the act.

'At once, sir! That book, please!' thundered the master. 'I—I—' began Bertie, trying to thrust the book under his desk. 'Your punishment will be heavier, sir, for every second you retain that book.' Bertie lifted his left hand and placed the book on the desk. Mr Scragg looked at it, then at Bertie's half-written exercise, and then at the boy himself. 'I am ashamed of you!' he said. 'You are a dishonourable lad! Come and be punished!'

In after life Bertie used to say, 'That thrashing saved me'. Never had he felt such a disgrace, as with burning cheeks he returned to his seat. At the end of morning school Mr Scragg ordered him to remain in the schoolroom to rewrite his exercise without the use of a key; and as the boys flocked out the tears rushed to Bertie's eyes.

A hard feeling came to his heart, a feeling that he would rebel and not do his exercise, when a firm hand was laid on his shoulder and he looked up to see Mr Scragg's keen eyes looking on him through his spectacles.

'Come, Bertie, buckle to like a man, and do your exercise; it would have been easier, no doubt, to do it in school; but now the least you can do is to work hard.' 'Please, sir', stammered Bertie, 'I am ashamed of myself'. 'Ah! and you ought to be too', said Mr Scragg. All through the dinner hour Mr Scragg sat by him, helping him.

and are outside the building wearing your hat, do not forget to lift it when you greet your teacher.

17. Do not be late to school nor absent from school unless it is necessary. When you come late or are absent you give other people trouble, and giving other people trouble when it is not necessary to do so is bad manners.

18. Do not be in a hurry to tell tales about the misdoings of other people, but be in a great hurry to tell when you yourself have made a mistake or have done something wrong. You are probably sorry. Do not be afraid or ashamed to say so.

The Children's Hour seldom refers to one of the most common aspects of moral training—punishment. From time to time mention is made of the consequences of certain actions: 'Don't tell a lie; if you do no one will believe you when you speak the truth'. But the ways in which adults punished children are rarely referred to. However, reading between the lines of 'Do's and Don'ts' one can well imagine what befell those who flagrantly disobeyed or rejected the codes, or who simply 'forgot their manners'. A simple, yet effective punishment was to be made to feel ashamed and guilty, unloved and rejected, for having brought disappointment, or worse, disgrace, on school or family. But the corporal punishment which teachers and parents undoubtedly resorted to ('spare the rod and spoil the child') and which children grew up to both expect and respect, is rarely mentioned in the *Hour*. Yet we know that in times past the disciplining of children by those in authority was considered just as important as the development of self-discipline.

But if horse whips, straps, canes or big sticks lay waiting behind kitchen and shed doors, or in schoolroom cupboards in readiness for malefactors, we are given few glimpses of them in *The Children's Hour*. But even though in this book we seldom hear sobs of remorse or yells of pain, we may be sure that between 1889 and 1930 there were damp pillows and sore behinds a-plenty!

CHAPTER SEVEN

WHAT ARE LITTLE GIRLS MADE OF?

> Give unto me made lowly wise
> The spirit of self-sacrifice.

> How well the girls have acted up to their motto this year! You will all be pleased to learn that we have been able to send to the Queen's Home, through Lady Tennyson, two hundred and forty-six pillow-covers, one pair of sheets, and one bed-jacket—and still they come! Since sending the fourth parcel about fifty more have come to hand, so that will bring our number up to about three hundred.

Such industry was reported in the 'Column for Girls' in *The Children's Hour* of June 1902. In July the column recorded the gratitude of the matron of the Queen Victoria Home who declared:

> We have not one pillow-cover in the house except those which were made by the school children. It was a splendid way of getting them—to ask every girl who could do so to make one, we are very thankful for them.

The first hospital especially for women was a milestone, not just in medical care, but for the women of South Australia too. *The Children's Hour* readers seem to have supported the home very willingly, and the opening day was of special importance to the whole community.

The first feminists were already emerging in Australia before *The Children's Hour* began. In South Australia in the 1880s, for example, were women like Catherine Helen Spence, and her niece Lucy Spence Morice, who formed the first union of working women, holding meetings in the front parlour of their house at Glenelg. But the general politics of feminism were neither well understood nor widely discussed. In fact, few things remained so undisputed as the clearly defined, and almost universally accepted roles of male and female. Equally understood was the class system which, while it pointed to different expectations of the male and female roles for rich and poor, nevertheless supported similar stereotypes.

It is perhaps the role of women, as one sees it in *The Children's Hour*, which provides the most startling contrast between the past and the present.

April 1902.

COLUMN FOR GIRLS.

DO THE NEXT THING.

DO you know that the 'Queen's Home' is nearly finished, and will soon be ready to open?

What about those pillow-covers? I am pleased to hear that a good number are being made, but am so anxious to see them finished. A tiny girl showed me a piece of hemming the other day, and said, 'Do you think I can sew good enough to make a pillow-cover for the sick mothers?' Every little girl who can hem nicely ought to be able to make one in this way: Instead of a 'seam and fell', or 'run and fell' at the bottom, simply turn down a neat narrow hem the whole width of the calico, then fold the calico in two and 'top sew' the hem.

I have just heard of a school where the *best girls* are allowed to make a pillow-cover as a reward of merit, the teacher in many cases supplying the calico, so that those who have not money to give can give their time, which is, when one comes to think of it, a very precious gift. I feel sure that a great deal of love will be sewn into these pillow-covers, and am more than ever convinced that the girls will not disappoint me. 'I believe you will get hundreds', some one said to me a few days ago, and I believe I shall.

The distinction of being the first girl to send me a finished pillow-cover belongs to Dora Lilly, of the Magill School. Next to her come Ruby Mary Wheaton, Plympton; Berril Harris, Magill; and Mabel Mundy, Magill; Frances Parr and Lizzie Vessey, Magill (First Class), are also amongst the first. Only six so far, but next month I hope to see that modest six multiplied by a number for which we must 'find factors'.

Be as cheerful as you can in well-doing. There is a double grace in good actions when they are done cheerfully and brightly.

1895.

SIX THINGS THAT A BOY OUGHT TO KNOW.

1. That a quiet voice, courtesy and kind acts are as essential to the part in the world of a gentleman as of a gentlewoman.

2. That roughness, blustering and even foolhardiness are not manliness. The most firm and courageous men have usually been the most gentle.

3. That muscular strength is not health.

4. That a brain crammed only with facts is not necessarily a wise one.

5. That the labour impossible to the boy of fourteen will be easy to the man of twenty.

6. That the best capital for a boy is not money but a love of work simple tasks, and a heart loyal to his friends and his God.

As already mentioned, some books and magazines made their way to the households of 'the privileged' in South Australia, who enjoyed such diversions as *The Child's Pictorial* and *Aunt Judy's Magazine.* Most of the English weeklies and annuals of the time were designed specifically for either boys or girls. *The Girls Own Paper*, *The Boys Own Paper*, *Chums* and *The Boys of England*—'A journal of sport, sensation, fun and instruction for the youths of all nations'—were some of them. Girls are known to have enjoyed the boys' stories, but the reverse is unlikely to have happened, for there was a great difference between them. Boys were given a fairly unchanging diet of stories centred on adventure, heroism, travel in foreign lands, with hunting and sporting prowess given prominence. The 'manly' virtues of honesty, courage, strength and 'gentlemanliness' were emphasised. Girls, by contrast, were treated to stories and articles almost exclusively based on what were considered to be the 'womanly attributes'—gentleness, virtue, constancy, selfless devotion, modesty and grace.

It is characteristic of the editors to have had the initiative to start the 'Column for Girls' within a few years of the *Children's Hour*'s commencement. The lead had of course been given by the English publications for girls; in fact the first such articles in the *Hour* very much resembled them, or were simply reprinted from them.

It would not have occurred to the editors—nor indeed to anyone at that time—that a section of the *Hour* especially for girls was discriminatory! But there were books in which boys were given unattractive characteristics while girls were endowed with the pleasing ones. This was so well established as to go quite unnoticed one suspects. For example:

What are little girls made of?
Sugar and spice and all things nice . . .
What are little boys made of?
Frogs and snails and puppy dogs' tails . . .

In *The Girl's Own Book of Amusements, Studies and Employments*, published in 1877 (considerably enlarged and modernised by Mrs L. Valentine), a game is described:

> THE BUTTERFLY AND THE FLOWER.
>
> This game may be played either by young ladies and gentlemen, by little girls and boys, or by little girls alone. If there are gentlemen and boys, they always take the part of insects, ladies and girls take the names of different flowers.

The same book offers this firm advice:

> All fancy work should be regarded as mere amusement and never suffered to encroach on duties, or on more important employments. The early hours of the day should never be given up to it, there is so much to learn when school and teaching ends—so much self-culture waiting for the leisure of bright, earnest, energetic youth.

Such advice was, of course, intended for the daughters of the comfortably-off English gentry. It was from this kind of social background that many women came to be the first settlers in South Australia. Contrasting the tone and flavour of *The Girl's Own Book* with the reality of the life these women faced in the new colony, and considering their background, one recognises the degree of adjustment and adaptability required of them.

The women and girls who accompanied settlers as servants, and those who came (more bravely) under employment schemes, were assured of jobs, particularly if they were good reliable workers. There are frequent complaints in the letters and diaries of early colonists about the difficulties of acquiring adequate domestic help. Some servants found the life unbearable and returned to England; others accompanied husbands and together they struck off into the country to make their own lives, recognising the opportunities for independence that could never be theirs in the 'old country'.

A warning came from the chairman's report to the London Labour Office in 1851:

> Care must be taken by philanthropic individuals only to send such as can labour hard for a living, bush work is no child's play, masters work hard and expect their employees to work hard also. A man with his own land wants a wife who can manage while he is doing the business of the farm.

Just what was meant by 'a wife who can manage' was shown in the proud, compassionate and dignified words of Dame Mary Gilmore in her 'Ode to the Pioneer Women':

> For these women also, fell the responsibility of providing the continuity of life in a harsh land—they bore children, gave love, warmth and security to their households, enabling all to surmount an endless succession of difficulties, challenges and privations as a united little community.

Despite the early inadequacies of domestic help, the colony soon established a social life of a surprisingly high standard in elegance and formality. The social life of Adelaide and of the 'landed gentry' developed along the lines of the English middle-class life so familiar and dear to many of South Australia's first settlers.

1897.

FANCIES.

WHY', asked a lady of an old judge, 'Why cannot a woman be a successful lawyer, I should like to know?'

'Because', said the judge, 'she is too fond of giving her opinion without pay'.

1897.

Speak gently! it is better far
  To rule by love than fear;
Speak gently! let not harsh words mar
  The good we might do here.

Seek to be good, but aim not to be great.
Better to be lovable than lovely.
Better a fair fame than a fair face.
Better be alone than in bad company.
Better buy than borrow.
Better to be sure than sorry.
Better three hours too soon than a minute too late.

November 1894.

FOR BOYS.

A boy should learn.
To be neat
To be honest
To make a fire
To be punctual
To do an errand
To sing, if he can
To sew on a button.

1927.

ALL BOYS SHOULD LEARN.

1. To run.
2. To swim.
3. To carve.
4. To be neat.
5. To make a fire.
6. To be punctual.
7. To do an errand.
8. To cut kindlings.
9. To sing if they can.
10. To help their mother.
11. To hang up their hats.
12. To respect their teacher.
13. To hold their heads erect.
14. To sew on their own buttons.
15. To wipe their boots on the mat.
16. To cultivate a cheerful temper.
17. To speak pleasantly to an old person.
18. To remove their hats upon entering a house.
19. To laugh. A good laugh is better than medicine.
20. To help and not tease boys smaller than themselves.

1897.

COLUMN FOR GIRLS.

WORK to do and a will to do it well are sure to cause cheerfulness and contentment.

Be obliging. We never know when we shall need the assistance of others, often of those weaker than ourselves. Girls never know how much pleasure and satisfaction they can give their elders by doing even the smallest services for them. I noticed a little girl in a tramcar the other day who seemed to be enjoying herself by the open window watching what went on in the streets through which we passed. A lady sitting near shivered very slightly, and in a moment this thoughtful and obliging little girl said, 'Would you like the window closed?' 'Please', said the lady; 'I have a bad cold'. It was only such a trifle you might say—not worth noticing. Perhaps it was a trifle, but, like straws that show which way the wind blows, it showed that girl's character.

Another day I noticed a tiny girl carrying a can of milk. She had to go through a wire fence, and seeing an old lady coming in the same direction, she put her can on the ground and held the wire down for her to go through. When I heard the old lady say 'Thank you, my dear', and noticed the happy smile on the tired face as she went on her way, I thought to myself how much pleasanter it would be if there were more polite and obliging children in the world, who were always on the watch to perform some deed of courtesy.

Kind hearts are more than coronets.

1897.

COLUMN FOR GIRLS.

GIRLS WHO ARE LOVABLE.

In all things mindful not of herself,
But bearing the burden of others.

GIRLS who have not too great a love of liberty. Girls who will let themselves be guided. Girls who feel the love of a daughter for their mother. Girls who know that all day and every day cannot be devoted to holidays and holiday-making, without any duties coming between. Girls who accept their roses with girlish pleasure, and when they are denied them submit without grumbling. These are the girls whose company gladdens the old, and whose sweetness and obedience to authority makes life so pleasant to those in whose charge they are.

1897.

BE A WOMAN.

Be a woman of smiles, not a woman of tears,
Be a woman of hope, not a woman of fears
Be a woman of joy when sorrows assail;
Be a help, not a clog, when misfortunes prevail;
Be true to yourself, and true to your God.
But neither a weakling, nor only a clod;
Be a home, joy, a solace, the best that you can.
Oh, be what God made you, a helpmate to man.

Selected by Nellie Kelly
Lefevre Peninsula School.

The little girls who read the 'Column for Girls' in the *Hour* in the 1890s and the beginning of the 1900s were, in many instances, the daughters of women whose livelihood came from supporting and maintaining that way of life. The future held much the same prospects for many of them, too. Domestic service, whether it be as a weekly laundress, or as cook, housemaid or nurserymaid, for many years offered employment opportunities to women, and training to young girls that was rivalled only by factory work. Moreover, being a really competent domestic servant could be an occupation with some dignity and status.

1899.

Highest duties oft are found
Lying on the lowest ground;
In hidden and unnoticed ways,
In household work on common days.

A growing fashionable society aroused in most women an awareness of—and for those belonging to it, a serious preoccupation with—the duties and responsibilities of entertaining and the requirements of fashionable dress. The clothing favoured in Adelaide during the first fifty years or so of settlement closely followed the English fashion trends, however inappropriate to the South Australian climate. It brought this advantage: the elaborate furnishings of the houses, and the formal attire of men, women and children required the services of large numbers of seamstresses, embroiderers, dressmakers, milliners, hatters, tailors and mercers. Trades and industries grew up in South Australia in answer to the demands for such apparel, providing employment for women and girls in particular. Moreover, boot factories, glove makers, lace makers, corsetieres found a market in the everyday life of the community, as well as in higher society. Women and girls were generally engaged by the owners of shops which supplied such goods—drapery and haberdashery were even considered suitable areas of commerce for ladies of 'genteel' background to be associated with. There were certain other occupations which befitted maiden ladies and widows of 'small means', for whom the labour of the factory, the drudgery of domestic duties and the 'vulgarity' of commerce and trade were considered inappropriate. They included schoolteaching, governessing, dressmaking, and 'taking in paying guests', which sometimes meant running a boarding house. To run a small tea-room could be acceptable and to give private lessons in music (mostly the piano, but sometimes singing or another instrument), elocution, dancing, drawing or painting, provided an income for some women, who, without the financial support of a husband, would have had to rely on the generosity of relatives.

In 1914 the *Hour* described a new school being set up where the training was of a practical nature:

> Cooking and laundry work are taught to girls who, no doubt, with the knowledge they will gain of these important subjects, will be better fitted to make comfortable homes when they are married. They may also learn dressmaking as well as tailoring.

In South Australia large families were common in the past, and some of the daughters of a family were required to help run the household.

Not every girl was free to go 'into service' or 'out to work'. The management of even the simplest household was a constant job. When one realises that everything was done by hand and performed at home, one can appreciate that 'a woman's work is never done' was a well-justified cry! The care of clothing was very time-consuming. Many women, often with the help of older daughters, made all the clothing for the family, except for the heaviest coats and suits for men. Laundry was tackled in coppers over wood fires, combined with zinc tubs and wooden and glass wash boards. Ironing with 'box irons' (where hot coals from the kitchen fire were shovelled into a metal box surmounting the flat plate of the iron) and 'flat irons' (which were placed in the top of the wood stove until they reached the required temperature) was particularly arduous, needing patience and skill, as for many years fashion favoured starched garments and pleats, flounces and frills of exasperating detail! Monday was devoted to the laundry, as, being the day after 'the day of rest', women were more likely to be strong enough for the physical demands of the task!

The 'Column For Girls' in the *Hour* always included advice collectively known as 'Household Hints'. They covered an intriguing range of items, and it would be foolish to dismiss them all as useless to today's daughters—'Place onions under water when peeling them and so save your tears'. The importance of these little scraps of information would have been well appreciated by the girls of the time, for they realised all too well, and seemed to accept without much complaint, that to rule a domestic domain would probably be the highest attainment in life for most of them.

1899.

COLUMN FOR GIRLS.

TABLE-LAYING COMPETITION.
PRIZE, UPPER DIVISION.

As my table is set for six people only, it need not be a large one. I have arranged to have two at each side, one at the top, and one at the bottom. My damask is snowy white, and my glassware shining: No table is completely laid without either. Next to that I am most particular about the flowers. It is most essential that flowers should always be fresh.

1899.

COLUMN FOR GIRLS.

IT is now about two years since our last competition, and as I have by this time recovered from the effects of the work entailed in reading over the few hundred papers I received, I think my constitution is strong enough for another effort in the same direction.

I have so often seen girls—not very young girls either—who knew simply nothing about setting a table for a meal, that I thought it would be a good plan to have a little light thrown on the subject. In some of the London schools there are regular lessons given in housekeeping to the elder girls, and I saw some time ago several pictures of girls at work with their teacher making beds, washing dishes, and setting the table for dinner. Small cottages are attached to some of the schools, and these are furnished for the purpose of teaching housekeeping and cookery. However, as we cannot do just as the London school girls do, let us try to do the best we can.

I will give two prizes, one to those under twelve and one to those over twelve, for the best description, clear and brief, of the correct way to set a table for, say six people. Of course it will be only a plain family dinner of two courses: Meat and vegetables and pudding. Tea is not necessary at dinner-time, so there will be no cups and saucers. What I want you to tell me is—What articles are to be put on the table, where they should be placed, where the vegetable dishes should be, and the proper position of the knives and forks and spoons? Begin with the laying of the cloth. Some people do this so carelessly, that it quite takes away one's appetite for the meal. Let me know how you would lay a cloth just fresh from the mangle. If I were you, I think I should set the table *first*, and *then* sit down and write exactly what you did. Be sure you do not forget anything. It is not nice to have to jump up from the table to get the mustard, or another salt spoon, or an extra plate. No matter how plain a dinner you have, you cannot be too particular in the setting of your table, and always try to have a few flowers, or a growing plant in a fancy pot. When describing *your* particular table, say what kind of flowers you use, and where you place them. As this is Autumn, or almost the beginning of Winter, be careful not to decorate your table with *Spring* flowers, which, of course, no one would be able to get now. I shall look forward with a great deal of pleasure and interest to reading these competitions.

Now to commence the setting of my table. The table-cloth should always be folded in three folds lengthwise, so that when it is laid on the table the centre fold will be exactly in the middle of the table. After laying my cloth, I place my centre-piece of white linen (drawn thread), then put the cruet in the centre, and at each end I place a bowl of flowers. I have chosen pale-pink roses, white chrysanthemums, pink ivy-geranium, a few pieces of pretty plumbago (the blue goes so beautifully with the pale-pink) and some delicate green tendrils of bridal wreath. My cruet of five bottles holds freshly-mixed mustard, vinegar, pepper, catsup, and Worcestershire sauce.

After that I place the mats for the meat and vegetable dishes. Then I place two salt cellars and saltspoons at each end of the table, and two tablespoons at each salt cellar, to be used for the gravy and vegetables. I then place the knives and forks for two at each side of the table, and one at each end, and at the left-hand side of each person I place a dessert-spoon and fork. Table-napkins, folded in the shape of a diamond, are placed at the right-hand side of each person, and a small piece of bread is laid inside the napkin. Of course a carving-knife and fork is placed at each joint, and outside of the knife and fork used by the carver.

I put a sirloin of beef with scraped horse-radish at the top of the table, and a leg of mutton, boiled, with caper sauce, at the bottom. The vegetables to go with the beef are baked potatoes and cabbage; and with the mutton, boiled potatoes and mashed turnips. The vegetable dishes are placed near the joints, but nearer to the centre of the table. A glass is placed at the right hand side of each person, and a glass jug of filtered water placed as near to the centre of the table as possible.

After the first course is finished, the joints, plates, knives, and forks are removed, and I bring in my apple pie and custard, and place them at the top end, and in the same place as the meat occupied. At the bottom of the table I place a small but rich plum pudding and sauce. Pudding-plates must be put near each dish.

I have tried to tell you as clearly as possible the correct way to set a table, and I have endeavoured to word it as briefly as possible.

Edith Isabel Fitzpatrick
Willunga Public School.
Age 13 years.

PRIZE, LOWER DIVISION.

The first thing is to see that the saltcellars and cruet are properly supplied, and arrange everything required upon a tray, so that it may be readily carried into the dining-room. About half an hour before dinner-time, arrange four vases, two fairly tall ones and two low ones, with white daisies, yellow chrysanthemums, and maidenhair fern. Then dust the table and neatly spread over it, the cloth, taking care that the centre fold or pattern be exactly in the middle of the table. Arrange prettily a centre cloth or drape, then, on it, arrange your four vases of flowers, the taller ones between the centre and top and bottom of the table, the two low ones, one at each side.

The tray should then be taken into the dining-room, and the things transferred from it to the table. In placing the various articles, first place the saltcellars at each corner of the table if there are four, if only two, one at the right-hand corner at the top, and the other at the corresponding corner at the bottom; place the cruet in the centre, and the two rests for the carvers at the bottom. Then place a dinner-knife and fork, a dessert-spoon and fork, one of each, at each end of the table and one

Above: *1910. The Way to Produce Short Sight, Curvature of the Spine, and Narrow Chests.*

Below: *Correct Position for Writing.*

1896.

A USEFUL PAPER-CUTTER FOR FATHER.

BUY an ordinary garden trowel, which will cost about ninepence, and enamel it any colour you like; then, if you are clever enough, paint a tiny spray of rosebuds or forget-me-nots on the blade, and finish it off with a neat little bow of narrow ribbon tied on the handle. This will be found much better for cutting newspapers and magazines than either a penknife or a hairpin.

1897.

COLUMN FOR GIRLS.

In all things mindful not of herself,
But bearing the burden of others.

THIS month the prize-winners in the 'washing-up' competition will receive their prizes. The upper division girl will get a book of poems, and the lower division girl a small work box. When I have had time to recover from the effects of the last competition I should be glad to get suggestions for another one.

The following names were, by mistake, left out of last month's list:—Commended—Ada Wilson, Jane A. Noyce, Sarah Noble, Susan Ellery, all of Clement's Gap school.

1896.

HOUSEHOLD HINTS.

TO renovate black kid gloves.—Mix a few drops of good black ink in a teaspoonful of olive oil; apply this with a feather, and dry them in the sun.

To prevent flies from alighting on picture frames, &c., rub the articles over with a little oil of lavender.

A little salt sprinkled on a hot stove will remove any disagreeable odour while cooking.

at each side, the knife to the right and the fork to the left, the dessert-spoon and fork crossed in front, the handle of the spoon to the right and the bowl to the left; the fork with the handle to the left and the prongs to the right.

Then put the carving-knife and fork at the bottom of the table, outside of the dinner-knife and fork, with the points resting upon the rests. Place two table-spoons by each saltcellar, with the handles to the right. Place a water decanter, or water-jug, one in the middle of each side of the table. Place a tumbler to the right of each place, a serviette and a piece of bread to the left of each place. Then place a chair for each person.

When everything is ready bring in the meat-plates, meat, and vegetables, placing the meat-plates and meat at the bottom of the table, and the vegetables at the top. When the first course has been partaken of, remove the meat-plates, meat, and vegetables, also cruet and saltcellars. Then place on the table the pudding-plates, the cream, and sugar, placing the plates at the top of the table; then bring in the pudding, which is also placed at the top.

Evelyn Jubeletta May Howell
Hynam School.
Age 11 years 11 months.

HOUSEHOLD HINTS.

Fat in which there is salt should never be used for greasing cake tins; it makes the cake stick to the tins.

To Clean Floorcloth. Melt half an ounce of beeswax in half a pint of turpentine in a cool oven, and do not use until next day. Use only a very little and afterwards polish the oil cloth with a clean soft duster.

1897.

WASHING UP.

UPPER DIVISION PRIZE ESSAY.

Washing up is generally looked upon as, perhaps, *the* most disagreeable part of household duties, but if performed in a systematic manner a great

1916.
Cooking in the Kitchen.
The Mount Gambier District High School.
Teacher—Miss Needham.
Taken at the opening of the Summer School, September 21st.

part of its unpleasantness disappears. In the first place it is necessary to have a supply of glass, knife, and tea cloths, every kind being plainly marked, so that each may be kept for its proper use. The dishcloth is frequently a cause of annoyance by being found greasy when wanted to wash teacups, &c., but this can easily be prevented by sprinkling a little soda, pouring hot water on it, and rinsing well before putting away. To those who wish 'to take care of their hands', and avoid having them constantly in water, an excellent substitute for the dishcloth is found in a 'mop', which can be bought for a very small cost from any ironmonger. It is a good plan to have several, such as one for glassware only, a second for china, a third for dinner-plates, dishes, &c., and a fourth for saucepans, being careful to keep them strictly for their respective uses. Having provided ourselves with these requisites, let us proceed to wash up the dinner things.

The first thing to do (in order to protect our dress) is to put on an apron made of rather coarse linen, with the skirt large enough to meet behind all the way down, and a bib reaching to the neck. For those who are particularly careful a pair of loose sleeves, made to slip over the dress as far as the elbow, may be added. All the greasy plates and dishes should be collected in one pile at the end of the table, the knives placed in a jug with a little soda and water sufficient to cover the blades only; they should be dried at once, not left in, and the handles washed quickly in warm water without soda. The spoons and forks should be put all together. The glasses must be washed in cold water (if warm is used they will have a smeary appearance) and dried immediately, being rubbed with a coarse glasscloth, and then polished with a soft leather or old cloth. The spoons and forks should be attended to next. If washed in soft warm water, with plenty of soap, and rubbed (like the glasses) with a leather, they will always look bright and shining, and require very little (if any) extra polishing. The water they are washed in may be used, by increasing the heat, for the plates and dishes, care being taken that the dessert and pudding plates receive the first attention. It is well to have a pan of cold water in which to rinse the separate articles after they have been thoroughly washed in the hot water.

Having finished all the actual dinner things, we must see to the saucepans. These need not be considered such 'dirty articles' if properly kept. As soon as they are emptied they should be filled with water and left on the fire till they can be attended to. If the contents have not been at all greasy the water can be poured off after it has boiled and the pan wiped round with a cloth, when it may be put away. The others should be well scrubbed with a saucepan-brush, and occasionally some sand, and have the soot all brushed off the outside, so as to avoid the next thing cooked in them being spoiled and burnt. When they are washed stand them in front of the fire for a few minutes, to get thoroughly dry inside before putting away, to prevent rust. The fryingpan should not be scrubbed, as it roughens the bottom, and so makes it liable to burn the contents. It should be washed in hot water with a little soda; and if done before the pan has cooled there will be no difficulty in wiping it dry with a cloth. The two washing up dishes, when finished with, should be sprinkled with soda, rinsed with boiling water, and carefully dried before putting away for future use.

The management of the breakfast and tea things, especially the latter, is far more simple than those used for the midday meal.

Crockery looks dull from various causes. If the contents of the teacups are emptied into the water being used, or there is a pile of greasy plates at the bottom of the pan, we cannot expect china to be bright. It is

April 1929.

WASHING UP.

A HOUSEHOLD PROBLEM FOR GIRLS.

MOLLY'S mother had been poorly all the week. On Saturday morning Daddy woke Molly.

'Come along', he said, 'you and I will see to things to-day and give Mother a rest. While I get the breakfast you wash all the dirty crockery in the scullery.'

When Molly saw the number of things that had been left over from the previous day scattered about the scullery table, she felt quite frightened. There were plates, glasses, cups, saucers, spoons, knives, and forks. Which should she do first?

In what order would you have washed them?

Answer.

When 'washing-up' always remember:—

To clear the plates of any pieces left over by scraping them into the sink tidy or dust-bin.

To sort the different kinds of articles, placing plates in one stack and saucers in another, cups together, and knives, forks, and spoons. Greasy articles must be kept separate.

Wash the glasses, cups, saucers, and spoons first, using warm water, then add hot water and wash plates, knives, and forks, taking care not to put the handles of the knives in the hot water.

Last of all, wash the greasy articles in nice hot water and a little soda.

Dry them all as quickly as you can and put them away into their proper place.

(*The Teachers' World.*)

1899.

HOUSEHOLD HINTS.

TO clean a stove really well, rub it all over first with a rag dipped in a little kerosene. This will remove every spot of grease.

The ivory handles of knives, when stained, should be rubbed with a piece of damp flannel dipped in salt, and the stains will soon vanish.

To make a lamp burn brightly, add a teaspoonful of salt to the oil.

Fruit or tea and coffee stains on linen should have boiling water poured through them at once before the articles are washed, and in almost every case they will instantly disappear.

1899.

COLUMN FOR GIRLS.

Nothing great is lightly won,
Nothing won is lost;
Every good deed nobly done
Will repay the cost.

THIS time we have a longer motto than usual, and I have chosen one sent to me by a boy, which shows that some boys, at any rate, take an interest in the girls' column, as well as an interest in poetry. Some of the mottoes sent were much too long, though otherwise good; some, though very nice verses, were not quite suitable for this column, and some were not poetry at all.

Since the boys have to read all of *The Children's Hour* as well as the girls, it is just as well to have a motto which they too can take to heart.

1897.

HOW TO BE HAPPY.

IF you expect to be happy you must keep busy. No idle girl was ever happy, and but few idle people are innocent long.

If the girls who look much into mirrors reflect as much as the mirrors do they will look into them less.

When in haste avoid short cuts.

It is a good plan to say as little as possible about that of which one knows nothing.

best to have a basin at hand into which to drain all the cups and jugs. The plates should be put aside till the smaller things are finished. When all the pieces have been collected and thrown away (if no fowls are kept) wash the plates in hot water—not lukewarm—give them one rinse in a pan of cold water, and dry them at once. If they are very greasy a little soda may be added; and, most important of all, we must not be sparing of our water, but change it frequently.

Emily Elizabeth Russell Oborn
Wirrabara Forest School.
15 years old on
November 29th, 1896.

1898.

COLUMN FOR GIRLS.

Little maiden, time is precious;
Work well done brings joy for aye.

A country girl wrote to me the other day asking if I would describe some kinds of fancy work in this column, but I am afraid I should not be able to give any very *clear* directions without the aid of pictures. It is rather difficult to understand new stitches, for instance, without illustrations. The girls in the large schools are taught so many different kinds of fancy work that I am afraid there is nothing new that I could tell them; but with country girls it may be different, though many of them, too, may be taught in school to manufacture some of the pretty articles that were to be seen at the last show. Have any of you ever tried to make useful little hanging cupboards out of empty cigar boxes? These, if neatly lined inside with thin silk or coloured paper, and nailed side by side or placed one on the other, make charming little cupboards for holding small books or medicine bottles, or, in fact, any odds and ends that you wish to have at hand.

Take, say, three boxes and nail them to a piece of board the size of the backs of the three boxes, or perhaps it would be better to screw them with small screws. Leave the lids on, of course, and to keep them closed screw on a tiny button of wood, such as is used to fasten gates, &c., or you might buy a small brass knob (I think they are to be had for about 3d), which will look neater. Lastly, rub the wood with sand-paper, and then give it a coat of enamel, any colour you fancy. Hang up the cupboard by a cord like a picture, or screw into the top of the

1914.
Skipping, Sevenhills School.
Photo: Morton Studio.

piece of wood, at the back, two of those picture screws with rings, and slip them over small nails in the wall. I have a cupboard something like this, which is used for holding small bottles. It is a pretty blue, and is touched up with a little gold paint; so it is not only useful, but pretty as well. You will say this is not fancy work; but if it is not fancy work it is useful work, and not too great an undertaking for any girl who reads *The Children's Hour*.

The conditions of women have improved very much since the early days of the *Hour*. The limited opportunities and the indignity of the lives of many women have been recognised by society during the last century, with discrimination against women becoming a prominent social issue. The ground was already being prepared as early as 1874 when the Adelaide University was established, for by 1879 the first woman student had completed a course and graduated. In 1891, the first woman graduated from the faculty of medicine, and a few women graduates in arts and science were proving themselves in positions previously considered to be the province of men. Many women graduates became teachers, and this was in some sense an extension of the 'training' role traditionally bestowed on women. A great proportion of the earliest Australian books for children, dating from the first years of the colonies, were written by women of varied literary ability. *The Children's Hour* relied on the contributions of women on various topics, not just for the 'Column for Girls'.

It is interesting to see that women were already able to rise to senior positions in education, within both the State and the independent school systems, in the late 1800s. In about 1900 there was an obituary to Inspector Blanche McNamara printed in the *Hour*.

The evidence and example of women in professions must have been an inspiration to those girls who longed to go on to the Adelaide University on leaving school. But fees were required to attend a university, which meant that only those who were well off or who were exceptionally clever and could win the few scholarships available, could hope to take a degree. For most women, their traditional domestic occupations were broadened by the experience of companionship and service to the community, offered by church and charitable organisations, to which all but those from the poorest levels of society belonged—church guilds and fellowships, hospital auxiliaries, homes for the destitute, orphanages and free kindergartens, country women's associations. The charitable work of women reached great heights during the Great War of 1914–1918. Indeed that war brought changes to the lives of women in many respects.

At the time of South Australia's centenary in 1936, Marie Carola Galway, who had frequently written to *The Children's Hour* readers when her husband had been the Governor of South Australia during the war years, wrote her recollections of that time for inclusion in the book *Women in the First Hundred Years*:

> The war was the turning point in the life and outlook of the woman citizen . . . it is, I think, unquestionable that it was the intensive training which women and girls were rapidly passing in order to fill the great variety of vacated posts and the opportunity afforded for particular talent to prove itself, which transformed theory into reality . . . Difficulties and a certain amount of prejudice still block the advance of women along

1900.

INSPECTOR BLANCHE McNAMARA.

IT is with sincere sorrow that we have to inform the readers of the *Children's Hour* that, just as the May numbers were being printed, Miss NcNamara passed peacefully away to heavenly rest, after having taught and examined the children of our schools for about twenty-five years. Although Miss McNamara was never very strong bodily, she was blessed with a strong active mind, and a sweet gentle soul, which enabled her to do all her work well. Only a few hours before her death, in speaking to the writer, she specially spoke of the happiness she had enjoyed in her work, both as teacher and inspector, and expressed the regret she felt, when she first knew she would meet the teachers and children no more.

IN MEMORIAM.

INSPECTOR BLANCHE McNAMARA.

When faith and love, which parted from thee
never,
Had ripened thy just soul to dwell with God,
Meekly thou didst resign this earthly load
Of death, called life, which us from life doth
sever.

John Milton (1608-1674).

1896.

COLUMN FOR GIRLS.

Be good, sweet maid, and let who will be clever.
Do noble deeds, not dream them all day long.

WOULD any of the girls who read *The Children's Hour* like to help to select a new motto for the heading of this column? I should be very pleased if any of you would do so. For nearly a year we have had the same motto, and, as 'variety is charming', I think it would be nice to have a new one for the new year. Those of you who are fond of reading will no doubt find great pleasure in looking up something suitable—say a couplet, or a verse of four lines, not more, in which good advice is conveyed to girls, as in our present motto.

Your selections should be sent in *not later* than December 12th, so as to be in time for the January number.

Each girl may send one selection, and the most suitable lines will be used as the heading of this column for one year. Sign your full name to your paper, and write only on one side. Be sure to give the name of the author of the lines, and the name of the poem from which they were taken. For example:

Her kindness and her worth to spy,
You need but gaze on Ellen's eye.
Scott. 'Lady of the Lake'.

The name of the girl whose motto is most suitable will be published.

Address 'Motto'
Post Office
Norwood.

this or that path, but looking back upon the conditions of even a generation ago, the opportunities have increased beyond the dreams of the pioneers.

The education of girls became more seriously considered after the First World War. Subjects hitherto regarded as intellectually beyond them, or simply as inappropriate, became available to them, so that their education was no longer confined to a preparation for domesticity. Women became typists and worked in offices and banks, whereas previously they had been employed only in shops and factories, or domestic service, nursing and teaching.

As the editors of *The Children's Hour* changed and others took their places the direction of the *Hour* altered too, as might be expected. But there were other influences of change, particularly social change. Its pages bear out Lady Galway's comments on the changing nature of women's lives in particular.

Articles and columns exclusively for girls began to disappear. The editors produced a paper which was for 'children'—boys or girls, in line with the broadened attitudes towards girls' education.

The readiness and ability of women to contribute more freely to the needs of society, and their desire to enrich their lives with learning and experience, were beginning to emerge with a quiet strength which, in years to come, asserted itself with force and power, and demonstrations of anger and violence.

In the early days of the *Hour* a competition was held to find an appropriate couplet or verse to head the 'Column for Girls'. There was perhaps a glimpse of feminist struggles ahead in the opening couplet for 1899: 'Nothing great is lightly won/Nothing won is lost'. But militant women were then in a very small minority. Such fighting words were tempered by the next lines which were perfectly attuned to the female model for 1899, and, indeed, that of many years to come: 'Every good deed nobly done/Will repay the cost'.

1914.
Maypole Dancing, Sevenhills School.
Teacher—Mr H. W. Fielding.

CHAPTER EIGHT

AFTER HOURS

Although the aim of *The Children's Hour* was explained in simple and specific words, 'to encourage a taste for reading', it was soon clear that the paper's role was not going to be confined to that. In a short time almost every aspect of South Australian life, and a great deal besides, was accepted into its pages. Reading was of course a leisure activity in itself, but many other pastimes were suggested, and instructions were given on how to enjoy them. In the case of games, each new one was no doubt added to a vast collection most families already possessed. Nowadays some people find it hard to imagine how earlier generations amused themselves without radio, television, cinema, electronic games, fast transport and fast foods! 'Whatever did they do?' they ask. One answer is: 'They played games!'

A book published in 1869, entitled *Manly Games for Boys*, by Captain Crawley who also wrote *The Handy Book of Games for Gentlemen*, is subtitled, *A Practical Guide to the Indoor and Outdoor Amusements of all Seasons*. It provides information about hundreds of games under such headings as: Games without Implements (about twenty of them); Games with Implements (sixteen, including marbles and tops); Miscellaneous Games (kite-flying being included among the twelve); Simple Indoor Games for Winter Evenings (suggesting knucklebones and spillikins, among others); Grand Ball Games (cricket being one of the thirteen listed); Games of Skill with Various Instruments; Aquatic Amusements; Gymnastics; Games of Skill and Science; and a section on Domestic Pets, offering advice on the keeping of rabbits, pigeons, silkworms, butterflies and moths.

Many of those games would have been familiar to readers of the *Hour* when it began in 1889, but nowadays they are not well known to most people. In the early days of settlement a great variety of games were played in groups, by both young and old, especially at parties and at holiday times. At Christmas, for example, the newspapers and magazines included many more puzzles and word games than at other times. They were eagerly welcomed, just as the games and competitions appearing in *The Children's Hour* each month, under the heading 'Puzzledom', were cause for excitement.

September 1899.

A NEW GAME.

AN American paper gives some useful suggestions for amusing children in summer. A favourite new game with American children is called 'Bubbles and Bundles'. Little gifts are prepared, each of which is placed in a box, or made up into a bundle, and tied up as prettily as possible in coloured tissue papers, with ribbons to match. These bundles are suspended by ribbons on a strong cord, or clothesline, suspended from tree to tree, in a manner to remotely suggest a cobweb. The children are provided with pretty terra-cotta soap-bubble pipes, tied with ribbons, and a huge bowl of soapsuds is brought upon the scene. A tablespoonful of glycerine added to the suds will prevent the bubbles from breaking easily. Two persons at a time take turns in blowing. The bubble must be thrown off the pipes into the air, and the children get under them and try to blow them against the packages that they wish for their own. If the bubble hits the bundle the latter is awarded as a prize, and when a child has secured one he does not try again. It has all the mysterious charm of a game of chance without its objectionable features, and should become popular with the children of Australia.

1902.

PUZZLEDOM.

Conducted by Cymro.

Contributions and solutions of puzzles to be addressed 'Cymro', Mount Gambier.

RULES.

Write your name on the top of your paper.
Put all your answers on *one* sheet of paper.
Put new puzzles on a separate sheet.
Leave a margin, and separate your answers by firm lines, as shown in the solutions.
Answers which do not comply with these rules will not be acknowledged.
All replies to puzzles in this number must be posted not later than Friday, January 30th, 1903, or they will not be acknowledged.

No. 817.—CHARADE.
William Wheatley, Gilles Plains.

My first syllable is short for company;
My second shuns company;
My third assembles B Company of Rifles;
My whole amuses a company of adults or children.

No. 818.—ANAGRAM.
William Wheatley, Gilles Plains.

Make one word forming the name of a battle won by the English during Victoria's reign from
Lo! best soap.

Cymro was responsible for 'Puzzledom'. In 1912, a tribute to him accompanied his photograph in the *Hour*:

> 'Cymro' is the pen-name of a teacher who has been conducting the column known as 'Puzzledom' since 1893. As he announced in the December number, he is now relinquishing his good work, which during twenty years, has had many readers who are now solving the harder problems of life.

It is hard to believe that he could have kept up the steady flow, month by month and year by year, of puzzles and problems with names like Numerical Charades, Enigma, Triangular Puzzle and Historical Acrostics! Some were almost certainly republished from English journals and annuals, but he made up many himself and encouraged the readers to send in original contributions. Their delight when these were published can be imagined.

Mental challenges were tremendously popular and appealed to the entire family, for many puzzles required concentration and intelligence, and a vocabulary and sense of logic often beyond the reach of most children. The answers were published in the following month's edition, alongside the names of those who had gained a score of six correct answers. Not everyone bothered to send in their solutions, but the rules were stated for those who did, and Cymro warned sternly: 'Answers which do not comply with these rules will not be acknowledged'.

Sometimes the 'Puzzledom' section must have been handy for trying out on guests and at family gatherings, when everyone assembled in the parlour for 'parlour games'. Such occasions are described in *Christmas in the Colonies* (Stapleton and Macdonald):

> When all were in a holiday mood, the digestive lull after the midday meal, or the convivial hours before bedtime encouraged family games and pastimes, often reserved especially for this time of the year. The English custom favoured the playing of 'Snapdragon' (played around the fire). In the colonies, however, neither the heat nor the light evenings favoured such entertainment and only the energetic played other traditional games, such as 'Hunt the Supper', 'Hide and Seek' and 'Blindman's Bluff'.

The Australian Town and Country Journal wrote in 1890:

> Christmas Time is the season for family round games and when our boys and girls are tired of tennis and cricket and such active sports, they are glad to form a family circle and join in some pastime, which will provide plenty of fun without much physical exertion.

By the end of the nineteenth century the needs of children were being not only recognised but, to some extent, met, with simply written stories and toys and games, designed not just for learning, but for fun as well. The principle of learning through play had won favour among some educators in England by the mid-eighteenth century, influenced by the theories of philosophers like Rousseau, and a century later by the teaching methods devised by Montessori. Toys, games and puzzles were introduced which required certain materials—boards, dice, coloured blocks, pegs, geometric shapes, rods, counters, cards, and more. In time they were adopted in the more advanced schools in South Australia. This gave working class children the advantage of 'learning games' until then only available to the 'well-to-do', whose relatives, still living in England, often sent them games and toys which were both beautiful and expensive.

The 'day of rest' was firmly entrenched in Victorian family life, and consequently in South Australian homes, and strict rules applied to the way in which it was spent:

> Haste! put your play things all away,
> Tomorrow is the Sabbath-day;
> Come! bring to me your Noah's ark,
> Your pretty tinkling music-cart,
> Because my love, you must not play,
> But holy keep the Sabbath-day.
> (*The Infants' Magazine,* 1868.)

Sunday was, in fact, mostly taken up with church-going and with reading moralistic and religious works, like *Youth and its Duties*, by the Revd Harvey Newcomb (1873), or simply Bible reading.

Despite the monthly replenishment of supplies of reading material with the arrival of *The Children's Hour*, it was still hard for some children to find enough. In the early 1900s the editor of the 'Column for Girls' apologises, in one edition, for not having been able to send more girls' magazines to the country and asks if more can be contributed for sending to those in need.

The State Library of South Australia (the Public Library as it was then called) had, as mentioned in an earlier chapter, been established originally as part of the South Australian Institute. In 1915 the *Hour* noted the opening of the Children's Library in a section of the library's own North Terrace Building:

> At one end of the building—the end nearest to North Terrace—a room has been fitted with shelves and table and chairs, as can be seen in the picture, and a lot of books have been bought for the use of any children who may like to go in and read . . . There is a librarian in charge of the room, who will be able to show you how to find the books, and to help you in choosing the best for your purpose . . . of course the library will be most useful to children living in Adelaide, but many children come at some time or other from the country to visit Adelaide, and they will always be just as welcome as those from the city.

In 1918 and 1919 readers were reminded of the convenience of the Children's Library and that it was open on Tuesdays, Fridays and Sundays, from two to five o'clock. Looking ahead to the hot summer holidays, the editors pointed out that the library was 'a very cool room in which to spend an hour'.

At the turn of the century, school was at the centre of the lives of most children, for social life and leisure were generally limited to the areas of school, church, community and family. Sundays being very restricted, only Saturday remained for relaxation and fun. School hours were long and many children spent hours going to and from school, most of them travelling on foot, so that there was little time left for play during the week. School terms were long and holidays, in consequence, short, so that the recreation and social life children did have was important to them. This was particularly the case for country children.

1897.

No. 489.—LETTER CHARADE.
Thomas Rogers, Riverton.

My first is in the, but not in how;
My second is in lamb, but not in cow;
My third is in can, but not in bottle;
My fourth is in tub, but not in bubble;
My fifth is in man, but not in son;
My sixth is in woman, also in London;
My seventh is in cook, but not in daughter;
My eighth is in book, but not in water;
My ninth is in plain, but not in snow;
My tenth is in rain, but not in show;
My whole is a town in South Australia,
Which gives its name to an animal.

NO. 490.—ENIGMA.
H. Willmerton, Yorketown.

In the merriest eyes, in the sweetest flower,
In the busiest flies, in the coolest bower;
In the hottest clime, in the brightest dream,
In the swiftest time, in the silver stream,
In them I am found, but not in the ground.
What am I?

No. 491.—HIDDEN FRUIT.
Ruby Cowley, Wintanerta.

1. Pass me that map, please.
2. I hope Arthur will come soon.
3. I saw our gardener Adams on a bicycle.
4. The Ohio range is a good one.
5. I saw a turban, an Arab, and a camel.
6. The Frenchman got six ounces of gold.

No. 492.—ARITHMETICAL PUZZLE.
Sylvester Hilbig.

Multiply 1010101 by a certain number less than 200 so that the answer will be all sevens.

1899.

PUZZLEDOM.

No. 625.—LETTER CHARADE.
A. C. Somerville, Hindmarsh.

My first is in hat, but not in bonnet;
My second is in mouse, but not in rat;
My third is in plant, but not in weed;
My fourth is in lizard, but not in centipede;
My fifth is in house, but not in shed;
My sixth is in month, but not in week;
My whole is a mighty river.

No. 626.—NUMERICAL CHARADE.
Mabel Allen, Copper Hill.

I am a word of ten letters. My 1 2 9 is an article used every day in the kitchen; my 4 6 7 1 gives light; my 1 5 10 is a deep hole; my 1 8 2 3 4 is a precious article found on northern coasts of Australia; my whole is a place where most men would like to be.

Cymro.

No. 627.—WORD SQUARE.
Dora Liebing, Angaston.

1. Deep mud.
2. A strong hard metal.
3. A highway.
4. Terminations.

No. 628.—DECAPITATION PUZZLE.
Bessey Pomroy, Cross Roads, Moonta.

My whole is often used in war; behead me and I am a delicious fruit; behead me again and I am part of the body. What am I?

No. 629.—TRIANGULAR PUZZLE.
Mabel Brown, Wallaroo Mines.

1. An ornament for the neck.
2. A title of courtesy.
3. A round figure.
4. An instrument of cutting.
5. To regard with affection.
6. Beer.
7. A short way of writing 'company'.
8. A vowel.

1906.

PUZZLEDOM.

No. 1386.—DIAMOND PUZZLE.
Mabel Goldfinch, Glenelg.

1. A consonant.
2. 2240 lbs.
3. A small bag to contain money.
4. Seeing, beholding, viewing.
5. The largest county in England.
6. A flower named after Dr Fuchs.
7. To flow gently; to slip along with ease.
8. Part of the verb 'to be'.
9. A vowel.

No. 1387.—WORD SQUARE.
Marjorie H. Johanson, Bramfield.

1. A South African animal allied to the horse.
2. A girl's name.
3. To shut the eyes quickly.
4. Pertaining to the kidneys.
5. The chief joint of the foot.

No. 1388.—ARITHMETICAL PUZZLE.
Sidney Smith, Angaston.

If it takes a clock three seconds to strike 3 o'clock, how long will it take to strike 7 o'clock?

No. 1389.—CHANGE-LETTER PUZZLE.
Ella Lloyd, Gilles Plains.

Change 'head' into 'feet' in three moves, each word to be an English word, and one letter to be changed each move.

No. 1390.—HIDDEN ISLANDS OF THE WORLD.
No Name.

1. They suddenly heard a shot. 'Hist?' Leslie exclaimed.
2. Tom and his brother had a great adventure today.

A feature of school life in a country town was the annual Schools Exhibition. This would be of interest to people living in neighbouring towns as well, and everyone for miles around would turn out to view displays of work, sporting events and concerts, which sometimes stretched over several days.

The pride and goodwill that accompanied those occasions can be sensed in the following lines (although they are a little ambiguous): 'July 1894; Again the use of the Institute has been granted free of cost for four days. The residents [of Jamestown] will house the children from a distance, as they did last year'.

NORTHERN AND MIDLAND PUBLIC SCHOOLS' EXHIBITION.

November 1893.

The Northern and Midland Public Schools' Exhibition was held at Jamestown on the 31st of August and 1st of September. The weather was threatening on the morning of the first day, occasional showers falling, which however, did not prevent a large number of people visiting the recreation grounds, where in connection with the show, sports, including races, skipping, tug-of-war, scrambles, and other amusements were held. Fortunately towards noon and opening time the weather cleared, enabling many people who were doubtful as to coming to put in an appearance.

October 1892.

THE HOLIDAYS.

IT seems an easy matter to tire boys and girls with work, but a very hard task indeed to thoroughly tire them with play; they never seem to have enough of that. The Michaelmas Holidays form one of the pleasantest vacations in the year, probably because we can generally reckon on such beautiful weather, and probably too, because there has been such a long spell of work since the Easter recess. This year the weather, though stormy at both ends of the week, kept bright and beautiful for the greater part of the time, and so endless trips to the seaside and the hills made the few days pass all too quickly.

The crowd which collected round the doors of the institute to see the opening ceremony performed, and to hear the speech by the Minister of Education (Dr Cockburn) was immense. The hall was decorated very prettily with wattle blossom—the Australian flower—and flags. The exhibition of work was splendid. During the evening a pleasing and successful promenade concert, consisting of solos, choruses and various other items, was given by the Jamestown scholars. Nor must we forget to mention that the Laura band assisted before and during the concert, their playing giving great pleasure . . . altogether the show was a great success in the quantity and quality of the exhibits and the attendance of the public and parents, and to the latter it must have given a good idea of what the girls and boys of our public schools are able to do. In conclusion, I think the school's show at Jamestown was the best ever held in the north.

Rose Hill
Jamestown Public School.

Country schools went to great trouble to arrange for the children to visit Adelaide for occasions like the annual Public Schools' Exhibition. The children of the Gawler River School wrote with excitement of their visit to the exhibition in 1893, which included lunching at the rotunda by the Torrens.

September 1893.

EIGHT HOUR DAY.

The annual demonstration of the labouring classes of South Australia took place on the holiday September 1st, and proved to be the most important event of the day. The morning was occupied with the procession, which formed in Grote St and wound its way round Victoria Square along King William St, Currie, Morphett and Rundle Sts, to the old Exhibition Grounds. Fortunately the day was fine, and the public turned out in large numbers to see the sons of labour as they marched along behind their splendid banners, or plied their tasks in view of the great crowds. Special interest was added to the procession by the presence of miners from Moonta, who, with their friends and families to the number of about 1500, had taken advantage of the cheap fares allowed them to visit the city.

The Royal Zoological Society, formed early in the life of the colony, in keeping with the intellectual climate of the times, had established the Zoological Gardens during the 1880s to the delight of Adelaide's citizens. It was of a commendably high standard for a city of Adelaide's size and development. *The Children's Hour* published accounts of visits there from time to time.

1895.

A TRIP TO ADELAIDE.

Recently the Annual Industrial Exhibition was held at Adelaide, and Mr James Malcolm, JP, thinking it would be a great treat to the children of the Peninsula, made the necessary arrangements with the Railway Commissioners for an excursion trip to the city, tickets being 2s return, lasting for a week; and about seventy-five children availed themselves of the opportunity of seeing, to them, a sight of a life-time. Wednesday, the 10th April, was the day set aside for our departure, and our party being completed at Kadina, we were soon on our way to the city under the charge of Messrs J. Malcolm (Chairman of the Board of Advice),

1895.

AN EASTER TRIP.

THE 12th day of April being Good Friday, a party, including myself, left Port Wakefield on a visit to Clare. It was a beautiful morning, the sun shining brilliantly, not a cloud in the sky. We left the above-named place at 9 am and arrived at Balaklava, sixteen miles distant, an hour and a half later. After being refreshed with luncheon and rest we proceeded on our journey. Leaving Balaklava at 11.30 we passed through some beautiful country, that of the Devil's Garden and Skilly being most attractive. Further on we came to the well known estate of Mr Cadford. The way in which it is laid out is most pleasing and attractive, the avenues running for miles around, and there are fruit gardens in great variety, with streamlets winding in and out among the hills. All along the route to Watervale we had one of the most lovely drives in the colony, the fruit gardens and the work done there, giving evidence of the energy displayed by the inhabitants. At all places we were treated with the greatest hospitality, gathering as much information with regard to the places as possible.

At 6 pm we arrived at Watervale, as pretty a little town as you will find in the country, and surrounded by hills and valleys. Putting up at one of the hotels, we had tea, and, after spending a very pleasant evening with local ladies and gentlemen, we retired for the night. Of course, all of us were eager for the morning to come; so after a good sound sleep we arose at 7 am, when, after taking a good survey of the little town, we returned to breakfast. This over, we put the ponies in the carriage, and in an hour's time we were to be seen walking round the Seven Hills College garden. Here we were received with the greatest kindness, one of the brothers showing us round the ground and instructing us as to the work done there in late years. In the centre of the garden we came to the wine cellars, and, after being treated with some of its special contents, we wandered round the garden, helping ourselves to the walnuts, and various kinds of fruit therein. After purchasing a case of grapes and apples, we proceeded on our way to Clare. It was 4 o'clock before we reached Clare.

J. Evans (Mayor of Wallaroo), and the Rev. P. A. Enright. On our arrival at Adelaide the majority of us proceeded to the homes of friends, while the remainder went to see the Exhibition. Before we parted at the train on Wednesday afternoon, Mr Malcolm told us to meet on Thursday morning at the Museum, which was our appointed meeting place during our stay in town. Thursday arrived with the sun shining brightly, making everything cheerful and pleasant. When all had assembled at 10 o'clock we went into the Museum, where there was to be seen a great variety of stuffed animals, birds, and snakes, also the skeletons of animals, and in a shed outside was the huge frame of a whale. From there we made our way to the Botanical Gardens, where we spent nearly three hours in examining the beautiful scenery, and feeding the ducks and swans. We also had the opportunity of visiting the picturesque fernery, which we greatly admired. After lunch our destination was the Industrial Exhibition. Having gained access to the building, we were not long in finding something with which to interest ourselves. The works of art were numerous, and, taken on the whole, they were a fine lot of pictures. The incubator, an American invention, excited a great deal of interest. It is a machine for hatching chickens; it is a construction something like a table, with a drawer in which the eggs are placed, and after being there for a certain time the drawer is opened, and chickens instead of eggs meet the gaze, having been brought to life by artificial heat. We also saw a large variety of fancy work, lollymaking, etc. On Friday, at 10 am, we again met at the Museum, and after the roll call we marched to the railway station, where tickets were secured for us for Aldgate. The journey up we enjoyed immensely, the scenery on all sides being beautiful, and going through the tunnels was something that the majority had not before experienced. At Aldgate the first performance was to find a suitable place for luncheon. After having appeased our appetites, which the pure air had made very keen, we played, and gathered ferns until it was time to return to the city, where we finished the day by visiting the Zoological Gardens. The Zoo has, during the last few years, been greatly improved, and the collection of birds and animals is well worthy of any city. We arrived there just in time to see the animals receiving their food, which, considering the number of mouths to be satisfied, must cost a great deal. After having made a thorough inspection, some of our party indulged in a ride on the elephant, which they seemed to enjoy very much. We then went home, thoroughly tired with our day's exertions. On Saturday we visited the City Baths, the Art Gallery, and the Children's Hospital. At the Art Gallery we saw a number of lovely pictures, also several letters written by noblemen and others a great many years ago. At the Children's Hospital what we saw gave us an idea of the good work in which we took a small part by contributing our pennies towards the hospital funds. On Sunday I accompanied my cousin to the Norwood Wesleyan Church, where I heard an excellent sermon by the Rev. T. Lane, late of Moonta. Monday afternoon was spent at the Cyclorama. which, to those who had not previously seen it, was simply wonderful. A very interesting lecture on the Battle of Waterloo was very much enjoyed. On Tuesday we went to the Asylum for the Blind, and found the inmates all busy at brush, basket, rope, mat, and cage making. One would almost think to watch them, that their sight was perfect, they work so quickly and well. While we were watching the rope-making one of our party was so intent that her hair got entangled in the rope, which had to be untwisted before she could get free. In the afternoon we went to Semaphore, where we had a trip in the *Defiance*, which proved anything but enjoyable owing to the rough weather. We were to have gone on board the *Orlando*, but we had to forego that pleasure, which was a great disappointment. Wednesday morning found us assembled at the railway station, ready to start for home, after having had a pleasant week's enjoyment. The success of the whole affair was due, principally, to Mr Malcolm, who did everything in his power to make our trip a pleasant one.

Ella Taylor
Kadina School.

1928.

AT THE ZOO.

Who of our readers, if they were given the opportunity, would not like to take a ramble in the forests of other parts of the world—in Asia, or Africa, or America? But to most of us that opportunity will never come; we shall have to stay at home and do our work. Is it, then, impossible for us not to get a glimpse of the wild in far away countries? Shall we never see the stately elephants, the fierce lions or tigers, the cruel-looking crocodiles basking on a river bank, the lively monkeys, or the gorgeous macaws and other birds flying from tree to tree?

December 1930.

THE ADELAIDE ZOO.

THE Zoo will be the happy-meeting place of hundreds of children during the Christmas holidays. Everyone loves a day at the Zoo, even the grown-ups; and the day is all too short for the small people who want to feed and get to know the ways of all the friendly animals, to ride on the elephant, to have an excursion on the tiny train, and to see all the exciting things that the Zoo provides for visitors.

Its trees and gardens make it such a nice shady place for picnic parties, too.

Mr J. H. Gosse, who is the President of the Zoological Society, has just returned from a world tour, and he is so interested in Zoological Gardens that he visited all the great Zoos of Europe and America, so that he could compare our methods of caring for the captive animals and birds, with those of other countries. It is splendid to know that, after seeing so much abroad, he is convinced that the methods of those in charge of the Adelaide Zoo in looking after the welfare of beast and bird in every way possible, is excellent, and that they are made as happy as possible under the circumstances.

Mr Gosse made arrangements with other Zoological Gardens to exchange animals and birds with us, and already some of these have arrived, while others are arriving in the near future; so that you will be able to view them on your holiday visits.

Some interesting little animals that have already arrived are the Patagonian hares; two of these were obtained by Mr Gosse for us, and on the way here two little baby hares were born, so that the little family is now four, and such extraordinary little things they look, with their big heads and hare-like ears.

It is gratifying to know that these additions to our Zoological Gardens will not cost money, for other Zoos are anxious to get, in exchange from us, Australian birds and animals, particularly marsupials, many of which are little known in other parts of the world. Probably, later on, we shall be having bears from Canada. Mr Gosse saw many of these in Jasper Park, Rocky Mountains, running loose.

Above: *1928. The 'Zoo Express'.*

Below: *1928. 'Miss Bridget' Carrying Some Happy Passengers.*

1895.

SCHOLARS' CORNER.

A VISIT TO THE MUSEUM.

ON Saturday I visited the Museum and saw various kinds of stuffed animals and birds. One thing that interested me greatly was the bower bird and its nest. The bower bird lives in Australia, and generally picks a spot to build its home where it can enjoy the sun. They gather small twigs and branches, and, bending them over until the tops meet, form a sort of arched parade. They ornament their homes with bright feathers or even jewellery which they may come across. In fact, anything that is gay they will pick up to adorn their homes. Many other birds and nests are shown. I think birds show great skill in building their nests, and their whole pride seems to be in making comfortable homes in which to rear their young. Many skeletons of animals are to be seen. There are some fine specimens of minerals, as silver, copper, diamonds, rubies, sapphires, &c. There are large cases of very pretty shells from the Sea of Marmora and elsewhere. There is a fine collection of very pretty butterflies and many other insects. Many other things are to be seen which are too numerous to mention.

From the Museum I went to the Art Gallery, which is well worth going to see. There is a fine show of oil paintings. I saw, amongst many others, some views of Adelaide in the year 1854. A very natural picture is that of a horse in a burning stable, entitled, 'Under Fire'. Among some of the pretty paintings are 'Evening Shadows', 'Queen Esther', 'Homeward Bound', and many others. I enjoyed the visit to the Art Gallery very much.

Maggie Pearce
Rose Park School.

The efforts of those who fostered learning and the arts in Adelaide from its earliest days had their reward, however modest, in the occasional articles which tried to develop an awareness in such things through the pages of the *Hour*:

The British Pictures. September 1893. During the last week or two a fine collection of pictures lent by the British artists for exhibition in the colonies has been on view in the new Museum buildings on North Tce. The exhibition is well worth a visit, and indeed many visits as pictures seem to grow in favour when time is given to dwell on their various excellences. With so many different styles illustrating history, nature, mythology and events in human life, every taste must find some pleasure. Arrangements have been made by which scholars may be admitted at half-price, and it is hoped that teachers will arrange to secure this benefit for their elder scholars at least.

Statues in the City. 1892. During the last few weeks Adelaide has been adorned with two statues, which have been presented to the city by Mr W. A. Horn MP. The marble statue of Venus, the Roman goddess of love, stands near Government House under the watchful eyes of the members of the Permanent Force, who act as guard to the vice-regal dwelling. The figure is sculptured in pure white marble, and is a copy of one of the most famous representations of the goddess. Hercules, the old Greek hero—the Samson (*sic*) of classical writers, and the possessor of enormous strength of body—stands before the people of Adelaide in dark bronze, resting on his terrible club, from which there hangs a lion's skin, one of the trophies of his strength. This statue has been erected in Victoria Square, close to the office of the Commissioner of Police.

This article concludes by urging 'others of our wealthy colonists' to 'follow the good example and add to the beauty and attractiveness of our fair capital, many vacant spaces in which might well be filled with similar works of art'.

1896. Art. 'Sir John Millais'—Mr J. L. Bonython, of the Advertiser, has very kindly lent us a portrait of Sir John Millais, who has lately been made President of the Royal Academy, London. He is a very celebrated painter, and copies of one of his pictures:—'Little Miss Muffet' are in many of the schools. Most people know a very pretty advertisement picture called 'Bubbles' representing a handsome little boy blowing soap bubbles. This too was painted by Sir John Millais. The Royal Academy is a society whose members are thought to be the best artists in England, and it is a great honour to be elected as a member. It is a still greater honour to be elected president.

Outings to the Museum and the Art Gallery made items of interest in the *Hour* too:

December 1894.

SCHOLARS' CORNER.

THE MUSEUM AND ART GALLERY.

Most large towns have a Museum and an Art Gallery. The Museum is, as nearly everybody knows a collection of curiosities, such as stuffed animals, ancient weapons and tools. Its object is to enable us, by seeing these, to learn more than we could by merely reading about them. We cannot get many animals to live in the Zoological Gardens, and it is much easier to obtain them stuffed and place them in the Museum for inspection and instruction. The Adelaide Museum is situated on North

Terrace, facing the parade ground. It has a very good collection of animals, which have been obtained, no doubt, with some difficulty, from all parts of the world. Among these are several human skeletons, and lately an addition has been received in the shape of two Egyptian mummies. There are also exhibited many kinds of fish and birds, as well as different kinds of beasts. Also there are shown under a shed outside the building, the skeletons of two whales. Neither of them is of any great size, the larger being 23 feet long. It is very interesting to inspect and study the various specimens exhibited, and as no charge is made to anyone visiting the Museum persons interested in these studies can come and go as often as they please. The Art Gallery, a collection of splendidly executed pictures and statues to some people is even more interesting than the Museum. These works of art, got up at great expense, labour and patience, place before us in vivid reality scenes of history and romance, or represent places of beauty in our own and other lands. There is nothing so striking to the eye of the observer as the actor in a well-painted picture. In the Adelaide Art Gallery, which occupies part of the Exhibition Building on North Terrace, these is a splendid picture of a horse in a burning stable. The attitude of the horse under the influence of the fright is represented so perfectly that it appears almost real and if the representation were as large as an actual horse it would positively be difficult at first sight to distinguish it from one. Perhaps that is a slight exaggeration but the picture is certainly, as far as effect goes, almost perfect. There are many other good pictures in our Art Gallery, amongst them some very good reproductions of South Australian scenery. There are also several very interesting pictures of battles. A little of the material in a picture always adds to the effect. We look proudly on 'our gallant defenders' even if we do make them the means of exhibiting our wit. However none of these works of art and natural exhibits can be painted by words and it will not cost anything to any person in Adelaide to see all for themselves by paying a visit to the Museum and the Art Gallery.

Annie E. H. Adey
Woodville.

It was about ten years later that the *Hour* took a more serious interest in art education by introducing stories of the lives of famous artists—Michelangelo, Raphael, Turner and William Morris. In the 1920s, reproductions of old masters on the covers of the *Hour* brought works like 'Angel Faces' by Sir Joshua Reynolds, 'The Blind Girl' by Millais, and, at Christmas, the 'Virgin and Child' by Bouguereau (which is in the collection of the Art Gallery of South Australia) into the lives of many people for the first time. Attention was drawn to sculptural pieces in the same way. Experience of art at first hand was limited for children. Drawing lessons were generally tightly structured and inhibiting.

Opportunities for creative expression came mostly from crafts, which became many and varied. From time to time photographs in the *Hour* showed boys absorbed in carpentry. Most boys were encouraged to be able to do more than simply 'knock a nail in', but facilities varied from one school to another.

The choice of 'fancy work' for girls covered a diverse range, and some beautiful objects were made by hand, especially in embroidery, a traditional female occupation. An eighteenth century book for girls assures them that 'the art of embroidery is easily acquired by those who are diligent and patient' and that crocheting 'is a style of

Top: *1906. This picture shows a section of the East Adelaide School Juniors and the drawings they did in the presence of visitors at the Public Schools' Exhibition. They had only worked at the new drawing course for a few months.*

Middle: *1917. Yahl Paddock School, a Successful Class at Carpentry.*
Head Teacher—Mr Geo. Brown.

Right: *1928. Real Australians at School.*
Boys at Carpentry, Point McLeay School.

1915.
Quorn School Girls Hemming Handkerchiefs for our Wounded Soldiers.

work which can be applied most usefully, and as it is quickly learnt little girls can manage it easily'.

The same book claims, that 'unless a girl becomes a good needlewoman before the age of sixteen she very seldom cares for, or attains any proficiency in needlework and therefore the use of the needle should be begun in childhood', advice that was put into practice in South Australian schools.

Country children were not the only ones to benefit from excursions. Adelaide children discovered pleasures beyond the city on weekend

1913.
A Picnic Party in the Flinders Range.
Photo: Mr Albert Canning.

outings and holiday visits. People thought nothing of walking long distances. Many people in the inner suburbs walked to the city daily, and weekend walks were customary. Photographs in the *Hour* showed groups posed casually and happily on fallen logs in National Park, Belair, and walking in Waterfall Gully and Morialta. During holidays they moved further afield, for camping trips were certainly undertaken with delight.

1910.

CAMPING AT PORT
NOARLUNGA.

Geo. C. Davies.

The idea of a holiday spent camping out in the bush or at the sea generally appeals to the ordinary boy, but nevertheless a great many lads have never experienced outdoor life, and consequently do not like to try it.

Perhaps it is because they are afraid of 'roughing it', or that they fear the bath in the cold and frosty mornings, or maybe they don't like washing greasy dishes, or eating coarse food, or doing the dirty work which has to be done by someone in every camp; yet I believe that

Top: *1914. Bathing in the Onkaparinga. Balhannah School boys having a swimming lesson. Teacher—Mr W. T. Stone. Photo: Mr Stone.*

Right: *Four Girls from Little Swamp School (near Port Lincoln) Enjoying Their Holiday at the Seaside.*

1910.
Our Camp at Port Noarlunga.
The River Onkaparinga is in the foreground.

if they would only try the experience for a couple of days they would soon be craving for another such holiday, when they saw the many benefits they would gain from it.

During the last Christmas holidays I, with a party of other boys, spent an enjoyable three weeks camping at Port Noarlunga. Close to the camp was the Onkaparinga River, in which we enjoyed many swims. The first photograph shows the camp, and the second the campers.

Behind the sandhills, shown in the first photograph, is the sea, and a long, clean, sandy beach, over which I had many pleasant strolls, picking up coloured shells, stones, seaweed, and the other interesting things strewn along the shore. On the other side of the jetty are the rocks, with one rather peculiar one, which is the feature of the shore. It is known as the Flat Iron Rock, and is almost covered with such shells as chitons, limpets, and zebra shells, and with crabs.

There was practically no difficulty in obtaining firewood, for as we had the free use of the two boats seen in the first photograph we could row a short distance up stream and get several days' supply.

Three times we rowed six miles up the river to the town of Noarlunga, not for firewood, but for the pleasure of the row, and also to telephone home. Once or twice whilst rowing we were in trouble on the sand banks, and in the strong currents, which usually ended in everyone having to get out and push until all was clear again.

Every morning we all enjoyed a swim, either in the sea or in the river, the latter being preferable, because it was deeper, and free from sharks, stingrays, jelly fish, etc. Frequently there was a heavy surf breaking on the shore, and then we would race over the sandhills to the beach and soon be plunging into the mighty, white-crested waves, which came dashing and splashing all around us, and invariably lifted us off our feet and carried us tumbling and rolling up towards the sandy shore.

As fish were fairly plentiful, almost every day we had fish for breakfast. One morning early three of us caught over five dozen garfish, and at other times we were equally successful.

1907.

A TRIP IN THE *GOVERNOR MUSGRAVE*.

DURING the Christmas holidays eighteen of us were able, through the kindness of the South Australian Government, to take a trip for four days in the steamer *Governor Musgrave*.

2. We were able to see the islands—some of them very seldom visited—which lie at the entrance of the two great gulfs which run into the South Australian coast.

3. We left Port Adelaide at 10 on a Monday night, and by 5 o'clock next morning had dropped anchor off Cape Jervis.

4. The lighthouse—which looks from the sea very much like a pepper-pot—was painted white. At night it guides the ships up and down St Vincent's Gulf and in and out of Backstairs Passage.

5. This passage is a deep channel, about eight miles wide, between Cape Jervis and Kangaroo Island. The land behind the lighthouse is very hilly.

Our meals were exceedingly good considering we cooked them all ourselves. The following was the usual bill of fare for the day:—Breakfast—Porridge, fried fish, bread and jam, and cocoa. Lunch—Tinned or boiled fish, lettuce, tomato and onion salads, bread and jam, and raspberry vinegar. Dinner—Tomato stew, or soup and vegetables, bread and jam or butter, biscuits, and tea.

We had many other amusements, such as visits to the ochre pits in the neighbourhood, reading in the cool shade of the rocks on the beach, carving lumps of ochre and the backbones of cuttlefish, rabbiting, and swimming. The last we enjoyed most frequently of all; sometimes we had five swims in a day, not because we wish to wash so much as to cool ourselves.

We all enjoyed excellent health in the camp, the nearest to anything like an illness being that we were all well sunburnt. We returned home healthier, stronger, and wiser from our pleasant experience of camping.

In 1907, the South Australian Government gave eighteen schoolchildren an enviable trip on board the steamer the *Governor Musgrave*. The cruise took them around Spencer and St Vincent gulfs and Backstairs Passage for four days—a treat many children would have longed for in those days, as they would today.

A climate like that of South Australia invites an open-air life, and this advantage of living in the colony was very quickly recognised and appreciated by the first settlers. Picnics were immensely popular and enjoyed by almost the entire community. Outings arranged by

Top: *1907. The Steamer* Governor Musgrave.

Right: *1915. A Combined Schools' Picnic.*
A procession of children attending the following schools:—Lameroo, Hundred of von Doussa, Bews, Wilkawatt, Hundred of Cotton. The picnic was held on September 18th last.

Top: *1914. The Edwardstown, Brighton, and Sturt Schools on the Beach at Brighton, February 12th.*

Left: *1915. Children, Parents, and Teachers on the Brighton Beach.*

the well-to-do were generally most elaborate—linen cloths, glasses and silver spread out; food hampers overflowing with hams, pies, tongues, puddings and tarts; and wine and water provided in stone bottles. Very often 'billy tea' completed the feast. The 'picnickers' were dressed with an elegance to match the provisions. While some reclined under the shelter of awnings and tents others took part in races and games and even dancing. Most people were content with something more casual—happy simply to be in the open air.

It was the custom for State schools to hold an annual picnic, very often at the beach. Sometimes several schools combined, parents and families joined in, and the event was looked forward to all the year.

When the Edwardstown, Brighton and Sturt schools enjoyed a day together at Brighton in 1914, Union Jacks and a school band added to the festive atmosphere.

July 1894.

OUR PICNIC.

OUR teacher gave us a picnic on the 23rd of May. We marched round the town, each boy carried a flag and each girl an evergreen bough. We sang several pretty marches. We started from the school to a well-prepared piece of ground near the railway station where racing and other sports were gone through during the day. Over seventy children sat down to a well-spread table for dinner and tea. A quantity of fruit and sweetmeats were given away during the afternoon not forgetting a large, beautiful, iced and decorated cake, presented by a kind friend. Each child received a piece and we all spent a very pleasant day. Our parents and friends were with us, and I am sure we all feel very thankful to our kind teacher. I hope each scholar will long remember her kindness in giving us such a nice picnic. Some nice prizes were won during the day. Then we all returned to our homes in the evening, thinking of the pleasant time we had spent.

Charles E. Gwynne
Eurelia.

Parents and children are pictured reassembling at the end of their day at the beach. Some of the party are starting back in little clusters from far down the beach. It is a picture of absolute peace with dogs and babies' prams adding a homely touch. These picnics took place in February, but despite the midsummer weather the women are wearing long-skirted and long-sleeved dresses and of course, hats, and even the children are well covered and are wearing long socks and shoes. Perhaps protection from sunburn, as well as decorum, required so many clothes!

In later years the *Hour* was supportive of attempts to reduce the many drowning accidents that occurred in those days. Instructions and diagrams on swimming were published, and the results of swimming competitions, which were introduced between the schools, were reported. An annual award, the Clouston Shield, was competed for at the City Baths. In 1925 the winning team of four boys from the Port Adelaide Central School had their photos displayed in the *Hour*.

Top: *1915. The Breast Stroke.*

Right: *1910. Fig. 1.—Ready to push off.*

1906.

SWIMMING.

Charles Bastard.

It is hardly necessary in a climate like we have in Australia to ask why we should learn to swim. We all wish to be strong and healthy; we all wish to have clean bodies; we all run the risk during some period of our lives, and generally when we are young and inexperienced, of losing our lives by drowning. Learn to swim and your bodies will be developed; you will know the pleasure of being clean, and may be able to save your own life or that of some other human being from a death by drowning.

What Australian boy or girl would not like to have a strong body—to have muscles like steel. To be able to stand fatigue, so that you may be strong workers, you must strengthen the body by exercise. Australians believe in games that exercise the body. What is the best exercise?

If you ride a bicycle you will mostly strengthen the muscles of your legs; cricket will develop another set of muscles; football another; but those who have studied the matter agree that no pastime is so effective as swimming in bringing all muscles of the body to a state of perfection. In swimming you use your legs, your arms, and the muscles of the neck and back.

And now let me say that to learn to swim properly you must begin when you are young; then the muscles are soft and pliable.

In my work I find it much easier to teach a child than to teach a person over 16 years of age. Past that age the muscles begin to set, and it is then very difficult to get the pupil into the right strokes for swimming.

There was once a wise man who said that 'Cleanliness is next to godliness'. It is hardly possible for a person who is habitually dirty to be a good man or woman. A dirty body will soon become a diseased body. Perhaps you know how offensive it is to sit near an unclean person; no doubt you have wished such a person miles away. People who learn to swim cannot be unclean.

During the summer months we are often saddened by reading in the newspapers accounts of deaths from drowning. Often it is a boy who, if he had been able to swim a few strokes that would have sent him the length of your schoolroom, would have saved his life; or perhaps a child falls into a creek while a party are out picnicking, and an elder boy, unable to swim, tries to rescue the child, and both are drowned.

If you counted up the deaths in a year from drowning you would be astounded. At the beginning of November I enquired of the Government department which keeps a record of such deaths. Let me give you the figures. We went back twenty years, that is, to 1886. For the first ten years from 1886 there were 500 people accidentally drowned in this State; for the last ten years there were 412 people drowned. There are to-day 374 398 people in South Australia; ten years ago there were 346 716. I wish you to notice there has been a decrease in drowning though the population has increased by over 27 682. I have good reason to say that this is due to the efforts of myself and other teachers of swimming. More boys can now learn to swim, and although there is a larger population there are fewer deaths. Still it is sad to think that every year over forty-one persons, mostly boys, have met their death by drowning in South Australia.

1920.

HINTS TO BATHERS.

AVOID bathing in quiet or secluded spots, as should an accident occur, and no help be near, it is very clear what may happen to you.

The most suitable time to bathe is about an hour or two before a meal, when food taken at a previous meal will have become partially digested.

On no account bathe shortly after a hearty meal, or when exhausted from vigorous exercise, or when the body is cooling after perspiration, nor on the other hand, when shivering. Do not stand or wait at the water's edge until the warmth of the body has passed off.

Cleanse the mouth and nostrils before entering the water and breathing will then be easy. Do not gasp or catch the breath suddenly, or take short, quick breaths. Breathe freely, naturally, and regularly.

Persons unaccustomed to cold water bathing should not stay in too long at first.

Avoid bathing altogether in the open air if, after a short time in the water, it causes a sense of chilliness with numbness of the hands and feet.

Persons subject to giddiness or faintness, or who suffer from palpitation or other troubles of the heart, should not bathe without first consulting a physician.

Those subject to ear-ache, deafness, or running of the ears, should carefully plug their ears with greased cotton-wool or cover them with waterproof caps before entering the water. In such circumstances deep diving should be avoided.

In cases of accidentally falling into deep water, it should be borne in mind that weight of clothes will not hurriedly drag one under, nor cause one to sink sooner than if undressed—in fact, the air in one's clothes will help to buoy up as well as enable one to resist the effects of cold water for a longer time than if quite naked. Of course, one cannot swim fast with clothes on.

March 1915.

LEARNING TO SWIM.

THIS is the way in which Digby Heathcote, a boy of nine or ten years of age, was taught to swim by an old boatman named Toby.

One fine day they went out in a boat together, and Digby had his first lesson. When they were some little way from the shore, Toby said, 'Pull off your clothes, master'.

Digby did as he was told. 'Now, jump overboard', added Toby. Digby stood up; but as he looked into the water and could see no bottom, he was afraid to plunge in.

Toby had passed round the boy's waist a band with a rope fastened to it, but Digby had hardly noticed this. Suddenly he felt himself pushed, and over he went into the water.

'Oh, I'm drowning, I'm drowning!' he cried out, when he came to the surface.

'Oh no, you're not, master; you're all right', said the old man. 'Strike out for the shore, and try to swim to it.'

Digby did strike out, but wildly, and not in a way that would have kept him afloat.

'Catch hold of this', said the old man, pushing an oar overboard. 'Now, strike away with your feet, right astern; not out of the water, though—keep them lower down.

'That's the way to go ahead. Steady, though; strike both of them together. Slow, though, slower. There's plenty of time; you can learn the use of your hands another day.

'Draw your legs well under you. That's it. Now, as I give the word, strike out. That will do splendidly. If you keep steadily at it, you'll learn to swim in a very few days.'

Digby felt rather tired when the boat at length reached the shore. He had, however, learned a very important lesson. Before he went home, Toby showed him how to use his hands in making the breast-stroke.

1908.

SELF LIFE-SAVING BY FLOATING.

Mr F. Lyon Weiss, of Western Australia, has requested us to publish the following:—

Most persons desire to save their own lives or the lives of others; few know how to do so. Far more lives are saved in water accidents, &c., by floating than by actual swimming. Still, swimming is a very valuable help, the best of exercises, and a delightful, health-giving pastime. Water is a supporting, not a depressing, medium. Very few swimmers can swim for a long time and distance, whereas even non-swimmers can, with obedience to this advice and a little courage, float for a long time, probably till assistance arrives. Yet comparatively few swimmers can float properly. If you are so unfortunate as to be a non-swimmer, and to find yourself in water beyond your depth and without anything to support you, act at once as follows:—

1. Throw yourself at once on to your back, the head especially being bent well backwards. These actions will bring your mouth and nose uppermost to air, and your legs will rise when straightened.

2. Shut your mouth. Draw in air by quick gasps through the nose, breathing this air out slowly through the nose, and never allowing the lungs to get quite empty. But very little (if any) water will thus be swallowed.

3. Spread yourself out, clothed or unclothed, as flat as possible on the surface of the water, the arms and legs being extended fully, the arms beyond the head, feet and hands gently moving a little backwards and forwards (not upwards or downwards or with jerks) at the surface, the chest thrust upwards.

4. Do not raise any part whatever of your body—except the mouth, nose, eyes, and the top of the chest—even for an instant in the slightest degree out of the water. If you do you will at once sink.

5. Keep your eyes open; the water will not hurt them.

6. Don't keep struggling and screaming, which only tend to exhaust, sink, and drown you. At intervals call 'Help!' in a loud, high-pitched voice.

7. Keep your feet towards the wind.

Swimmers also might advantageously follow this advice to rest themselves.

If you follow these instructions (which I have proved the value of in rough water in the presence of scientists, experts, and thousands of gentlemen and ladies), you can float for hours, even in a rough sea, and you will, in all probability, be saved, and be able to save others. Please keep this paragraph, and circulate this advice, not only amongst those dear to you, but also among your acquaintances, schools, clubs, &c., and send me (at Perth, Western Australia) information of any rescues, attempts, instances, &c., that you hear of. This return will be a kindly, grateful act that will probably benefit your fellow men and women.

There is evidence in some very early editions of the *Hour* of the great loves of Australians—football and cricket. In 1892 there was a report about the rival football teams of the time—South Adelaide were the winners and 'The Ports' were runners-up. However, not

1892.

FOOTBALL.

THE football season is at an end, at last, and the South Adelaides have regained the premiership after several years of hard fighting. The Ports were the runners up, followed by the Norwoods, Medindies, and Adelaides in the order in which the names occur. The season has not been a satisfactory one on the whole; the South Adelaides too early gave evidence of their superiority, so that the excitement of a close finish was wanting to draw large crowds to the matches. The worst features of the season were the weaknesses of the umpires and the roughness of the play. The latter being largely the result of the former. As we have already spoken strongly on this subject we shall say no more at present, except to express the hope that the season of 1893 may be characterised by what every true lover of sport wishes to see—a close struggle for top place, carried with first class play and fair, honourable and manly conduct.

Top: *1915. A Swimming and Life-saving Class for Girls. Streaky Bay Public School. Head Teacher—Mr J. S. R. Oborn.*

Left: *1920. A Swimming Lesson at Port MacDonnell School. Teacher—Miss Agnes Reddan. Photo: Mrs C. E. Edwards.*

everyone was happy with the umpiring! In 1893 the Test match taking place in England was commented on each month, and in 1894 the sports editor exclaimed:

> Adelaide has been in a great state of excitement during the past week, owing to the cricket match between Stoddart's English Eleven and The South Australian team. It is not too much to say that this match is the greatest ever played in Adelaide and it is certainly the finest display ever made by our cricketers.

Sport in those days fitted in with the ideals of manly vigour and the gallantry of an honestly fought contest. Expressions like 'playing the game' and 'it's not cricket!' belonged to a generation who regarded a sense of honour in sport as beyond question.

1893.

CRICKET.

The Australian Eleven have taken their departure carrying with them the best wishes of all who are interested in cricket. South Australians feel a special interest in the team, as we have twice as many representatives as we have ever had in an Australian Eleven. The team is a very strong one, and is expected to worthily uphold the honour of Australia in a land which has been the home of cricket for so long.

August 1893.

A CRICKET RECORD.

The Australian Eleven whose play has for the most part proved disappointing have raised a record for a score in first-class cricket matches.

1897.

CRICKET.

WE are all pleased to notice the success of one of our teachers—Mr J. C. Noack, of the Robe School—who scored 248 runs on the Adelaide Oval during the Christmas week. He headed the batting averages during the teachers' annual Easter tour, on each occasion that he played, with averages of 77 and 100 respectively, batting five times each trip.

Many of our teachers are cricketers, and if the strongest eleven were available a most formidable team could be placed in the field.

Some of our inspectors follow the game closely. Inspector Burgan is an old Oval player, playing for the Kents when the Oval was first opened.

Inspector Plummer was a member of the first teachers' cricket team, and it is reported that in jumping to make a high catch he scratched the moon.

Inspector Clark is an enthusiast, and has accompanied the teachers on two occasions. Inspector Neale, too, I believe, is an old cricketer.

Playing against a weak team of the combined universities of Oxford and Cambridge, they put up the enormous score of 843 runs on Portsmouth oval.

1897.

SPORT.

DR W. G. GRACE.

By Austral.

Many English papers recently have taken the fitting opportunity of sounding the praises of the greatest cricketing giant the world has ever seen—Dr W. G. Grace, sometimes known as the GOM of English cricket. He has just reached his half century in years, and, judging by his strong physique and general robustness, he bids fair to run well into the three figures. I am afraid to say how many hundreds of pages of print have been devoted to descriptions of the exploits of this great cricketer from his earliest infancy to the present time.

CRICKET.

(Sir Henry Newbolt, born in 1862, is a well-known poet who has written many stirring verses to teach English boys to admire their country and the great men it has produced. A few years ago, when an English team of cricketers were about to sail for Australia to play in the test matches, Sir Henry wrote the following verses to remind the members of the team that, whether they won or lost, they must keep up the high reputation of the most admired and cleanest of English field sports.)

Our countrymen of England who winter here at ease
And send abroad their cricketers to fight across the seas—
They long to win the rubber, but inwardly they know
The game's the game: howe'er the luck may go.

1911.
The Two Captains.
Left: *Mr Clem. Hill. (Australia)*

Right: *Mr P. F. Warner. (England)*

They know the English skipper may cry, 'A head! a head!'
And t'other, like a kangaroo, may toss a tail instead.
But cricketers can smile away the force of Fortune's blow,
For a man's a man: howe'er the luck may go.

To field upon a field of brick, to bowl beneath the blaze,
To bat and bat and bat and bat for days and days and days,
And then to lose—there's something wrong—but no! but no! but no!
The game's the game: howe'er the luck may go.

1902.

THE AUSTRALIAN ELEVEN IN ENGLAND.

Our cricketers have now nearly completed their tour through England. Perhaps no team has ever left these shores under such adverse circumstances. Many cricketers and supporters of the game in Victoria were exceedingly jealous of New South Wales, which supplied the majority of the players, and, through the medium of the press, did not fail to express their feelings.

However, the selectors of the team have thoroughly justified their good judgement in choosing an array of cricketing talent that has more than held its own against England's finest cricketers.

The present English season is one of the wettest ever known, and many of the fellows are making their first appearance on English grounds, where the pitches vary. As a rule they are slower than those of Australia; the dull light, too, differs so much from our own brighter light. On the other hand, these existing conditions are the almost every day experience of the English cricketers.

When we think of all these disadvantages, and read of the excellent results attained, we can sum up the team as the bravest, pluckiest, and most determined band of players that has yet visited England.

So far, only two matches have been lost; but, to crown all, the team has achieved that for which it was solely sent, ie, to retain the cricketing supremacy of the world, and this has been done. The test matches have been played, and the honours rest with Australia.

Well done, Australians! We are proud of you, and Darling and his merry men can feel assured of a very hearty welcome on their return home.

F. L.

Basketball came into fashion in about 1914. The *Hour*'s first mention of it came in the August edition with a description accompanied by a photograph of a game between Long Plain and Mallala—even the spectators seem to be in the picture.

Sport for girls took some years to gather momentum—but archery had been accepted for women in all the British colonial outposts, as had croquet. *The Girl's Own Book* advised, in 1877:

Of all things in the world health is the most important and exercise in the open air most conducive to it. Archery is therefore one of the amusements to be encouraged among young people . . . Calisthenics is the name given to a gentler sort of gymnastics suited to girls.

1897.

SPORT.

Austral.

THE Ninth Australian Eleven have arrived home, covered with honours.

True, they did not win two out of the three last matches, which may be safely attributed to the rain, which completely spoiled their chance. Still, they achieved excellent results, and fully upheld the traditions of Australian cricket. No county could withstand this powerful eleven, and thousands upon thousands watched the progress of the three great fights against England's finest cricketers. The success of the team was enhanced by the kindly feeling existing between the individual members; they were indeed a happy family.

Many sights were visited, historic and otherwise, and the cricketers are brimful of the kind treatment received at the hands of the Englishmen.

On the other hand, the work was hard, trying, and, at times, wearisome—one day playing at Gloucester, then travelling nearly all night, and next day to play at Bradford, Manchester, or Birmingham. One of the members told me he could well stand a month of continuous cricket, but after that he began to get stale, and really had to put himself to it.

Probably the prolonged spell of cricket is the cause of the comparatively poor performances of the wanderers in batting in the recent intercolonial matches. We all regret the poor show made by South Australia in the fight for the Sheffield Shield. They have themselves to thank, and they cannot expect to win till they have learned to catch. Many boys are fond of a hit, and of bowling a little, but they are not so keen on fielding. How seldom do we see a batsman score 100, or even 50 runs, without a chance of some sort. I cannot urge too strongly the importance of being smart and accurate in the field. The catches dropped by our men were almost innumerable.

During the progress of one match the catching was so bad that a little boy walked out of the grand stand on to the field and handed to Captain Giffen a large-sized handbag, much to the amusement of the spectators. The players themselves could not refrain from joining in the hearty laugh that followed the suggestive joke.

August 1914.

BASKETBALL.

MR Anthoney, of Long Plain School, has sent us some photographs and a letter praising basketball as a suitable game for schools. His own school and also Mallala School play it, and we know that it is a favourite game among pupils in several Adelaide schools.

Basketball comes from America, where it was invented about twenty years ago. It may be played in the ordinary school yard and also in a large room. At each end of the playing space is fixed a pole, from the upper end of which projects a metal ring holding the net-bag. The ball is filled with air like a football, but it is perfectly round, and must be played with the hands only. Kicking is not allowed.

Five a side is the proper number for a team, though seven is usually the number in South Australia. The object of each team is to throw the ball into the 'enemy's' basket or goal, and to guard their own goal from the opposing team.

The game costs little, is played by a team either of boys or girls, and teaches quickness, unselfishness, and skill to the players, and is an excellent exercise for the body.

But by the 1920s girls were playing sport competitively in basketball, and the photos of teams were featured in the *Hour* from time to time. By 1930 the girls' swimming classes at Victor Harbor were making news, and the tennis team at the Gum Vale School was 'mixed'—three boys and three girls!

Top: *1914. Basketball. Long Plain Against Mallala. Scores—Long Plain, 10; Mallala, 9.*

Right: *1930. Girls' Swimming Class at Victor Harbor. (Picture taken last summer by their teacher, Miss K. B. Shannon.)*

Bottom: *1902. Visiting Day, East Adelaide, Girls' Pole Drill.*

The *Hour* rarely mentions dancing, either as an art or as a school activity, or even as a pastime, but in 1927 the girls at the Yurgo School were being introduced to eurhythmics—rhythmic movement to music—which had been developed in Geneva by Dalcroze. A photograph shows the dry hard ground of outback South Australia, where Miss Aunger Evans skips to the sounds from a portable gramophone which is perched precariously on a wooden fruit case. About a dozen pupils are joining in, their feet sensibly bare, but Miss Evans has not parted with her shoes and stockings, nor indeed her hat.

The rhythm of the lives of new settlers altered as they adapted to the different life-patterns evident in the seasons, and particularly in nature, in this country. But rhythm came with them in the familiar form of music. To begin with, it enabled them to express their nostalgia, their longing for home. Any emotion could find an outlet in the universal language of music—tragedy, humour, gaiety, sadness, celebration, religious worship, pomp and ceremony: all of which occurred in daily life. Year after year memories of the old world were kept alive through sea shanties and folk songs of the British Isles; sentimental ballads of the Victorian era; melodies of Schubert, Schumann and Brahms; favourite operatic arias from the works of Verdi, Puccini and Gounod; swelling choruses and clear harmonies from the oratorios of Bach and Handel; and the lofty Imperial Marches of Elgar.

The diaries of the early colonists make mention of their pianos. Many of them brought this almost essential piece of furniture with them, or at least a similar keyboard instrument. It became a symbol of civilised and cultivated life. It was not long before pianos were available to many people, and were in wide use. They became the focus of family entertainment, and social occasions of every kind were centred around musical performance. Practically everyone had a 'party piece'—either a recitation or, more commonly, a piano solo or duet, a song, or perhaps a solo on violin or flute.

There were strong musical influences in early South Australia, some of which grew out of the choral traditions of Wesleyan religious revival, associated particularly with the mining communities, where hymn-singing played a prominent part. Added to this was the heritage of *Lieder* and Lutheran chorales, from the first German settlers, which ensured that country life, as well as city life, was enlivened and cheered with music.

Many children learnt to play the piano and sat for the schools' music examinations, and it is astonishing to read in the *Hour* in 1918 that:

> During the last four years nearly 700 musical certificates have been gained by children attending our public schools. Children who wish to become teachers should note the Elementary certificate is the standard in practical music for the Junior Teacher's Entrance Examination, and is also one of the compulsory examinations for students in training.

That children of musical ability should consider becoming teachers is not surprising in view of the part music played in South Australian life. The musical element in *The Children's Hour* was so prominent

June 1915.

SCHOOL SONGS NO. 3.

Arranged by F. L. Gratton.

DURING the school year the pupils in II and III classes are expected to learn at least five songs. Sometimes teachers have a difficulty in selecting the songs, or when they are taught some pupils are absent. To get over such difficulties Mr F. L. Gratton has kindly selected several songs which will be published from time to time in *The Children's Hour*. If teachers prefer other songs they may teach them.—Ed.

1914.
Operetta—'Princess Tiny Tot'.
Rhynie School.
Teacher—Mrs Dvorak.

and so deeply implanted in the lives of schoolchildren, that it deserves an exclusive study. It is possible to write of it only superficially here—a cause for regret. The earlier editions of the *Hour* were inspired, in the musical sense, by Inspector Clark, and the songs he selected leant heavily towards the patriotic—a trend which continued into the era when Mr F. L. Gratton promoted music in State schools with great vitality and success. Songs like 'The Bugle Call', 'The Flag for Me', and 'God Save our Empire', or 'Strike Hard and Strike Again' were characteristic choices. The National Anthem recurred every few months, and 'The Song of Australia', a South Australian work, with words by Mrs Carleton and music by Carl Linger, was so often included that there could not have been a single South Australian who did not know it after so many years of exposure!

The musical tastes of early colonial society were reflected in the songs taught in schools. The sol-fa method of reading music was introduced into the *Hour*, and this made singing more accessible to children, as they learnt to work out melodies without a piano, if necessary.

School choirs became very popular and sometimes presented highly accomplished performances. The annual 'Decoration Society Concert' was an innovation of 1891, designed to cultivate a love of good music. The occasion was always popular and well attended. The word 'decoration' referred to the pictures and photographs which schools acquired to improve the appearance of their classrooms, and which they purchased from the proceeds of the concert. The *Hour* published the songs chosen for the programme well in advance, and they were learnt in the State schools, ready for performance in the Exhibition Building, where children from all over the State joined together to enjoy music. In 1892 it was decided to combine the concert with the Annual Schools' Floral Society Exhibition, and from then on it bore the cumbersome title, 'Decoration and Floral Society Concert'. This was a very successful venture and led to the 'Thousand Voice Choir', which was held in high regard in the State for many years.

June 1911.

DECORATION SOCIETY'S CONCERT—SONG NO. 6.
'THE GOLDEN VANITY'.
UNISON SONG.

Doh = C. Words compiled from several versions.

s	d'	:d'.,d'	d'	:m	.,f	s.,l:s	.,m d	:r .m
1. O,	I	have a	ship	in	the	North	coun - tree,	And she
2. And	then	up -	start -	ed	our	lit - tle cab - in	boy,	Say-ing
3. I will	give	you	gold,	I	will	give you of	my store,	And my
4. The	boy	beat his	breast	and	he	jump'd in-to	the sea,	Tak-ing
5. He	bored	with his	au	- ger	two	holes in	a trice,	While
6. He	swam	back a -	gain	to	the	*Gol - den Van - i -*	*ty*,	Say-ing
7. 'I'll	not	take thee	up	nor		give you of	my store,	My
8. The	boy	swam a -	round	to	the	star - board	side,	Say-ing

f	.m	:f	.s	l	.t	:r'	.d'	t	.s	:s	.s	s	:s	.s
goes		by	the	name		of	the	*Gold*	*-en*	*Van*	*-i*	*-ty;*	I'm	a -
' What		will	you	give	me	if	the	gal	-ley	I	de -	stroy,	Will	you
daugh-ter		you	shall	mar-ry		when		we	re -	turn	to	shore,	If	you
with		him	an	au-ger		from	the	*Golden-en*		*Van*	*-i*	*ty*,	And	he
some	were	play-ing		cards,		and		some	were	play-ing		dice,	And	he
'Mas-ter,		take	me	up,		I	am	drown-ing		in	the	sea,	For	the
daugh-ter		you	shall	not		Mar-	ry	when	I	come	to	shore,	I	will
						p							*slower*	
'Ship-mates		pick	me	up,		I	am	drown-ing		with	the	tide,'	And	they

d'	.t	:d'	.r'	d'	.s	:m	.f	s	.l	:s	.m	d	:r	.m
fraid	she	will	be	tak -	en	by	some	Turk	-ish	gal -	li -	lee,	As	she
give	me	of	your	trea-	sure,	if	I	sink	the	gal -	li -	lee,	If	I
sink	the	Turk-	ish	ship		to	the	bot -	tom	of	the	sea,	If	you
swam	un -	til	he	came		to	a	Turk-	ish	gal -	li -	lee,	As	she
let	the	wa -	ter	in,		and	it	daz -	zled	in	their	eyes,	And	he
Turk -	ish	ship	is	sunk,		from	all	per -	il	we	are	free,	I	have
kill	you,	I	will	shoot	you,	I,	will	send	you	with	the	tide,	I	will
						pp								
laid	him	on	the	deck,		and		then	a -	las	he	died,	And	they

f	.m	:f	.s	l	:t	d'	:-	|-	:
sails	a -	long	the	Low -	lands	low,			
sink	her	in	the	Low -	lands	low,			
sink	her	in	the	Low -	lands	low,			
lay		in	the	Low -	lands	low,			
sank	them	in	the	Low -	lands	low,			
sunk	her	in	the	Low -	lands	low,			
drown	you	in	the	Low -	lands	low,			
sank	him	in	the	Low -	lands	low.			

1914.
Snowtown School Band.
Teacher—Mr C. J. W. Mundy.

It owed its existence to Mr Gratton, who became the major influence in establishing a strong musical element in State schools; it was he who selected suitable songs and answered requests for help and advice from teachers of limited musical training who were anxious to encourage musical experience for both city and country children. A repertoire was built up of folk songs, carols, rounds, descants, part-songs, operatic excerpts and national songs, in which the *Hour* played an important part.

1892.

PUBLIC SCHOOL CONCERTS.

During the last week of the quarter two concerts were given in the large hall of the Exhibition Building by some of the city and suburban schools. These concerts were started last year to raise money for pictures to be hung in the schools to which the young singers belong. The united choirs amounted to no less than 1200 voices, and the vast audience must have been immensely delighted by the appearance as well as the music of such a crowd of bright and happy children. Evidently no pains had been spared by the managers, headmasters, and other teachers, for the whole display gave evidence of genuine enthusiasm, both in the completeness of the arrangements, the steadiness and obedience of the children, and the style in which the various songs and actions were performed. Inspector Clark, one of the most enthusiastic of solfa-ists, acted as conductor for the combined schools, and he must have been delighted and satisfied with the whole affair. The attendances were enormous and the takings very large.

As well as choral groups, schools began to form bands, usually wind ensembles of fifes and flutes and sometimes trumpets, with drum accompaniments. The heights to which they aspired is clear from the photographs in the *Hour* which were included regularly, year after year. Many schools adopted a band uniform, and in country communities the players were included in local concerts, and took part in public festivities and any special occasions. The names of schools with bands began appearing, along with their photographs, in 1915—Kadina, Mount Gambier, McLaren Flat, Quorn, Oakbank, Burra, Williamstown, Lockleys, Nailsworth, Murray Bridge, Uraidla, Rendlesham, Kingston, Oodla Wirra, and many more!

Musical performances were described—a Japanese concert at Yongala Vale, an operetta entitled *Cinderella*, by the Loxton Public School, and *A Japanese Love Song* by the Compton Downs School in the Mount Gambier Institute Hall, in 1917. The enthusiasm for musical performance was in keeping with the traditions of Adelaide and South Australia, which had developed a lively amateur musical and theatrical reputation over the years. This vitality continued and became part of a matrix of accepted values and high ideals from which Adelaide has derived its civilised character.

October 1893.

CONCERT AT KANGAROO FLAT.

Minnie Kippin sends the following account of this entertainment: On Friday evening, September 8th, we held a concert in the schoolroom. There were several action songs, such as 'The Chinese Umbrellas' and 'The Spanish Gypsies' which were both rendered very nicely by the Misses

M. and O. Clark, as was also, 'England and Ireland' a duet by two gentlemen from Gawler. Beatrice Hocking recited 'The Crow's Children'. I recited a piece called 'The Milkmaid'. I also sang a song 'I'm the Life of the Young and the Old'. My sister Elsie recited 'The Dead Doll' and sang 'America's Emblem'. George Nottle gave a recitation 'The Frog's School'. There were several choruses by the scholars. The proceeds are to be donated to the school prize fund.

May 1893.

ENTERTAINMENT AT MODBURY.

The concert was held in a large room belonging to Mr Powell, which he kindly lent for the use of the children and which had been very prettily decorated for the occasion. On the minute of 8 o'clock Miss Potter began the overture, a very pretty piece of music called 'The Mocking Bird', which I liked very much. Then followed a song by one of the girls and a chorus 'The Rose Queen' in the middle of which Dora Hugall was crowned Queen of the Roses. After a duet and another song or two, a dialogue called 'Good Old Times' was acted. I think everybody in the room nearly had fits when the boys sung (*sic*) the vocal march (that's what they call it on the programme) 'Mulligan Guards'. After a short interval Miss Potter played another piece which some people seemed to think grand, judging by the way they clapped, but I could not make a tune out of it, and it hadn't even got a name, unless 'opus 70' is a name . . . . After Mr Haines had made a speech, we gave three cheers for Mrs and Miss Potter, and then sang 'God Save The Queen' and went home.

Thomas C. Angove
Tea Tree Gully School.

It takes no more than a glance at the institutions along Adelaide's North Terrace to recognise this city's long-established respect for the arts and learning—a characteristic which has contributed to a way of life in which the human scale has not been lost in the visions, nor in the realities, of 'progress'. *The Children's Hour* reflects this sense of proportion.

One such institution is the Children's Literature Research Collection where books—including copies of *The Children's Hour*—are cherished for the pleasure they bring and, perhaps of more importance, for the insight they offer into Australian and South Australian life. Among the treasures of this collection are toys and games generously donated, in recent years, by the descendants of the pioneer Lucy family. The gift comprises one hundred and sixty toys and games.

Another precious collection, donated in 1968, was the gift of the Gilbert family who came to South Australia in 1839 and settled at Pewsey Vale where they became respected as pastoralists and as citizens through subsequent generations. There are two hundred books and fifty games, all beautifully preserved, in this magnificent collection. Such pioneer families helped to develop the flavour of life in Adelaide and South Australia as surely as did the buildings, the industries, the business organisations and the developing arts and sciences of later years.

In 1957 Miss Dorothy Gilbert wrote, describing their childhood at Pewsey Vale:

> For the children the high point of the day came when after [five] o'clock tea they were brushed and washed and tidied by nurse and sent to the drawing room for the children's hour . . . The tinies were allowed to romp for a while till captured by nurse and popped into bed, the older children learned to do things with their hands while they listened to reading aloud stories from history or Shakespeare and the old classics, stories of adventure and just stories . . . These were all chosen because they were written in good English and without being preachy were soundly moral in tone.

Perhaps that seems a very different 'children's hour' from *The Children's Hour*. Yet, not so different. For both 'hours' sought to bring enriching qualities and influences into the lives of children.

Every generation retains, modifies, even discards inherited customs, depending on its aims and values, and sometimes its needs. *The Children's Hour*, with changing and unchanging styles and emphases, reflected the views of society. On reading excerpts from these old publications some of us may deplore and deride the values which were then upheld. Others may regret that we have renounced some of those values.

I hope that some, like me, will acknowledge with gratitude the many simple, yet honest attitudes that were bequeathed to us by earlier generations of South Australians, and recognise with respect the significant part played by *The Children's Hour* in establishing them.

1889.

THE CHILDREN'S HOUR.

Between the dark and the daylight
When the night is beginning to lower,
Comes a pause in the day's occupations,
That is known as the Children's Hour.

I hear in the chamber above me
The patter of little feet,
The sound of a door that is opened,
And voices soft and sweet.

From my study I see in the lamplight,
Descending the broad hall-stair,
Grave Alice and laughing Allegra,
And Edith with golden hair.

A whisper and then a silence:
Yet I know by their many eyes,
They are plotting and planning together
To take me by surprise.

A sudden rush from the stairway,
A sudden raid from the hall!
By three doors left unguarded
They enter my castle wall!

They climb up into my turret
O'er the arms and back of my chair:
If I try to escape, they surround me;
They seem to be everywhere.

They almost devour me with kisses,
Their arms about me entwine,
Till I think of the Bishop of Burgen
In his Mouse-Tower on the Rhine!

Can you think, O blue-eyed banditti,
Because you have scaled the wall,
Such an old moustache as I am
Is not a match for you all?

I have your face in my fortress,
And will not let you depart,
But put you down into the dungeon,
In the round tower of my heart.

And there I will keep you for ever,
Yes, for ever and a day,
Till the walls shall crumble to ruin,
And moulder in dust away!

Longfellow.